WE WERE
EACH OTHER'S
PRISONERS

AN ORAL HISTORY OF WORLD WAR II
AMERICAN AND GERMAN PRISONERS OF WAR

LEWIS H. CARLSON

BasicBooks
A Division of HarperCollins*Publishers*

FIRST EDITION

Designed by Nancy Singer

Maps by University of Wisconsin Cartographic Center

Library of Congress Cataloging-in-Publication Data

Carlson, Lewis H.
    We were each other's prisoners : an oral history of World War II American and German prisoners of war / by Lewis H. Carlson.—1st ed.
        p.   cm.
    Includes bibliographical references.
    ISBN 0-465-09120-2
    1. World War, 1939–1945—Prisoners and prisons, American. 2. World War, 1939–1945—Prisoners and prisons, German. 3. Prisoners of war—United States. 4. Prisoners of war—Germany. 5. World War, 1939–1945—Personal narratives, American. 6. World War, 1939–1945—Personal narratives, German. 7. Oral history. I. Title.
D805.U5C29   1997
940.54'7243—dc21   96-39116
                                                                                    CIP

97 98 99 00 ❖/RRD 10 9 8 7 6 5 4 3 2 1

Contents

Acknowledgments

THERE ARE SO MANY individuals to thank. Peter Steinbach of the Free University of Berlin first suggested the subject and has been a continuing source of inspiration and support. German historian Norbert Haase, with whom I collaborated on a German edition of this book, conducted two of the interviews found in Chapter Five. As he has so frequently done in the past, Stefan Sarenius cheerfully and competently provided bibliographical expertise. John Rieben contributed constant encouragement, as well as helping locate German and American ex-POWs who now reside in Wisconsin. John J. Fogarty helped uncover German ex-prisoners living in the Midwest, as did Herb Breitbach. Whenever my enthusiasm waned, Keith A. Long reminded me of those youthful, halcyon years we spent together in Germany. David L. Rozelle read parts of the manuscript and offered helpful criticism. Roger Bell very generously sent me copious amounts of information on German-held British prisoners, as well as many unique photographs. Jim Shiley and Ernst G. Richter transcribed several of the interviews. Frank Unger checked several of my German translations. Kenneth D. Schlesinger and other staff members of the Military Reference Branch of the National Archives were most helpful. Joseph and Linda Dietz and A. G. and Ann Thomas provided lodging during extended research trips, as did Alexander and Maria von der Osten.

I am particularly grateful to Western Michigan University for a faculty research and travel grant and for a year's Sabbatical leave. President Johann W. Gerlach of the Free University of Berlin provided two months' lodging and a generous stipend which allowed me to spend additional time interviewing former German prisoners of war. I also want to thank Linda Kahn, my editor at Basic Books, for her penetrating insights, helpful advice, and ongoing encouragement. I am most grateful to Jane Jordan Browne of Multimedia Product Development, Inc., for introducing this project to Linda Kahn.

Above all, I thank the former German and American POWs who so willingly told their stories. Without them, of course, there is no book. Among the many, I especially want to single out Phil Miller, Robert Engstrom, and George Rosie, three American ex-POWs who got me over some early hurdles by supplying names, addresses, and moral support and who continually asked me about the state of my research.

Finally, I have to thank my wife, Simone Conrad Carlson, for her patience and her willingness to believe this would honestly be the last time I would undertake a project of this magnitude.

Introduction

I

I count my own fortune now in the treasury of lives opened to me in trust. They live in me, resonate in me, teach me every day that no age or event can of itself prevent the human spirit from outstretching its former boundaries.

GAIL SHEEHY, *PASSAGES*

DATING AT LEAST BACK to Patrick Henry's famous regret that he had but one life to give for his country, most Americans believe that to die for one's country is the ultimate heroic act; to become a prisoner of war, however, is something quite different. Most noncombatants are not as blunt as was the wife who wrote her husband in 1944, "I still love you even if you are a coward and a prisoner," but in the public mind, there is nothing heroic or ennobling about becoming a prisoner of war.

In early June of 1994, Americans celebrated the fiftieth anniversary of D-Day. Numerous television and radio documentaries, articles, books, and other testimonials paid fitting tribute to the brave men who poured onto the Normandy beaches on or after June 6, 1944. Over the next ten months, Allied forces inexorably pushed the German forces out of France and into eventual surrender. Endless rows of white crosses serve as grim reminders of the thousands of Allied troops who were killed during this campaign. Briefly mentioned, if at all, were the thousands whom the Germans captured, especially during the Battle of the Bulge.

The 1995 Victory-in-Europe fiftieth anniversary celebrations inspired an even greater outpouring of public gratitude to the men and women who defeated Hitler and his Axis power. VE-Day also marked the anniversary of the liberation of the 95,000

American prisoners of war held by the Germans. In 1945, these men received no ticker-tape parades and were quickly forgotten by their government, the media, and the general public, but the experience has continued to affect their lives, even a half century after the fact.

And what of German soldiers and POWs? Their inclusion in this book is not an attempt at revisionist history—Hitler and his Nazi henchmen remain the essence of an evil nightmare that cost the lives of at least forty million human beings. But the common man, whether German or American, seldom picks his nationality, and he has few options when his political leaders determine he must serve his country. The experiences of such ordinary men, who did most of the fighting and dying and who dominated the prison camps on both sides of the Atlantic, illustrate that national distinctions fall away when human beings are trapped by circumstances they neither control nor fully comprehend. Through the telling of their stories these men achieve a dignity and importance not found in traditional history books. To be a soldier and a POW, and to survive to tell the story, is an act of heroism. These men's testimonies deserve attention, especially from those of us whose information has come either from the detached objectivity of scholarly discourse or from the commercial and myth-laden stories so frequently found in popular fiction, movies, and television.

American and German World War II prisoners shared much in common. All were lonely, bored, and no longer capable of controlling their individual destinies; most indulged in introspective examinations of self; all suffered indignities, but many experienced an incident or two that reinforced their belief in human decency; all had to learn patience and a degree of tolerance; some became very self-confident after realizing they could handle extreme adversity; others suffered what has become known as post-traumatic stress disorder (PTSD). Almost all agree that their imprisonment, along with the war itself, was the central experience of their lives.

But there were also differences between the experiences of the two groups. Most German prisoners in the United States were reasonably well treated; after all, they looked like the majority of Americans, and they shared a common heritage with many of their captors. German POWs had plenty to eat, a warm place to sleep, and even such niceties as toothbrushes, soap, and sufficient clothing. Many took classes, including some for college credit; others played in orchestras, frequented camp libraries, and engaged in sports. Those who worked outside the camps gained an intriguing perspective on everyday life in America. Of course, camp guards could be hostile, insulting, and, in a few cases, physically threatening. German prisoners also had constant worries about their families and loved ones back home, especially as news of lost battles and devastated cities reached their prison compounds. They anxiously wondered what kind of country awaited their return and who would still be alive to greet them.

A few German POWs encountered terrifying threats from their fellow prisoners. Initially, hard-core Nazi officers ran many of the camps, sometimes with the full and admiring support of American military authorities. These ardent fascists demanded total discipline and unwavering allegiance to the *Führer*, and often brutally attacked fellow prisoners whom they suspected of anti-Nazi activities or of collaborating with American authorities. In several instances they even killed the alleged offenders. After the war, the U.S. government executed fourteen German POWs, each of whom was convicted of killing a fellow prisoner. Most prisoners, however, were apolitical, especially as the war ran down, and eventually American authorities attempted to isolate the more zealous Nazis in segregated camps.

For many German prisoners in America the greatest surprise and shock came at the end of the war. They naturally expected to be repatriated to Germany, but fewer than 75,000 of the 380,000 German POWs in the United States were sent home in 1945. Those remaining continued to work in the United States, at least until July 1946, when the U.S. Government returned its last German prisoner to Europe. Unfortunately, because of negotiated agreements among the Allied Powers, the majority of those shipped in 1946 ended up in France and England where they spent up to three additional years as POWs.

The most pressing problem for most American *Kriegies* (short for *Kriegsgefangenen*, the German word for prisoners of war) was obtaining sufficient food, warm clothing, minimum health care, and adequate shelter, especially during the frigid European winter of 1944–1945 when many died of pneumonia. Some POWs were deliberately and flagrantly abused, but in general American and British prisoners received much better treatment than did their Russian counterparts or the tens of thousands of slave laborers or concentration camp inmates. Once they were on the ground and safely in the hands of military authorities, U. S. Army Air Corps personnel suffered least because Hermann Goering's *Luftwaffe* recognized a certain honor and respect among airmen.

Whatever the conditions inside or outside the camps, a prisoner's cultural attitudes could influence his general outlook and his willingness to adapt. The British, with their sense of tradition and imperial superiority, and the Americans, with their belief in their own higher mission, both considered themselves vastly superior to their enemies; consequently, they believed there was little to be learned from their captors. In World War II, this attitude was most blatantly directed toward the Japanese, although Germans could also be held in contempt. Allied prisoners delighted in baiting and ridiculing their guards, referring to them as "Goons,"[1] while seldom making any attempt to study the language or customs of their captors.

German prisoners could also be insufferably arrogant, but many of them sought opportunities to study life outside the camps, eagerly learned English, and took a wide variety of classes, some even for college credit. Similar educational opportunities existed in several of the German prison camps, at least for the officers, but few Americans took advantage of them.[2] A large number of the nonpolitical German prisoners brought positive feelings about the United States with them to the prison camps. Many had

---

[1]According to historian Arthur A. Durand, *Stalag Luft III: The Secret Story* (Baton Rouge: Louisiana State University Press, 1988), 89, the term "Goon" evidently stemmed from a comic strip in the London *Daily Mirror* "that depicted 'goons' as low-browed, primitive apemen of great strength and stupidity." Americans also referred to Germans as "Krauts."

[2]One notable exception was future Attorney General Nicholas Katzenbach who while a prisoner of the Germans completed much of his work for his subsequent law degree. Most Americans who tried to learn German either had studied the language in school or came from families where German was spoken; see Durand, *Stalag Luft III*, 226.

read Karl May's Westerns[3] or thought they knew about America from Hollywood films, popular music, and travel literature.

Naturally, many American prisoners also transcended cultural provincialism. Some attempted to make friends with guards who treated them well. Sympathetic Air Corps prisoners even came to understand the outrage of German citizens who had wanted to kill them when they hit the ground. Finally, the more perceptive prisoners understood that like themselves, the common people, including their military counterparts, were also suffering the ravages of history's most devastating war.

II

Oral history is a tool to democratize the study of history.

RONALD J. GRELE

METHODOLOGY

The inspiration for this book came from two very different sources. The first was Professor Peter Steinbach, one of Germany's leading experts on the historical resistance to National Socialism, who several years ago told me about the Nazi/anti-Nazi conflicts that occurred in several of the United States prisoner-of-war camps. Knowing of my interest in oral history, he suggested interviewing some of those involved. The second person to suggest a study of prisoners of war did so inadvertently. In 1991, I met Dimitri Borisovich Lomonosov at a Russian/American student writing conference in Moscow. A former World War II POW, he

---

[3]Between 1875 and his death in 1912, Karl May wrote seventy books on the American West. These highly romantic tales have sold millions and can still be found in many German bookstores. Although May never traveled outside of Germany, many German travelers to the Great Plains, including not a few of the prisoners, insisted they recognized the landscape from May's literary descriptions.

insisted he owed his life to several American prisoners who had generously shared with him their own meager food rations. He asked if I could possibly find some of his American benefactors so he could write and thank them. I wrote his story for the *American Ex-POW Bulletin*. Unfortunately, no one remembered him personally, but several former POWs knew of similar incidents and contacted me. Their response triggered my interest in extending my study to American POWs who were incarcerated in the Third Reich.

Over the past five years I have interviewed more than 150 American and German ex-POWs who were interned in the homeland of the enemy. I made two trips to Germany and also traveled extensively in the United States, interviewing both former American prisoners and a number of German ex-prisoners who returned to the United States and eventually became American citizens. Locating and interviewing these subjects presented certain challenges. For years after the war, many of the American ex-POWs were unwilling to talk about their experiences, even to family members. However, the nation's increased understanding of what the Vietnam veterans experienced, both during and after that most unhappy of wars, the outpouring of sympathy for the 1979–1980 Iran hostages, the shocking media portrayal of new POWs taken during the Gulf War and in Somalia, as well as the additional time for reflection afforded by advancing age and retirement, encouraged many of these men to reconsider their silence.

Some eventually discovered that sharing their experiences made it easier to deal with their own pain. Nevertheless, talking to these men was often a very emotional experience. Often they broke down in tears when particularly agonizing memories surfaced. Sometimes we simply had to stop the interview. One former prisoner, whom I interviewed just before Christmas, complimented me on the timeliness of my arrival: "Over the last couple of years," he announced, "I have attempted to commit suicide during the holidays." Another confessed that during one of his uncontrollable rages he had tried to murder his son. Two men, who had initially fully cooperated, later wrote asking that I destroy the audiotapes and anything I might have written about them.

Most of the men wanted their stories told, however. Indeed, the very urgency with which they related their experiences left me feeling an awesome responsibility as collector and editor of their narratives. I will never forget one of them saying, "Lew, my story is now in your hands."

The American Ex-Prisoners of War organization is of paramount importance for anyone attempting to locate or work with former prisoners from any of America's recent wars. Its major publication, the *Ex-POW Bulletin*, contains timely articles on related medical, military, and political concerns, as well as memoirs, membership lists, photographs, news of various reunions, and sundry other personnel matters. Even today, more than fifty years after the end of World War II, veterans continue to join its national, state, and regional chapters.

There were numerous other helpful veterans' organizations. My experience with the 101st Airborne Division Association, many of whose members were captured after they jumped behind German lines on or before D-Day, was typical. At its 1994 national convention, one member, whom I had already interviewed, put a note on the bulletin board asking any other former prisoners to meet with me. For an entire day I had men standing in line ready to share their experiences.

I discovered one American ex-prisoner while turning the pages of a 1945 *Life* magazine. The haunting photograph of a living, but nameless, skeleton who had just been liberated by Allied forces jumped out at me. Clearly he had been badly mistreated or was deathly ill. I asked many of the men I interviewed if they had ever seen this photograph. A few had, and finally one suggested the prisoner in question might be Joe Demler. Fortunately, there was a Joseph Demler in the American Ex-Prisoners of War Directory. I wrote, Joe answered, and his story and his then-and-now photographs appear in this book.

Of course, there are still those former prisoners who refuse to join veterans' organizations or to talk about their experiences. Two wives, who learned of my project, wrote and pleaded with me to try to get their husbands to talk. Unfortunately, I was not successful. Such experiences made me realize that the painful memories revealed by those I did interview are shared by thousands of others who have chosen to remain silent.

Locating former German prisoners presented different kinds of challenges. At a *Volkstrauertag* (*People's Memorial Day*) celebration to honor German prisoners who had died at the wartime prison camp at Fort Custer, Michigan, I met several former German POWs whose stories appear in this book. There is no national organization of ex-prisoners in Germany, although there certainly are many veterans' organizations. On my trips abroad, friends and colleagues interested in the project provided me with names and addresses of former German prisoners who in turn introduced me to others.

One of the most fascinating discoveries was made by German colleague Norbert Haase, who at the time was doing research at the *Gedenkstätte Deutscher Widerstand* (The Museum for German Resistance to National Socialism) in Berlin. Haase uncovered the names of several former American-held POWs who, because of their Communist activities in the 1930s, had been forced into Hitler's notorious *999 Strafbatailon* (999 Penal Battalion). Once on the front lines many simply deserted or were quickly captured. After their eventual liberation they disappeared into the German Democratic Republic where the new Communist authorities distrusted them for having been "contaminated" by Western ideas. With the reunification of Germany in 1989, many of these men were now able to talk freely, and two of their stories appear in Chapter Five.

Sometimes it was simply chance that led me to German ex-prisoners. In 1992, my wife and I were the only non-Bavarians on a German tour bus heading to Prague. One of our fellow passengers was a fascinating German priest with whom we soon became friends. He had been taken prisoner in Norway, and never made it to the States, but he did tell us an extraordinary story about a German officers' eugenics experiment that featured beautiful Nordic women. He also told me to interview Josef Krumbachner, whose story appears in Chapter Five. My daughter Ann, who lives in Austin, Texas, suggested I might want to interview her German cabinetmaker who had spent time in Texas as a POW. Guenther Oswald appears in Chapter Three. Since completing this manuscript, both friends and strangers have suggested additional names.

The oral historian prefers to work with the largest possible number of subjects; unfortunately, considerations of time, location, and financial resources force a certain selective process. Although I deliberately attempted to get a cross-section of various ranks and branches of service, I confess an affinity for the enlisted men, whose individual stories too often have been reduced to impersonal statistics in traditional military histories. Of course, I could not ignore the thousands of U.S. Army Air Corps officers and noncommissioned officers who were shot out of the skies. I sought a variety of personalities and points of view, but I must admit I was unsuccessful in identifying former German prisoners who had retained their enthusiasm for National Socialism. Such men, of course, still exist, but few are willing to attest their allegiance for publication.

From my more than 150 interviews I selected thirty-four narratives to appear in this book. Some of these men had also written about their experiences. A few kept diaries during their incarceration, which was a difficult and even dangerous thing to do; others recorded their memories well after the war. Two of the men published books about their experiences, and several have been the subject of newspaper or magazine articles. Although my oral interviews remain central to their narratives, I also occasionally drew on their own writings and related articles to augment their stories.

Using these individual accounts, the chapters of this book take the reader through the entire experience of being a prisoner of war. Beginning with the front-line soldier, the stories reveal the shock of capture, the uncertainty and confusion of the first days of captivity, the enervating and often debilitating conditions found in the permanent camps, and, finally, the joy and relief of liberation and repatriation, which all too often were followed by painful, even crippling memories. Some repetition is inevitable in such narratives, because prisoners share so much in common, but ultimately each story is as unique as the man who lived it.

THE ORAL HISTORIAN

Oral history, as Ronald J. Grele states in his superb *Envelopes of Sound*, "is a way to get a better history, a more critical history, a more conscious history which involves members of the public in the creation of their own history." Furthermore, writes Grele, oral history examines "the dialectical relationship between changing consciousness and social, political and economic movements."[4]

---

[4]Ronald J. Grele, *Envelopes of Sound: The Art of Oral History*, 2nd ed. (New York: Praeger, 1991), xvi, 3.

This is as important as it should be obvious. For example, the experiences of the Vietnam veterans, reported in several superb oral histories, greatly affected the willingness of World War II soldiers to talk openly about their experiences in graphic and candid terms. To do so, they had to overcome the popular and military stigma against surrendering and becoming prisoners of war.[5]

Oral historians ask their subjects to individualize or personalize events and experiences. Our subjects tell us not only what happened but what they thought happened; that is, what they have internalized and interpreted from their experiences, as well as from the surrounding culture. This often leads to a conflict between individual and collective memory, the former based on what one actually experienced and the latter on what society creates as an acceptable past.

Oral history can be a liberating force. This is very important for POWs or for members of any disenfranchised group, who are victimized by a profound sense of guilt about their individual condition. For example, many of the POWs I interviewed seem to have blanked out their moment of capture. After all, John Wayne was never captured. John Rambo was, but only in order to escape and exact his bloody revenge. The individual must develop a sense of history, if for no other reason than to escape or at least illuminate the myths that affect his judgment of his own existence.

Studs Terkel, whose *The Good War*[6] is but one of his many fine oral histories, argues that the common man is conditioned not to have a sense of history or has learned the wrong history—a history without blemishes, contradictions, or pain. While popular culture often reduces the masses to a level of banality, passive ignorance, or comic relief, oral histories often illuminate in the ordinary person a raw intelligence, complexity of character, and intuitive understanding of historical forces that scholarly writers might well envy.

---

[5]U.S. military officials consistently opposed any attempt to grant formal recognition to World War II POWs. Finally, in 1985, Congress created the Prisoner of War Medal and subsequently many states have issued free license plates with "POW" inscribed on them.

[6]Studs Terkel, *The Good War: An Oral History of World War II*. New York: Pantheon, 1984.

In the final analysis, the people we interview become our teachers. Interviewing soldiers and POWs, for example, teaches us just how cheap life is in war. American males are taught always to appear brave, yet the capricious whims of Dame Fortune do not consistently recognize or reward courage. Unlike most fictional portrayals of war in which courageous soldiers create their own destinies, in real war it is chance that often dictates one's fate in combat or in a prison camp.

Interviews with ex-soldiers also teach us how thin our veneer of civilization is, and how quickly it is stripped away in conflict or captivity. Had compelling oral histories such as Studs Terkel's *The Good War* been available in 1950 or 1963, would Americans have been so willing to send their children off to Korea and Vietnam? The answer is probably yes, because popular myths about sacrifice, courage, and national glory are so deeply ingrained in the nation's psyche. Nevertheless, our national hesitancy to become involved in a land conflict in the Gulf and now in Bosnia has certainly been affected by our increased understanding of what war does to those who fight and die, and to those who survive the carnage.

DATES AND NUMBERS

Of the approximately 95,000 Americans who became prisoners of the Germans,[7] the first sizeable numbers of ground troops were taken during the five-month North African campaign which began in November of 1942. The invasion of Italy, which began September 3, 1943 and lasted well into the summer of 1944, pro-

---

[7]The estimated number of American POWs captured by Germany has grown over the years. On July 15, 1944, just five weeks after D-Day, the War Department reported 28,867 German-held American POWs, of whom 16,593 were airmen and 12,274 were ground troops. On April 13, 1945, just over three weeks before Germany's formal surrender, the *New York Times* estimated there were 85,000 Americans in German hands. By November 1, 1945, the War Department had raised that total to 92,965, of whom 32,730 were airmen and 60,235 ground troops. In 1980 the Veterans Administration put the total figure at 95,532; see David A. Foy, *For You the War Is Over: American Prisoners of War in Nazi Germany* (New York: Stein and Day, 1984), 12–13.

duced the next large group of American POWs. Thousands more became prisoners in the first weeks after the June 6, 1944, Normandy invasion, but the largest single group of American land troops—more than 23,000, including 4,000 on one day—were captured during the five-week Battle of the Bulge, which began on December 16, 1944. Most of these men were young, untested soldiers who in the heat of battle were often without effective leadership. This lack of discipline and training greatly affected their state of mind at the time of capture and during their subsequent incarceration.

Approximately 33,000 American prisoners were Army Air Corps personnel shot down over enemy territory. The first American air raid over Germany took place on July 4, 1942, but not until 1943 did the Allied raids occur on a regular and massive scale.[8] Daily missions involving hundreds of planes did untold damage to the Third Reich, but also resulted in thousands of Allied casualties. For example, during the October 14, 1943, raid on the Schweinfurt ballbearing works, the Germans shot down sixty B–17 bombers carrying more than 500 airmen.

With casualties so common, the possibility of capture was not alien to airmen. But most did not foresee the hostile reception that often awaited them on the ground. German civilians, inculcated with propaganda about *Terrorflieger* (terror fliers), readily believed the German press which accused the American airmen of being *Luftgangster* (air gangsters) who were paid $50,000 for each mission.[9] When *SS* Commander Heinrich Himmler assured citizens, "It is not the task of the police to intervene in altercations between Germans and landed English and American *Terrorflieger* who have bailed out," he left the door open for civilians to take revenge into their own hands.

In spite of such dangers, American prisoners held by the Germans had a much better chance of surviving than did their fellow countrymen who were captured by the Japanese. Fatality

---

[8]At the January 1943 Casablanca Conference, British and American leaders designed a massive air campaign not only to destroy Germany's military, economic, and industrial might but also to crush the morale of the German people.

[9]Foy, *For You the War Is Over*, 21–22.

rates among Japanese-held prisoners approached forty percent. For those captured on the European continent, less than four percent died in captivity.[10] But German-held Russian prisoners died by the tens of thousands. Hitler had total contempt for what he called "the Mongol Half-Wits,"[11] and Josef Stalin scorned and rejected his own soldiers for having been captured. Stalin's refusal to sign the 1929 Geneva Convention also meant Russian prisoners had no access to Red Cross parcels or international guarantees of decent treatment. More than three million Russians perished in German prison camps, in large part because of their nationality, and other Slavic captives fared little better.

Beginning in late 1942, the Allies shipped almost 380,000 German prisoners to the United States. The first large numbers

---

[10]The exact number of World War II American prisoners who died in captivity remains unknown. For example, E. Bartlett Kerr, in his *Surrender and Survival: The Experiences of American POWs in the Pacific 1941–1945* (New York: William Morrow, 1985), 335–40, writes that 10,600 or 41% of the Japanese-held America prisoners died in captivity. Robert C. Doyle, in his *Voices from Captivity: Interpreting the American POW Narrative* (Lawrence, Kans.: University Press of Kansas, 1994), 25, puts the figure much lower. The same problem exists in estimating the actual number of American prisoners who died in the German camps. Doyle's own estimates appear contradictory. He suggests that approximately 4 percent of British and American POWs died in captivity in Europe (p. 25), but later he writes that only 1,121 Americans, or something over 1 percent, died (p. 303). The "Med-Search" column in the May 1983 *Ex-POW Bulletin* used this same figure of 1,121 for the number of American deaths. Complicating these calculations is the fact that of World War II's 78,773 American MIAs many certainly died as POWs, especially during the long, forced marches during the final months of the war when the Germans no longer could maintain a precise accounting of their prisoners.

[11]Propaganda Minister Joseph Goebbels insisted, "The Russians are not people, but a conglomeration of animals," and Hitler told his armed forces, "This enemy consists not of soldiers but to a large extent only of beasts;" quoted in Gordon Wright, *The Ordeal of Total War, 1939–1945* (New York: Harper and Row, 1968), 126. Not surprisingly, until their labor was badly needed in the last years of the war, the Nazi leadership made little or no effort to keep Russian prisoners alive.

were from Rommel's Africa Corps.[12] Most were well-trained, bat-
tle-tested veterans, and many were ardent admirers of Hitler and
National Socialism who remained convinced Germany would win
the war.[13] The next large contingent was captured during the
Sicilian and Italian campaigns. Although some of these men had
been fighting since 1939, most still considered themselves loyal
soldiers, and many remained convinced Germany would prevail.
Such was not the case with the majority of German prisoners captured after the Normandy invasion, and especially not among the
enlisted men. Many were exhausted and discouraged after six
years of hard fighting; others were teenagers who had been
rushed into the front lines without adequate training. The
German losses were appalling, food and other supplies were in
short supply, and morale was at low ebb. These were beaten men
who knew the war was a lost cause.

German prisoners eventually arrived in one of the 155 base
camps or over 500 branch camps in the United States.[14] More than
100,000 ended up working in private industries such as logging,
mining, food processing, and agriculture where their labor greatly alleviated war-time shortages. Their general treatment was
unquestionably better than that experienced by American POWs
in the Third Reich. There was always sufficient food, medicine,
clothing, and shelter. There was also no danger from errant air
raids or angry citizens ready to exact personal revenge. By the
end of 1944 the American press and not a few politicians, hearing
rumors of the harsh treatment of American POWs in Germany,

---

[12]The surrender of 170,000 German troops on May 13, 1943, in Tunisia
was a disaster of such proportions that some Germans secretly referred to
it as "Tunisgrad."

[13]For a good account of these early German prisoners, see Arnold
Krammer, *Nazi Prisoners of War in America* (New York: Stein & Day,
1979), 16. Krammer's superb history is the only comprehensive study of
World War II German prisoners in the United States.

[14]For security reasons two-thirds of the base camps were located in the
South and Southwest. Another one-fifth were in the Midwest. Eventually,
there would be POW camps in forty-seven states; see Krammer, *Nazi
Prisoners of War in America*, 21–22.

accused their own military authorities of coddling German prisoners. They certainly were not coddled, but as the accounts in this book make clear, many of them found their American incarceration to be an interesting, if not enjoyable, experience.

THE GENEVA CONVENTION

Because of its obvious importance to prisoners of war, the Geneva Convention plays an important role in their stories. On July 27, 1929, forty-two nations, including Germany and the United States, signed *The Geneva Convention Relating to the Treatment of Prisoners of War*. Its ninety-seven articles governed all aspects of military captivity, including such items as interrogations, the privileges of rank, the quantity and quality of food, clothing, and housing, sanitary conditions, medical care, disciplinary measures and allowable punishments, mailing privileges, allowable work assignments, prisoner representation, and even the location of the camps themselves. In addition, it called for International Red Cross inspections as well as those by a neutral power (Swiss teams periodically inspected both German and American camps). It also attempted to spell out the terms of liberation.

The Geneva Convention recognized the privileges of rank and class. It called for the segregation "of different races or nationalities," as well as separate compounds for officers, noncommissioned officers, and enlisted men. High-ranking prisoners were allowed the services of orderlies and aides-de-camp, who were expected to make the officers' beds, wash their clothes, and perform necessary duties around the camp, including cleaning the officers' latrines. Officers usually enjoyed better food, including the more frequent distribution of Red Cross parcels, better recreational and cultural facilities, and superior health care. Officers were not to work; work was optional for noncommissioned officers but mandated for enlisted men. Working was a mixed blessing for the EM. It did take them out of the camps, reduced boredom, and sometimes allowed them to forage for food. But it also could mean danger from bombing raids or irate citizens who not surprisingly saw in them the enemy who was raining terror from the skies.

Living space and a semblance of privacy were also very important. According to the Geneva Convention, prisoners were entitled to the same amount of living space as were the soldiers of the detaining Power. In the United States' camps this meant that each German enlisted man was supposed to have forty square feet of living area, while each officer was to receive 120.

The Code was to be posted in each camp in the language of those incarcerated so that prisoners might know their rights. Unfortunately, there were no binding provisions for enforcement, and both sides were guilty of violations. Hitler had contempt for any law that did not suit his needs, and the *SS* and the *Gestapo* blatantly ignored the Geneva Convention when handling prisoners. Allied prisoners were often forced to work under hazardous conditions or on tasks directly related to the war effort, both of which were violations, and medical treatment and general care often fell short of that prescribed by the Convention. For the most part, the *Luftwaffe*, which administered the Air Corps camps, did an adequate job of adhering to the Code's provisions.

Hoping that German authorities would treat its prisoners accordingly, the American government did implement and enforce most of the provisions of the Code. However, after the war and the safe return of the American POWs, the United States violated at least the spirit of the Geneva Convention when it did not return its prisoners to Germany with "the least possible delay."

In spite of transgressions on both sides of the Atlantic, the Geneva Convention did assure prisoners held by Germany and the United States that they would fare better than those interned by the U.S.S.R. and Japan, neither of which recognized the Geneva Convention.

THE MYTH OF THE AMERICAN MALE

Well before the fall of communism, an old Russian cynic was heard to say, "We know the future; it's the past that keeps changing." His contrary view of the past applies particularly well to the myths that dominate so much of popular history. Society's current values, assumptions, and expectations, as well as its antipathies, illusions, and anxieties, greatly determine how it chooses to depict its past. America's popular perception of prisoners of war is no exception.

The myth of the individual dominates American culture. Unlike most fictional heroes, however, the common man—and especially the POW—must rid himself of the notion that he is an independent agent. If he is to survive the hostile and often dangerous world of captivity, the prisoner must accept and welcome the support of his fellow captives. This need for a certain amount of humility and dependency may appear obvious, but it is a difficult lesson for most American men, who have been raised to believe it is a sign of weakness to need the help of another human being.

America's cultural heroes are always self-sufficient, larger-than-life individuals who stand tall in the saddle, no matter what the odds. Consider the Marlboro Man, alone, astride his horse, silhouetted against the sunset, ready to take on all comers. Or John Wayne, almost singlehandedly fighting a two-front war against the Axis powers. Nothing puts the lie to imagined individual heroics more quickly than the reality of modern war, where the individual becomes a faceless nonentity, battered by forces he often never sees and certainly does not control.

In a culture that embraces the individual as an independent agent, the concept of control dictates one's sense of self. Imprisonment, of course, quickly exposes this notion for the illusion it is. One of Kurt Vonnegut's other-worldly characters in his whimsical POW novel *Slaughterhouse-Five* put it best: "I've visited thirty-one planets in the universe, and I have studied reports of one hundred more. Only on Earth is there any talk of free will."[15] Prisoners of war, of course, talked little about free will, whether real or imagined. They were caught, as Vonnegut has described them, "like flies in amber."

SURVIVAL TACTICS

Although fictional portrayals of POWs have invariably focused on the excitement generated by attempted escapes, gloomy resignation and stifling boredom more typically characterized a prisoner's daily existence. Rather than undertaking unrealistic and potentially dangerous escapes, it was far more sensible for the prisoner to stay focused on his immediate environment and try to counter its negative effects. Keeping busy was all-important,

---

[15]Kurt Vonnegut, Jr., *Slaughterhouse-Five or the Children's Crusade* (New York: Dell Publishing Co., 1969), 80.

either through recreational, cultural, or educational activities or by just communicating with one's friends. Religion comforted some men, and especially for those who took a strong sense of spirituality with them into the camps. Many of those interviewed talked freely about praying, particularly when they felt alone and forgotten. Unlike the accounts published by former Vietnam POWs, however, they never seemed to blend religion, God, and America into some kind of holy trinity.[16]

Looking back, the most important survival factor seemed to be friendship. Perhaps because all experiences were magnified, possibly because there was such an obvious need for an active support system, and certainly because prisoners were an inescapable part of each other's lives, friendships became all important. Ex-prisoners can go years—even decades—without seeing a former prison buddy and then restart the friendship right where it left off in the camps. "Initially," said one former POW, "you tended to become very selfish because you spent so much time thinking about yourself and your own predicament. It was only when we got beyond that and started doing things for other people that we became less depressed."

But there were also times when a prisoner just had to lower the curtain and be alone with his thoughts—to seclude himself in his own little world. The key seemed not to be overly preoccupied with one single thing, whether that single thing was yourself or counting the barbs on the fence.

One former prisoner targeted the following characteristics for survival: a good sense of humor, fortitude, reliability, and a willingness to share. Another ex-prisoner suggested that "all people in positions of responsibility, politicians particularly, ought cer-

---

[16]Almost all of the Vietnam ex-POWs who have written about their experiences credit love of country, family, and religion for their survival. They emphasize the uniqueness of freedom in America, and, unlike the men interviewed for this book, they insist they are better human beings for their experience. For excellent analyses of the Vietnam narratives see Craig Howes, *Voices of the Vietnam POWs: Witnesses to Their Fight* (New York: Oxford University Press, 1993) and Elliott Gruner, *Prisoners of Culture: Representing the Vietnam POW* (New Brunswick, N.J.: Rutgers University Press, 1993).

tainly to have had schooling in the skills of being a good POW. It causes you to look after yourself being aware that someone else is looking out after himself and you mustn't damage him. You are both equal when all is said and done." Another insisted, "Afterwards you felt nothing was impossible. Whatever it was, you could do it, and you never allowed yourself to be bored again." This man also talked about discovering genuine goodness and courage in others as well as in himself.

The intensity of the POW experience brought out the best and the worst in human nature. One man related how a fellow inmate offered him a sweater to stave off the bitter cold of the 1944–45 European winter. When he told the would-be giver he had nothing to give him in return, his new friend said, "Just pass it on when you are finished with it."

Glossary of German Terms

Abitur	The final exam a German student takes to graduate from the Gymnasium or high school
Appell	Roll call
Arbeitsdienst	Service work
Arbeitskommando	Labor detachment
Der Ruf	*The Call*, a German POW newspaper
Dulag	Abbreviation for *Durchgangslager* or transit camp
Dulagluft	Transit camp for airmen
Gestapo	*Geheime Staatspolizei* or secret police
Hitler Jugend	Hitler Youth
Kampfgruppe	Fighting Group
Kommandant	Commander
Kriegies	Short for *Kriegsgefangenen* or prisoners of war
Lager	Camp
Luft Gangster	Air gangsters
Luftwaffe	German Air Force
Oflag	Abbreviation for *Offizierslager* or permanent officers' camp
Stalag	Abbreviation for *Stammlager* or permanent camp
Stalag Luft	Abbreviation for *Luftwaffestammlager* or permanent camp for allied air force personnel
SS	*Schutzstaffel* or "Protection Squadrons"
SD	*Sicherheitsdienst*, the Security Service of the *SS*
Strafbataillon	Penal battalion
Terror Flieger	Terror fliers
Wehrmacht	Regular armed forces

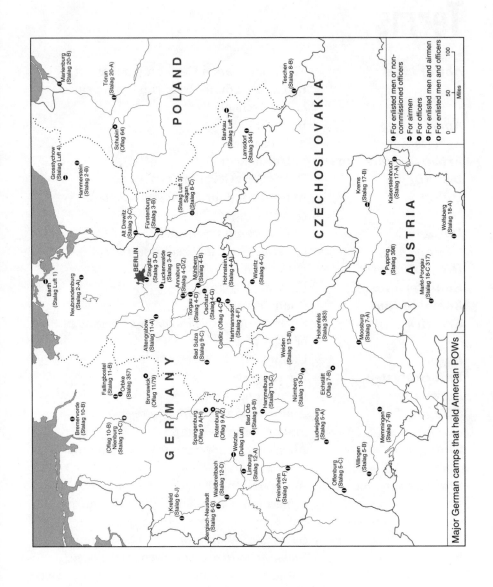

Major German camps that held American POWs

Marienburg (Stalag 20-B)
Torun (Stalag 20-A)
Grosstychow (Stalag Luft 4)
Hammerstein (Stalag 2-B)
Schubin (Oflag 64)
POLAND
Bankau (Stalag Luft 7)
Lamsdorf (Stalag 344)
Teschen (Stalag 8-B)
Barth (Stalag Luft 1)
Neubrandenburg (Stalag 2-A)
Alt Drewitz (Stalag 3-C)
Fürstenberg (Stalag 3-B)
Sagan (Stalag Luft 3) (Stalag 8-C)
BERLIN
Steglitz (Stalag 3-D)
Luckenwalde (Stalag 3-A)
Annaburg (Stalag 4-D/Z)
Mühlberg (Stalag 4-B)
Hohnstein (Stalag 4-A)
Wistritz (Stalag 4-C)
CZECHOSLOVAKIA
Krems (Stalag 17-B)
Kaisersteinbruch (Stalag 17-A)
Bremervorde (Stalag 10-B)
Oflag 10-B) Nienburg (Stalag 10-C)
Fallingbostel (Stalag 11-B)
Oerbke (Stalag 357)
Brunswick (Oflag 11/79)
Altengrabow (Stalag 11-A)
Torgau (Stalag 4-D)
Oschatz (Stalag 4-G)
Colditz (Oflag 4-C)
Hartmannsdorf (Stalag 4-F)
Bad Sulza (Stalag 9-C)
Weiden (Stalag 13-B)
Hohenfels (Stalag 383)
Moosburg (Stalag 7-A)
Pupping (Stalag 398)
AUSTRIA
Markt-Pongau (Stalag 18-C 317)
Wolfsberg (Stalag 18-A)
GERMANY
Krefeld (Stalag 6-J)
Bergisch-Neustadt (Stalag 6-G)
Waldbreitbach (Stalag 12-D)
Limburg (Stalag 12-A)
Wetzlar (Dulag Luft)
Bad Orb (Stalag 9-B)
Hammelburg (Stalag 13-C)
Rotenburg (Oflag 9 A/Z)
Spangenburg (Oflag 9 A/H)
Nürnberg (Stalag 13-D)
Eichstätt (Oflag 7-B)
Ludwigsburg (Stalag 5-A)
Villingen (Stalag 5-B)
Memmingen (Stalag 7-B)
Offenburg (Stalag 5-C)
Freinsheim (Stalag 12-F)

For enlisted men or non-commissioned officers
For airmen
For officers
For enlisted men and airmen
For enlisted men and officers

0   50   100
Miles

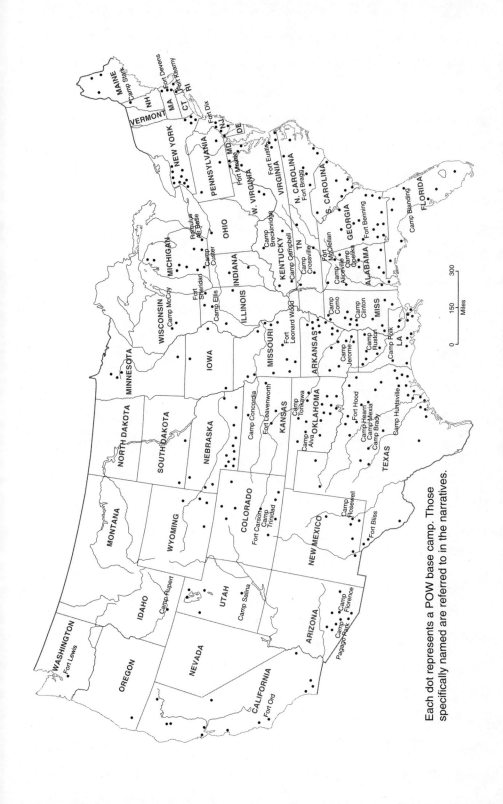

Each dot represents a POW base camp. Those specifically named are referred to in the narratives.

1
Soldiers and Prisoners

In their rememberings are their truths.

STUDS TERKEL

THE TWO LENGTHY NARRATIVES in this chapter are intended to introduce the reader to many of the experiences and themes that will be isolated and examined in greater depth in subsequent chapters. American Robert Engstrom and his German counterpart, Karl-Heinz Hackbarth, share much that is common to all prisoners of war—the danger and tensions of the front-line soldier, the anxiety and bewilderment of capture, the uncertain passage to an unknown internment camp, the challenges of everyday life in prison, and worries about loved ones back home—but there are also sharp differences. American prisoners such as Engstrom suffered greater physical hardships than did their German counterparts, specifically inadequate food and shelter, and because they were in a war zone, they were vulnerable to inadvertent attacks from "friendly" fire. Engstrom was also among those American prisoners forced by their captors into long and sometimes deadly marches to escape the fast-closing Allied forces at the end of the war.

For Karl-Heinz Hackbarth and other German prisoners, an ocean voyage to the United States removed the immediate terrors of war, and once in the States most of them enjoyed the same kind of food and shelter given to American soldiers. Physical mistreatment and undue hardships did occur—Hackbarth even helped stage a strike in a work camp—but they were normally the exception. However, their captivity did not end with the cessation of hostilities on May 8, 1945, as it did for German-held American prisoners. Many, including Hackbarth, were sent to England or France for up to three additional years of incarceration.

The filing time shown in the date line on telegrams and day letters is STANDARD TIME at point of origin. Time of receipt is STANDARD TIME at point of destination

WA200 44 GOVT=WUX WASHINGTON DC 22 547A

1944 JUL 22 AM 5 56

MRS FRIEDA KARRENBERG=

516 EAST 88 ST NYK=

THE COMMANDING GENERAL EUROPEAN AREA REPORTS THAT YOUR SON
PRIVATE WALTER D KARRENBERG WAS CAPTURED ON SIX JUNE MAIL
ADDRESS CANNOT BE FURNISHED UNTIL CONFIRMATION OF CAPTURE IS
RECEIVED THROUGH THE INTERNATIONAL RED CROSS WHEN ADDITIONAL
INFORMATION IS RECEIVED YOU WILL BE PROMPTLY NOTIFIED=

UL IO THE ADJUTANT GENERAL.

Telegrams such as this were a relief to family members who had previously been notified that their son was missing in action. *Photo by author.*

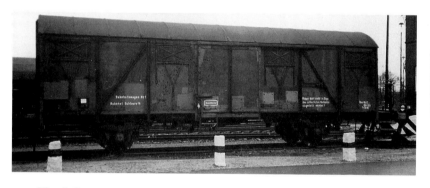

Used for transporting prisoners, this German boxcar was known as a "40 and 8" because it could carry 40 men or 8 horses. *Photo by author.*

The arrival of Red Cross parcels at Stalag Luft III. *Courtesy of the American Red Cross.*

Typical POW eating utensils. Notice the POW's initials on the knife handle. *Photo by author.*

Sample items found in an American Red Cross package. *Courtesy of the American Red Cross.*

More than seventy American prisoners of war were gunned down outside of Malmédy on December 17, 1944, by Colonel Jochen Peiper's SS troops. *U.S. Army photograph.*

German propaganda leaflet dropped over American troops. *U.S. Army photograph.*

BECAUSE, THEY LIVE IN PERFECT SAFETY.

BECAUSE, THEY HAVE THREE SQUARE MEALS A DAY.

BECAUSE, THEY RECEIVE MEDICAL CARE FROM AMERICAN DOCTORS AND DENTISTS.

BECAUSE, THEY ARE BEING ATTENDED TO BY AMERICAN CLERGYMEN OF ANY DENO- MINATION.

BECAUSE, THEY HAVE THEIR OWN THEATRES, THEIR OWN MOVIES, THEIR OWN JAZZ-BANDS.

BECAUSE, THEY HAVE SPORTING-GROUNDS AND GYMNASIUMS.

BECAUSE, THEY CAN CHOOSE TO WORK OR STUDY. EXTENSIVE LIBRARIES ARE AT THEIR DISPOSAL.

BECAUSE, ALL IN ALL, THEY MANAGE THEMSELVES.

AND LAST BUT NOT LEAST

BECAUSE, GERMANY STRICTLY ADHERES TO THE GENEVA CONVENTION.

NO WONDER, THEY ARE SITTING ON TOP OF THE WORLD, LOOKING AT THE WAR FROM AFAR, MINDFUL OF THE OLD AMERICAN SLOGAN:

SAFETY FIRST!

Newly captured German prisoners moving to the rear lines.
U.S. Army photograph.

German prisoners using the official Nazi salute at roll call in a U.S.
POW camp. *National Archives photograph.*

German POWs sewing American army uniforms at Fort Meade, Maryland. *National Archives photograph.*

German prisoners learning English. *National Archives photograph.*

Two German officers enjoying their American captivity. Enlisted men's quarters looked nothing like this. *National Archives photograph.*

German prisoners enjoying their 1943 Christmas dinner at Camp Swift, Texas. *U.S. Army photograph.*

German POWs perform a cabaret show at Camp Polk, Louisiana. *U.S. Army photograph.*

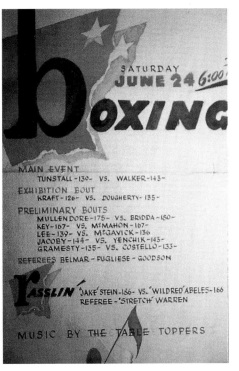

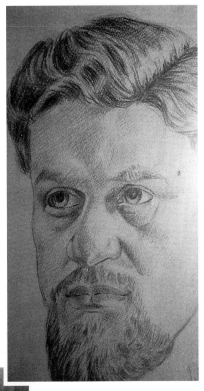

While a POW in Stalag 17, the camp later made famous by the play and movie of the same name, Daniel S. Abeles wrestled on the weekly card as "Wild Red." *Photos by author.*

American POW Angelo Spinelli used his secret camera to take this shot of a fellow prisoner trading with a German guard at Stalag 3-B. *Courtesy of Angelo Spinelli.*

Checking a German prisoner for telltale SS tattoo marks. *National Archives photograph.*

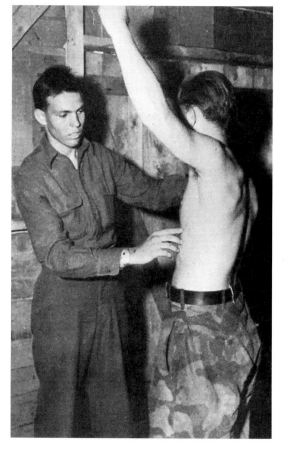

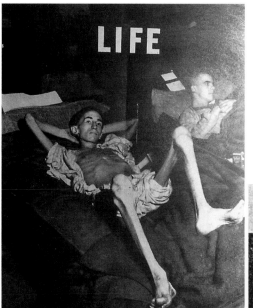

Taken on the day of his liberation, this unforgettable *Life* magazine photograph of Joseph Demler horrified many Americans. *Johnny Florea, Life magazine, ©Time, Inc.*

Joseph Demler weighed 155 pounds as an eighteen-year-old soldier. He would lose half his weight after three months as a POW. *Courtesy of Joseph Demler.*

Joseph Demler, fifty years after his shocking photograph appeared in *Life* magazine. *Courtesy of Joseph Demler.*

British and American prisoners released from Stalag 7A at Landshot, Germany, on May 7, 1945, await boarding C–47s that will ferry them to Le Havre and Brussels on the first leg of their trip home. *U.S. Army photograph.*

An American tank liberates Allied prisoners at Stalag 13-C outside of Hammelberg, Germany. *National Archives photograph.*

Captured at age 16, Oskar Schmoling was arguably the youngest German POW sent to the U.S. *Courtesy of Oskar Schmoling.*

Joseph Beyrle holding a POW photograph of himself which he liberated from the *Kommandant's* safe at Stalag 3-C. *Courtesy of the Muskegon Chronicle.*

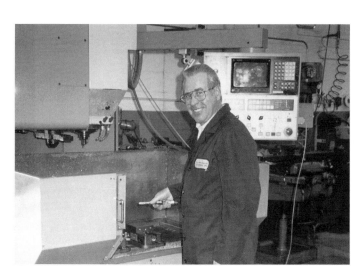

Fifty years after the end of the war Oskar Schmoling is president of his own machine shop outside of Detroit. *Photo by author.*

Young American soldier Robert Engstrom before his capture by the Germans at the Battle of the Bulge. *Courtesy of Robert Engstrom.*

Robert Engstrom has held on to his final day's bread ration for more than fifty years. *Photos by author.*

American POW Clifford Fox took this photo of Polish and Russian slave laborers who worked with him on a farm in eastern Germany. *Courtesy of Clifford Fox.*

Clifford Fox at home in Michigan. *Photo by author.*

Former prisoner Henry H. "Mac" McKee holding an autographed copy of *Mein Kampf* and a Luger pistol he liberated fifty years earlier from the German camp commander in Stalag 13-C. *Photo by author.*

At a 1992 memorial service at Fort Custer National Cemetery outside of Battle Creek, Michigan, Karl Hackbarth pays tribute to the twenty-six German prisoners who died while incarcerated with him at Fort Custer. *Photo by author.*

The funeral of German General Hans Schubert, who had been interned at Camp Clinton, Mississippi. *National Archives photograph.*

Alexander Jefferson, one of several Tuskegee Airmen who were shot down and captured by the Germans. *Photo by author.*

Karl and Stella Hackbarth, who met when Karl was a POW outside of Detroit. At the time, the FBI accused Stella of being a spy. Karl and Stella married in Germany after the war. *Photo by author.*

Former German POW Karl Hackbarth with author Lewis Carlson. *Photo by author.*

Liberation Day! U.S. Army photo taken at Stalag 9-B,
Bad Orb, Germany.

Five former German POWs return in 1991 for the annual
Volkstrauertag memorial service at Fort Custer. From left to right:
Helmut Dillner, Elmer Beck, Karl Hackbarth, Ernst Floeter, and
Oskar Schmoling. *Photo by author.*

ROBERT ENGSTROM

Bob Engstrom was a corporal and forward scout in the 32nd Cavalry when he was captured on December 17, 1944, during the second day of the Battle of the Bulge. Feisty, tough, resilient, and seemingly fearless, Engstrom survived an encounter with Jochen Peiper, the SS Colonel later accused of the massacre of more than seventy American prisoners at Malmédy, France, and some harrowing experiences in German POW camps. Near the end of his imprisonment, Engstrom began writing down everything he could remember, and he remembered a lot. Now a retired professor of art and a very successful designer and producer of fine jewelry, Engstrom becomes very emotional when recalling the painful memories of his incarceration.

Engstrom was one of those rare soldiers who was not only anxious for combat but was also good at it, including the killing. As a front-line soldier, he experienced the atrocities committed by both sides during the heat of battle, as well as the disorientation and shock that followed capture.

I WAS SENT TO England as part of a replacement unit—Repo Depots they called us. Of course, at the time it didn't really register on me this meant I would be replacing someone who had been either wounded or killed.

I landed on Omaha Beach just a few days after D-Day. Like so many of the guys who landed on June 6, we got dumped into water that was too deep to wade, and some of our guys couldn't swim. I just dropped my rifle and pack and scrambled onto shore. The front lines were only about a mile away, and the Germans were still shelling the beach.

I was on that beach for about two months. Finally, a corporal from the 32nd Cavalry got killed, and I was his replacement. Our main purpose was not to fight but to make contact with the enemy. I had a driver and a jeep, and we worked the point. When the Germans retreated to the next town or valley, our job was to drive down the road and make contact with them. Of course, the way to make contact with the enemy is to get shot at. As soon as we made contact, we'd fall back. We'd do this for two weeks and then get two weeks rest while the 18th Cavalry took over.

On December 16, we got a panic message to move up the front lines as quickly as possible. I thought it was just another false alarm, but we moved out. We came over a hill, and there were cars and trucks tearing by us from what was supposed to be the front. We couldn't figure out what was going on. Finally, I stopped and asked a truck driver where he was going and where his outfit was. He told me he no longer had an outfit. I asked him what he was talking about, and he said, "They're gone. They're all gone. I'm the only one left." Our lieutenant told us to retreat several miles to the village of Honsfeld, where there was a small Red Cross station, and to hole up somewhere until morning when he would decide what to do. That night he took my jeep and disappeared. I never saw him again.

Honsfeld was in the northern part of the Ardennes Forest just at the western tip of the Losheim Gap where the Germans blasted through that first day of the Battle of the Bulge. Of course, we didn't know anything about that then. We went to sleep that night in a small farmhouse. At the crack of dawn I heard a burp gun. About the same time one of the guys on watch was pulling on my foot, telling me there were some Germans outside shooting. I told him he was crazy, that we were at least ten miles from the front. One of our guys announced that he didn't care how many Germans were out there, it was his birthday, and he was going to have his breakfast. So he went into the kitchen and began making himself something to eat. The rest of us went outside and heard a little firing but not much. It was now lighter, and I noticed about 200 soldiers coming up from our rear. I told my buddy Lew,[1] "Hey, we're going to get some help." Right then he

---

[1] For reasons this narration will soon make clear, "Lew" is not his real name.

pulled up his rifle and *bang*, one of those advancing soldiers keeled over. I yelled at him, "Hey, you're shooting our own men." "Nope," he answered, "those are Germans." I didn't think it was possible, but during the night German paratroopers had dropped behind us and now were attacking from our rear. This meant the entire village was surrounded, and there was no way out.

I ordered my squad upstairs in the house so they could overlook the roads coming from town. Out in back, Lew and Tony were firing at Germans coming through a hedge. Every time a German would come through, they'd pile him up. Lew was a great killer who always shot everything he saw. I went back to the front of the house where I had left the cook and found him all crouched down under the window ledge. I asked him what was the matter. He said, "Hey, there are two German soldiers standing just down the road there. What do I do?" I told him, "Shoot the sons-of-bitches." And he did. Then he bent over and puked all over the floor. Later he got killed; in fact, most of our guys got killed. I think Lew, Tony, and I were the only ones to get out alive. Two South Bend Poles and a Michigan Swede.

There was no way we could match the Germans. We had a light tank with a 37-mm gun, and some canister ammunition for shooting snipers. It was like shooting beebies at those German tanks. They came down the street with their 88-mm cannons pointed right at us. They blew the back of the house right off. We had put the husband, wife, their ten-year-old son, and the dog in the basement. When we knew the end was near, we took out our wallets and burned our addresses. We hid our guns under the floorboards. We then went out and surrendered. That was December 17, 1944, the second day of the Battle of the Bulge.

The Germans searched us and then went down in the basement where they found the family. They lined them up and shot them. I guess they thought they had collaborated with us because we were in their house. But they hadn't. We had come in the middle of the night and just kind of took over. One daughter survived because she was out of town, but when she came back she never knew what had happened to her family. I'm probably the only one who knows what happened to them. I looked for her when I went back to that village after the war and visited that very same house, but I couldn't find her.

The reality of war really hit home when I got captured. They marched us out of town to an open field. There was a German sitting in one of our jeeps who looked familiar. His arm was shattered, and he had a tourniquet around it. He was a nice-looking kid, about eighteen or nineteen. He looked at me and we kind of recognized each other. We had first seen each other looking down a rifle sight. He said, "You know, we're kind of lucky. We don't have to fight anymore." I've never forgotten him. I just know I was the one who shot him.

I can also remember one of the Germans coming up to me and asking in perfect English, "Why did you come over here to fight me? I never did anything to you." I answered, "I don't speak German." Then he said, "But I am speaking English and you don't understand me." He spoke English as well as I did, but I expected him somehow to be guttural. I had no answer to his question, and I've thought about it since. I didn't know why I was over there in that mess or why he was in it with me. We were taught that Germans were monsters and baby killers, and when I discovered that this was not always the case, I had to ask myself why I was there.

Talking to those two Germans made me think of something horrible Lew and I had done just a few days before. We were behind German lines doing our usual scouting, when we captured these two Germans. We'd normally observe during the day and then travel at night, and we had stumbled across these two soldiers. I told Lew, "There's no way we can get back to our lines with these two guys." Lew agreed. He marched them off to a nearby barn, and I heard two shots. He came back and told me that everything was fine. We started to walk away, and Lew said, "You know, I forgot to look in their pockets. Maybe they've got something we want." So we both went back. When we got close to the barn, we heard this crunching and munching. There were pigs in the barn, and they were eating those two German soldiers. The farmer and his family had fled, so the animals had not been fed. There was not much left of our two prisoners, just their helmets and equipment.

[Engstrom breaks down in tears.]

So there I was, a prisoner, with all this on my mind, when a German officer came up the road followed by two guys with machine guns. The officer's face was beet red, and he was furious.

What had happened was a round from one of our 105-mm cannons had landed right in the middle of some German infantry, splattering them all over the place, and he wanted to know where those 105s were located. He looked at his watch and said, *"Vier Minuten."* Then he ran his finger under his neck from ear to ear. We understood exactly what he meant. When it got down to one minute, he told us to sit down. He was standing there as red as ever, just grinding his teeth. Tony was sitting next to me, and he motioned that he had a hand grenade hidden in his pocket. I took the grenade and thought to myself, "Well, if we're going, he's going too. I'll take that sucker right along with us." Then I thought, "This isn't the way to go. I'll be buried in a hole, and nobody will ever know it. My mother will get a Missing-in-Action letter, and she'll have no idea where I am." So I decided I wasn't going to die like that. I laid the grenade down in the snow, walked over to this officer, looked him right in the eye, and said in slow English so he could understand, "We're not fighters. We didn't shoot your men. None of us knows where that cannon is located. We're cooks. We have no idea where those guns are. If you don't believe me, down the road you'll find our mess truck with chocolate cake and cigarettes in it." A couple of days before our cook had baked a cake so I hoped some might still be in the truck. In the meantime, these two soldiers had set up their machine guns and were ready to shoot. He sent one of them down to the truck, and when he came back, he had the cake and the cigarettes. So he left one of those guys to guard us and away he went.

I don't know whether he was bluffing or not, but I think the fact I had the guts to go face to face with him may have made him change his mind about shooting us. I don't know how the words came out, but I know they were emphatic. I just decided I was not going to sit there and die. In such moments something just takes over. If you're meant to go on or not, something happens beyond your understanding. It was so close for me that I had to believe somebody was looking after me. For what reason, I don't know. Many times since then, I have looked at my wife and daughters and wondered if perhaps they are the reason.

That officer who threatened us turned out to be Jochen Peiper, the *SS* colonel responsible for the massacre of more than seventy American prisoners at Malmédy which was just down the road from where we were captured. Supposedly, Peiper was also responsible for the slaughter of hundreds of Belgian men, women, and children. At the time, I didn't know who he was, but his face was indelibly etched on my mind. I could never forget it. After the war, I was looking at a book on the Battle of the Bulge, and there he was, staring up at me from the page. He was tried as a war criminal and served ten years in prison. He later bought a château right outside of Paris where one night someone murdered him.

My second night of being a prisoner was really cold, and several of us traded our overshoes to the German guards so they would let us stay in a bunker where it was warm. That was a decision I later regretted. I also had a lamb's wool vest under my G.I. jacket. The next day we were being marched past a row of Tiger tanks that were going in the other direction. The German soldiers looked down at us, and this one guy noticed my vest. He pulled out his pistol and yelled, *"'raus, 'raus."* I knew what he wanted. But I thought, "Gee, I'm going to need this. He kept yelling, *"Schnell, schnell, schnell."* I said, "Okay, okay," but instead of unzipping it, I just ripped the zipper out and threw the vest at his feet and kept right on walking. I didn't know whether he was going to shoot me or not, but at that moment I didn't care.

[Engstrom begins crying again.]

You could see debris from past battles lying all around as we marched along. We were really hungry, and I spotted an old K-Ration on the other side of the ditch with a piece of cheese in it. I thought, "What the hell," so I got out of line and jumped across that ditch and grabbed the cheese. I turned around and I was looking down the barrels of about seven submachine guns. I didn't think it was that important. I got back in line, took a bite, and one of my buddies said, "Hey, give me some." That was the last I saw of that piece of cheese which almost cost me my life. I later picked up a dirty cabbage leaf that at least a hundred guys had walked on. I ate it with relish, dirt and all. I also found a wormy turnip, but I had to share it with a bunch of other guys. The only thing the Germans gave us during those first few days was some unseasoned barley soup.

[Being marched without food and sleep, seeing men shot, and suffering a brutal interrogation further broke down Engstrom's resistance. Life improved slightly in the permanent prison camps,

but the enlisted men's camps were poorly organized, with inadequate food and few if any of the all-important Red Cross parcels. To make matters worse, it was the coldest winter in fifty years, and Engstrom and his fellow prisoners had insufficient clothing and blankets.]

We were marched to just outside of Bonn, where about 100 of us were corralled in front of a farmhouse. A man gave each of us a form which he said to fill out so the Germans could notify the Red Cross that we were POWs. I thought, "Gee, that sounds good." They then took us one at a time into the farmhouse. Right inside the door was a big German soldier; he looked like Gargantua. The first thing he did was grab me by the front of the shirt and hit me right between the eyes. Oh, that hurt. Blood started running out of my nose. He picked me up and threw me to the bottom of the stairs where another German gave me a couple more whacks in the belly and in the face. By this time some of my teeth were loose, and blood was running out of my mouth. Each of us got the same treatment. I guess this was supposed to soften us up.

After that I was pushed into a room where a German officer was sitting behind a desk. He spoke excellent English. He asked me where I had been fighting, when and where I was captured, and what outfit I was in. I gave him my name, rank, and serial number. He asked me again, and I gave him the same thing. He said, "That's a good soldier. That's all I want to know."

[Engstrom again begins crying.]

He then told me he knew everything about us. He told me I had been captured on December 17, and that I was in the 32nd Cavalry. He even knew how many casualties we had suffered and how many of us had been captured.

We stayed in Bonn only one day. I was issued one-third of a loaf of bread and a half tin of cheese as a travel ration. We were marched about three miles to the railroad yards and put on a train. We were locked in these box cars called 40 and 8s for seven days,[2] and that travel ration was the only food we had. From the

---

[2]These railroad box cars were called "40 and 8s" because they allegedly could hold either forty men or eight horses.

time I was captured, I went eleven days with almost nothing to eat, very little sleep, and watching those around me get sick. One fellow got pneumonia and died two days later. The guards didn't even let us out of those freezing boxcars to relieve ourselves except briefly on Christmas Day. We spent Christmas Eve on a railroad siding looking out the little window covered with barbed wire, and we could see happy Germans walking by with food, drinks, and candles, getting ready to celebrate Christmas. One lady came up with some beer. We managed to push a little bucket through our window and she filled it with beer. Just once, though, and I didn't get any of it.

By the time we got to our destination on December 27, we were in bad shape. The guards broke the ice off the locks on the door, let us out, and then marched us off to Stalag 13-D, just outside of Nürnberg. We got a piece of bread and a small hunk of sausage that day and were issued one light blanket. We were all half frozen, especially our feet. By this time we just didn't care whether we lived or died. We were told to turn in all our money. I had a wallet that had a secret compartment, and I had a two-dollar bill in it that I carried for luck. I was determined to keep it. They had us fall out and strip naked. I remember there was snow on the ground, and it was cold. A couple of plain-clothes *Gestapo* types started inspecting us. There we stood, holding our wallets in our hands. It was too late then, so I thought here goes my two dollars and probably me too. I heard a shot and one guy went down. They got to me, and I thought I was finished for sure, but when they opened my wallet, they didn't see the secret compartment.

The next morning we got shaved. They used these horse clippers and shaved our entire body, and I mean every part. They did this to get rid of the lice. Then they marched us to the showers. There were already some German paratroopers taking showers. They looked at us standing there naked, and a couple of them started laughing. One of them went over to his clothes, got out his spring-loaded paratrooper knife, walked over to the guy standing next to me, shoved the knife into his belly, and released the blade. It went in maybe an inch. They all thought that was real funny.

We stayed at Stalag 13-D for maybe two months. Then they moved us to Stalag 13-C outside of Hammelberg. This was the camp where General George Patton sent that expedition to free his son-in-law, Colonel John Waters.[3] We were in one compound and the officers were in another. We could see Patton's tanks coming up this hill, and we could hear firing. The guards just took off so we felt real good. One of the guys even cut a hole in the fence and some of us went out scrounging for food. But then the firing stopped. It got real quiet. That night nothing happened. The next morning we looked out and saw several of those German Tiger tanks coming up the road on the low side of the hill. When they reached the crest, they began firing. Patton's tanks were all lined up on a ridge, but we couldn't see them. We later learned they were sitting ducks because they had run out of gas. They had taken a bunch of officers out of the compound and they were just sitting on the tanks. So the Germans just picked them off, one after the other. There must have been twenty tanks, and they were just shot to pieces.

Conditions were primitive at Hammelberg, at least for the enlisted men. We slept on the floor in a mule stable. We were so crowded no one could roll over at night unless everyone rolled over. There just wasn't enough room. We were stacked like sardines. The latrine was nothing more than a hole in the ground and a pail to sit on. The hole was periodically emptied by dipping the stuff with a steel helmet and dumping it into a horse-drawn wagon which was then taken out and dumped onto the surrounding fields as fertilizer. We called it the "honey wagon." Food was scarce. Each day we got one bowl of soup and a seventh of a loaf of bread. We became desperate for something to eat. One day some British POWs and their guards drove a horse-drawn cart up to our compound to load some cabbages from a shed behind our building. We stood there watching and drooling. After about the

---

[3]In a very controversial action, on March 22, 1945, General George Patton sent a small armored unit sixty miles behind enemy lines to rescue his son-in-law, Colonel John Waters, who was incarcerated in Stalag 13-C. Waters was wounded in the rescue attempt and never made it out of the compound. Several other officers were briefly liberated before German reinforcements arrived and quickly destroyed Patton's task force, with a loss of over thirty American lives; see, Richard Baron, Abe Baum, and Richard Goldhurst, *Raid! The Untold Story of Patton's Secret Mission* (New York: G. P. Putnam's Sons, 1981).

third trip one of the Brits tripped on purpose, spilling the basket of cabbages he was carrying so that they all rolled toward us. There were probably six cabbages that rolled underneath the rope behind which we were standing. I didn't get one, but we all thought that was just great. I waited a couple of minutes, thinking I really should have my own cabbage. I was really hungry. One of the guards went back into the storage room, and the other guy was just standing there looking off somewhere. That wagon was only about fifteen feet from me, and suddenly I got this uncontrollable urge to grab a cabbage. I darted under the rope and ran full tilt towards the cabbages. Just as I got there the guard turned around and saw me. I tucked a cabbage under my arm and ran like hell back to where I had been standing. I couldn't see the guard, but I heard a thump. He had grabbed his rifle by the barrel and took a swipe at me, but missed and hit one of the other guys standing there. It was an awful crack. I went scooting through the guys and ran back to the other side of our building. Later I found out that the other guard had come over to see what was happening. Evidently he took aim right at my back, but just as he was getting ready to fire, I rounded the corner of the barracks and went in the front side. By this time a riot had started. The guards got scared and started moving the wagon out, but there were prisoners everywhere. They had to put the horses to a full gallop just to get out of there. I was inside eating my raw cabbage. About an hour later the camp *Kommandant* came down with several officers and announced, "We cannot condone that kind of behavior. You will not do this ever again. If there's even the slightest infraction, we will line up and shoot several of you."

In a prison camp, the will to survive supersedes a lot of niceties, including the Golden Rule. Do unto others as you would have them do unto you? Bullroar! When it was my turn to reach into the pot with the food, I was not about to give it to somebody else. What was mine, was mine, and you better not touch it.

There was no real organization in the camps I was in. We were just leaves in the wind. We never had anything to use to bribe the guards like the air force guys did. We had no money and almost no Red Cross parcels. There was no leadership that I know of because the officers were off somewhere else. I don't even remember any staff sergeants. There was simply no one to take charge. When the bread came, we made up our own little group of seven men. It was very important that you got your fair share of the daily loaf of bread, and I offered to cut it into seven parts. Toward the end that's all we had to eat. In order to make it fair, we rotated the order in which the guys would pick their piece of bread, and I always took the last piece. Some guys would try to cut their piece into three smaller portions, to make three meals. Others ate it all at once so they were temporarily full. But nothing really worked. Anyway, that was as close to any organization that we had.

[Engstrom saved his last piece of bread and the primitive knife he used to cut it. See photograph.]

[The infamous Bataan Death March is well documented, but not so well known are the several marches forced on POWs in Europe to flee the fast-closing Allied troops. Engstrom and his fellow prisoners were moved by train from Hammelberg to Nürnberg from where they had to walk to Stalag 7-A just northeast of Munich, a distance of approximately 100 miles.]

About 1,500 of us started out from Nürnberg on April 1, 1945, on what would be a fifteen-day march. Many of us were pretty weak, and we would try to help each other. But there was one fellow we didn't help. He had been collaborating with the Germans. We knew about it in part because he had gained weight while the rest of us were losing. He'd disappear in the evening and then somehow get back to the barracks. Everybody hated his guts, but we just left him alone. No one talked to him or had anything to do with him. The guards told us during the march that if anyone couldn't make it, he would be disposed of, just like we later learned the Japanese did to their prisoners during the Bataan Death March. So this fat guy was walking along, and it wasn't too long until he was huffing and puffing and telling us he couldn't walk anymore. We told him we couldn't help him. So he fell off to the side of the road, and we heard a shot. That's all there was to it. Those Germans didn't have any qualms about shooting him, even after he had helped them.

We passed a field containing a pile of sugar beets which were only about 100 feet off the side of the road. They looked awfully good to me and evidently to some of the other guys. In back of me some guy broke and started to run toward them. Right behind him came a bunch of other guys, and soon there was a riot. This guard marching alongside me just lifted his rifle, took aim, and fired. That first guy just keeled over, and that stopped that.

Another couple of guys took off early in the march. The Germans unleashed their dogs, and they just tore them to pieces. That was to let us know they meant business. But it wasn't like that with all the guards. Some of them knew the war was over, and they really didn't care if we took off or not. I can remember a truck came along, and our guard stopped it. He and several of us hopped on. He even handed me his rifle so he could climb into the back. He opened the bolt to show me he had thrown away all his ammunition, and he kept saying, "*Alles ist kaputt, alles ist kaputt.*"

One evening we stopped by a farm, and I asked the farmer if a few of us could sleep in his barn. The next morning he came out, woke us, and invited us into the house. He told us to take off our shoes which we did. His wife then made some eggs and toast for us. I was quite surprised. In the middle of eating I saw this little girl looking in through the window. She then took off running and just a few seconds later a guard came to the house. We got ready to go back to the line, but he told us, "*Nein, nein.*" And he sat down and had some eggs and toast with us.

We stopped at another farm a couple of days later, and again discovered the German people weren't so bad after all. At this place the wife told us the horse had just died and that we could have the meat if we would skin it out and give the skin to her. I had some experience in the meat business so I cut out the tenderloin and ate it raw. We didn't cook any of that horse, and within twenty-five minutes there was nothing left but bare bones. Guts and all were gone. You just lived day by day any way you could.

Each day we became more and more just a straggling bunch of prisoners, and there was increasingly less control over us. I can remember a couple of us going into a bakery. We were really famished and we could smell the baking bread. We asked the baker for anything, just a chunk of bread. "*Nein, nein, nein,*" he said. He explained to us that he couldn't get more flour to make bread unless he had the ration coupon. About that time he turned around to take some bread out of the oven, and my buddy grabbed a loaf of bread and took off. So did I. We had our loaves of bread.

We finally arrived at Stalag 7-A in the small town of

Moosberg. We picked up the BBC on a radio somebody had made, so we knew that Patton was pretty close. Then we heard shooting from the sentry boxes near the gates. I can remember one of the guys climbed up on the barracks to see what was going on and got hit. Off he rolled. Imagine, getting killed the last day before being liberated.

There were Russian prisoners in Stalag 7-A, but we were warned we would be shot if we crossed over into their compound. But there were some holes in the wire between us, and at night we'd sometimes go over there. We'd trade food for little trinkets they made. I've still got a couple of their cigarette holders. They were pretty good guys, but they were tough. When we were liberated, we made the German guards who hadn't already fled tow our "honey wagon" around the compound. During our imprisonment we sometimes had to tow and dump the stuff out onto the fields. But now we thought it might be kind of fun to have the guards drag it around. We all cheered while they pushed and pulled it. The Russians then decided they would also have some fun. They lined up about ten of the guards just like we did, but they took the first guy and just slit his throat from ear to ear. They did the same thing to each of those Germans. I guess that was their idea of fun. Some of the Russians also went down to a nearby farmhouse and killed all the livestock and the farm lady and burned everything down to the ground.

A couple of us wandered out of the camp. I had picked up a bayonet, and we headed out to another farm. I noticed a chicken house out in back and a German lady on the porch. When she saw us heading for her chickens, she came running toward us, shaking her fist, and yelling, *"Nein, nein, nein!"* I told her to get out of the way. We were going to have chicken. We each got a chicken and started back toward the road. She came running after us, madder than all get out. But we had food, and nobody was going to take it away from us. I pulled the bayonet out and told my buddy, "She better get out of here because if she gets any closer, she's going to get it." I guess she got the message because she stopped. But by this time we were mad. There was a stump there in the front yard, and we killed both those chickens and gutted them right in front of her. Then we took them back and cooked them in the barracks. We needed that food. I still don't feel bad about what we did. We were just trying to survive.

After we were liberated we heard that many of the houses in Munich had Red Cross packages in their basements. The packages came in from Switzerland, and someone must have been intercepting them before they got to the camps. I think I received only a couple of Red Cross parcels, and those had to be shared. I can remember once getting a quarter of one which had some cigarettes in it. I was able to trade them for food and some Vitamin C tablets. On that long march from Nürnberg to Munich, five cigarettes netted me about six potatoes and a piece of fat raw bacon. That food and those vitamins helped get me through. Some of the guys would do anything to get a cigarette, including trading their food, and some of them died because their addiction was so strong.

An ironic final tragedy occurred when we were waiting to be flown out after our liberation. Hundreds of C–47s were lined up on what had been a grass fighter strip. It had been raining and the strip was kind of mushy. It was also short and there was a railroad viaduct at the end of the runway. About fifty of us and everything we had picked up after liberation were jammed into each plane. It was so crowded we didn't even have seats. A plane in front of us revved up and started down the runway. It got about three-quarters of the way down the runway when the pilot must have realized he didn't have sufficient flying speed to make it. I'm not sure what he did, but the plane veered to its left and crashed into a line of waiting C–47s which burst into flames. Maybe four guys jumped out, but the rest never did. When our pilot saw what had happened, he told us to throw out everything we owned—every bag, every souvenir, and all our equipment. We opened the side door and threw everything out. When we took off, the wings just vibrated from the weight of the plane. As we went over the viaduct we could look back and see those burning planes. All those ex-POWs had died in that last second before they were to fly home.

KARL-HEINZ HACKBARTH

Karl Hackbarth met his future wife while a POW near Detroit. Although fraternization between prisoners and civilians was strictly forbidden, Hackbarth and Stella Kohut became friends; in fact, so friendly the FBI investigated their relationship. In 1949, after Hackbarth had spent two additional years as a POW in Great Britain, they married in Berlin, Germany. Soon thereafter they returned to the United States where Hackbarth worked for thirty-three years at the Ypsilanti State Hospital in Ypsilanti, Michigan, just a few miles from where he and Stella first met. In 1987, he became a member of the board of directors of People to People International, an educational and cultural exchange organization dedicated to enhancing international understanding and friendship.

As a teenager, Hackbarth was not a member of the *Hitler Jugend,* but he was active for six months in the *Arbeitsdienst* (service work), before being called up for active duty.

I DID NOT BELONG to the *Hitler Jugend.* My father was a Social Democrat, and at that time in Berlin you could still belong to the *SPD* if it was not obvious. In February of 1939 everything changed. My boss suggested I immediately volunteer for the *Arbeitsdienst,* which I did. Then on January 1, 1940, I was drafted into an infantry regiment that was stationed in the Olympic Village in Berlin. I was put into the first company of the first battalion because of my height. We were supposed to be typical Aryans with blue eyes, blonde hair, and all that stuff, but when I look back at my regiment, there were also little fellows with black hair and brown eyes.

[Karl Hackbarth was captured in southern Italy on May 25, 1944.]

On January 22, 1944, the Americans landed just north of Naples and established their bridgehead at Anzio beach. In the middle of February I was part of a battle unit of some 6,000 men that was supposed to split the American bridgehead. We went in at 6:30 on the morning of February 16. Two heavy cruisers and four destroyers shelled us from the bay while planes bombed and strafed us from the sky. We did break through, but with terrible losses. My company went into the attack with 167 men and by 9:30 there were only eight of us left. Of course, we ran like hell. What else could we do?

By the end of February everything had come to a standstill. Hardly anything was going on. We were constantly exposed to freezing rain, and we couldn't use our foxholes because there was too much water in them. On March 2, I was hit by shrapnel in the leg and stomach and was in the hospital for four or five weeks. When I returned our unit no longer existed. We had been completely wiped out. We then reassembled in small fighting groups of fifty or sixty men called *Kampfgruppen*.

I'll never forget how American observer planes flew over and dropped cartons of cigarettes to lure us out of our bunkers. By then we were smoking tea leaves. One rainy day this plane dropped some five cartons of red Pall Malls. We didn't dare move, but one idiot ran out to get the cigarettes before they got all wet. It took the Americans about two minutes to zero in on us, and open up with mortars. For five cartons of cigarettes we lost eighteen men.

The *Waffen-SS* [the front-line fighting units of the *SS*] had the *999 Strafbataillon* [999 Penal Battalion] laying mines behind our position. This battalion was made up of guys who had been punished for one reason or another. Some were leftists or conscientious objectors. Others were criminals or had other problems. For example, an officer might get shot in the back, and if the authorities didn't know who did it, they would take ten or so of the soldiers and throw them into the 999. They had no weapons.

We had about forty soldiers left in our *Kampfgruppe*, and I was the oldest. Most were still teenagers. On May 25, we were supposed to be protecting the rear of a tank regiment. We happened to notice the 999ers placing T-mines in back of us. Our unit was obviously considered expendable, and headquarters had not even told us about these mines. I thought to myself, "The hell with it all." We held a democratic discussion about what we were going to do when the Americans came. We agreed we would take our weapons apart, bury them, and surrender. We actually voted to do this. We were trapped. The 999 Battalion had laid those mines behind us so we couldn't retreat and the American forces were in front of us. All of a sudden several Sherman tanks rolled up in front of us. We were lying low along the Mussolini Canal, but they raked us with machine gun fire. We lost fifteen of our men right away. One young man went crazy, jumped up, and started firing his submachine gun. They made a sieve out of him. All of a sudden the firing stopped. I was the only one who knew English. I was not very keen about going over the top to surrender, but I did. I took off my helmet and ammunition belt and shouted, "Stop firing, stop firing. We're surrendering." Some American yelled back, "Heinie, give up," or something like that. So I climbed out with my hands raised. This American master sergeant with gray hair came up to me and spoke perfect German: *"Mein lieber Freund, der Krieg ist vorbei"* ["My dear friend, for you the war is over"]. I said to him, "You're from Hamburg." He admitted he was, and I told him I was from Cuxhaven. Standing there on top of the Mussolini Canal we started hugging each other. I think this one moment saved our lives. He assured me we would be safe so the rest of the men surrendered and climbed out of the canal.

He took us back about 1,000 yards and told us he would wait there with us until some MPs could take over. He also assured us our personal belongings would be all right. In the distance we could see that the Americans had broken through our lines. German officers and men were wildly fleeing and getting shot down like a bunch of rabbits. I looked around and noticed there were dead German soldiers all about me, and some of their bodies had obviously been there for days. The American and Canadian dead had already been moved out.

The guards took everything away from us. I had a picture of my father in uniform standing next to my mother, and they took that as a souvenir. They left us with absolutely nothing. We were shipped south by truck to Naples. On the way the Italians threw stones and bottles filled with gasoline at us. We were lucky we had a sergeant who fired over their heads. Our first POW camp was right by the Adriatic Sea. It was a transition camp where we were interrogated.

The first thing they did was separate the Austrians from the Germans. They told us that the Austrians were no longer allies of the Germans. Even before we were captured we beat up some of the Austrians because they were trying to run away. They insisted we had forced them into the war, but we pointed out that Hitler was an Austrian. That first night in the transitional camp a German voice came over the loudspeaker, "Anyone interested in staying alive should come over to the gate. We will help you." The next night they repeated the message, telling us it was our last chance. The Austrians were the first to go. Most of us were still strongly nationalistic and thought Germany would still win the war. The SS types were in charge, and they immediately classified anyone who wanted to go over to the other side as a traitor. I know of a couple cases where suspected prisoners were dragged into the latrines, killed, and thrown into the toilets. They just disappeared. Such stories naturally had an effect on the rest of us.

Those of us picked to be interrogated were moved into a little circle around the only tree in the compound. We received nothing to drink for eight hours, but were told we would get something after they finished questioning us. I was the first to be interrogated. I stood at attention and gave my name, rank, and serial number. The major who interrogated me spoke fluent German. He put a package of cigarettes on the table and told me to take one, but I told him I didn't smoke. He then told me not to worry because all the things I was supposed to tell him he already knew. So I told him, "If you already know everything, I don't have to talk to you." That was the wrong thing to say. He shouted, "You know, we have to classify what kind of German you are, and we are classifying you a Nazi who should be shipped to the salt mines." I thought, "Oh, my, I said the wrong thing. Maybe I should have at least taken the cigarettes." So I asked him, "Can I smoke now?" He answered, "Not my cigarettes." So I took out my tin and started to roll one of my own, but he took it away from me and sent me outside. It was extremely hot, and I was ordered to stand there bare-headed in the blistering sun without moving. Every time I moved the MP jabbed me with the barrel of his machine gun. In the meantime, others came out and immediately went over to get a drink of water. Finally, after two hours, they brought me back in, and the major asked if I wanted to change my statement. I told him since I hadn't said anything there was nothing to change.

He told me he was putting me into a special battalion for hard-core Nazis and then sent me over to the main camp. Each day we were sent out to sweep sand off the main road with something about the size of a clothes brush. This was our punishment. Finally, someone asked if any of us spoke English. I raised my hand so I became the interpreter for the Lieutenant Colonel who was in charge of our group. So once again being able to speak English really helped me.

About the same time the Allies were landing on the beaches of Normandy, we were put on a Liberty ship and joined a convoy that included two POW ships, a hospital ship, and some thirty-five or so empty freighters. We knew we were sailing to the U.S., but we knew nothing about the state of the war except that every half hour we had air-raid and submarine alarms. We all were wearing our life jackets. There we were, all lined up, with half of us looking up at the sky and the rest looking down at the water. I thought to myself, "Wouldn't it be terrible if I made it this far in the war only to be sunk by one of our own submarines."

We landed in Norfolk, got our new uniforms with PW stamped on them, a blue fluffy hat, underclothes, and a pair of shoes. I was not terribly worried about anything. I was still a young man, and I had always been very independent, so the only person I really had to worry about was my mother. We left Norfolk on a train. We couldn't believe we were allowed to sit in upright seats on a Pullman car. There were a couple of guards in the front and back of each car. If you had to use the bathroom, you had to raise your hand, and a guard would escort you. We wondered what would happen if ten of us would have rushed them, because they wouldn't have known which of us to shoot.

The train went straight through until we hit Fort Custer, just outside of Battle Creek, Michigan. Our guards marched us into camp and encouraged us to sing German songs. They then assigned us tents because all the barracks were full. When we went to the mess hall to eat, we found eggs, white bread, jam, butter, and peanut butter, which we had never heard of. We ate like pigs. Some of the younger Germans came up and asked, "Karl, what do you think?" I told them, "Eat as much as you can because we never know what we'll get tomorrow. Remember, they told us they were going to ship us to the salt mines."

That night a couple of us were lying around in our tents when someone suggested we investigate the gallon jugs in the mess hall with "peanut butter" marked on their sides. We wanted to know what that meant and thought we should try some. So we sneaked in and took a couple of these jugs to our tent. There was oil floating on top of the peanut butter, but we didn't know you were supposed to mix it in, so we drank it. Well, that night the guards wondered why we had to make all those trips to the latrine.

Fort Custer was fantastic. In some of the other camps, such as those in Mississippi and Texas, the men had a terrible time picking cotton and doing other difficult and even dangerous jobs. Often they did not get enough to eat, and the weather and bugs were terrible. They were treated no better than the blacks who worked alongside them. We had two prisoners come to us who were just skin and bones. They had been forced to pick cotton and drain swamps in the Mississippi delta. They worked long hours every day and received very little to eat or drink. They looked like skeletons. We were able to give them some of our food. Of course, a lot of American POWs held in Germany also lost fifty or more pounds. So I never saw this mistreatment as something terribly one-sided. Both sides were guilty. It's just that we lost the war so people heard much more about the German mistreatment of Allied prisoners.

[According to the 1929 Geneva Convention, captors could require enlisted men to work, but occasionally they went on strike, and, like all prisoners, they enjoyed fooling their guards.]

About 600 of us were sent to Shelby, Michigan, to work in the orchards. A Captain Palmer was in charge, but he spoke no German; in fact, nobody among the Americans spoke German. In the evening people would drive up to our camp and try to talk to us over the fence. We would sing German songs, and sometimes the people would throw cartons of cigarettes over the fence. Everything went well for the first week, but some of the farmers did not treat us well. They wanted us to pick more cherries than we possibly could and then would complain to Captain Palmer who reported us to Colonel Edwin Reynolds, the commander of POWs at Fort Custer. All we had to drink while working was warm water. There were also a couple of other violations of the Geneva Convention which, of course, we knew by heart. One farmer tried to feed us corn, but we thought corn was for pigs. He didn't want to give us our morning and afternoon rest periods, which we did not accept. Captain Palmer threatened to reduce our beer and food ration. He told us we were a disgrace to the German army and then used armed guards to threaten us. I told him open arms in camp was a violation of the Geneva Convention.

We then picked even fewer cherries. It was passive resistance. Because I was the translator, Captain Palmer singled me out to punish. He put me in a detention tent and sentenced me to bread and water for a week. The medical officer examined and weighed me and told me to behave or I might have to serve an additional week. Our chief cook was Hans Croll, a fellow prisoner who told me not to worry about food. That first night I ate my bread, but I was still hungry. About two in the morning our camp dog, Fritz, came scratching at my tent. The guard was half asleep. Attached to Fritz's collar was a bag containing two pork chops and some liver sausage. I ate everything, but I didn't know what to do with the bones so I buried them in a hole under the bed posts.

This happened each night. On the third day the medical officer weighed me and was amazed to discover I had gained half a pound. After one and a half weeks I had gained another pound. So the doctor told me, "Well, this is not punishment. I'm going to tell Captain Palmer to release you." They never figured it out until we broke camp, and they discovered all the bones, but by this time it was October, and I was on a truck going back to Fort Custer.

Life was good at Fort Custer, although there were a couple of unpleasant incidents. There were wounded American soldiers in the camp hospital, and one of them hit a prisoner with his crutch and another drove his wheelchair into several of the POWs. It was a reaction and I could understand it. We were healthy looking, and these American boys were all shot up.

The worst thing that happened at Fort Custer was a terrible accident. A bunch of prisoners were returning on a truck from farm work when they were hit by a train. Sixteen of them were killed. We never heard anything about it until a couple of days later. Apparently it was foggy or rainy, and it was an unprotected railroad crossing. Either the truck stalled or the driver didn't see the train coming. Everyone was killed instantly. Every barracks had a memorial for those fellows. In fact, they are buried at Fort Custer in a corner of the U.S. Veterans National Cemetery with ten other German prisoners. Each November those who died have been remembered in a memorial service called *Volkstrauertag*

[People's Memorial Day] which is attended by both Germans and Americans.

[It is difficult to generalize about the guards' treatment of their prisoners. It was not a desirable job, and early in the war they were often poorly trained. Then, too, external events could influence their behavior.]

The guards were not overly nice to us, but there was a change in their attitude about the middle of December 1944 when the Ardennes offensive started [the Battle of the Bulge]. We didn't know anything about it, but all of a sudden we noticed this change on the part of the guards. They became real friendly and nice. One of them even said, "Hey, I got to be nice to you guys because one day I might be your prisoner." They couldn't do enough for us. But after the failure of the German offensive, they let us have the usual treatment again with both barrels.

[Both Hackbarth and his father were POWs in the United States, but rank and class prevented any chance for a meeting.]

My father was a noncomissioned naval officer. He was badly wounded and captured during the Normandy invasion. He was sent to America, and I found out he was at Camp Forrest, Tennessee. I applied a couple of times to visit him. I also tried to get a transfer to his camp, but the authorities would not let an enlisted man go to an officers' camp. So we never got together. There was much more political factionalism in the officers' camps than in ours. Hitler had personally created the navy, and so its officers and enlisted men tended to be strong supporters of National Socialism. On the other hand, these same men were among the first to know that Germany could not win the war. They knew the German navy was simply too small; for example, when the *Bismarck* went down it took with it almost 20 percent of the entire German navy. So at Camp Forrest they had many heated discussions on the subject. I later found out my father had been repatriated in August of 1945 as one of the first from the States to be sent home. He landed in Bremerhaven and had to walk on crutches all the way to Berlin. It took him more than two months.

[Prisoners were not allowed to fraternize with their captors, but, of course, many of them did.]

In March of 1945, 200 of us were assigned to the Romulus Air Force Base close to where Detroit Metro Airport is today. I was the camp spokesman and interpreter. We were assigned as orderlies, cooks, or handymen, and it was good duty. Colonel Rowl was the commanding officer. He looked and acted like a Prussian. He had a short haircut and drove a red Packard. When he drove on base, any soldier who saw him just disappeared. If the soldier wasn't fast enough, Colonel Rowl would get out of his Packard, inspect him, and always find something wrong. I was his orderly for four months. We had several long talks, and I really came to respect him. He was 100 percent American and professional soldier. He told us, "You are my prisoners, and you are my enemies. I didn't want you over here, but since you've been assigned to me, I will do everything I can to make it comfortable for you. I only ask that you do what you're told. If you don't, you will be punished." He lived by those words. He was a marvelous man. I even met his wife; in fact, I served as their bartender at some of their parties.

In Romulus we had contact with a German Lutheran church that was located in Detroit. Emil Schmitt was the minister, and he would come on post to direct our church services. One day he brought six big boxes that were supposed to be filled with Bibles and song books. He told us to take off the first couple of layers of books. Underneath were all kinds of foodstuffs and cigarettes. There were also several individual packages from members of his church. They even had their names attached to these packages. I decided to send thank-you notes to them, and I gave these notes to an American woman named Stella Kohut who worked at the base. I asked her to tell the parishioners, "The shipment has arrived."

[Karl's wife Stella takes up the story at this point.]

I was a civilian employee for the War Department working in Purchasing and Contracting at the Romulus Air Force Base. My mother had always told me about the handsome German soldiers of World War I, and that impressed me. I met Karl when he taught me to play three-ball French billiards. Of course, there was an anti-fraternization regulation, but we continued to talk. Evidently someone became suspicious and notified the FBI. The day the FBI showed up, was the day I had this list of Detroit families, all of whom had German names, and their telephone numbers. I rushed to the bathroom and tried to flush the list down the toilet, but it wouldn't flush. Someone yelled, "Come out immediately, or we'll break the door down." They thought they had caught some kind of Nazi spy who was undermining the security of America. The FBI kept me in confinement for three days, but I wasn't that worried because I was innocent.

I corresponded with Karl after he was sent to England. In August of 1948, I was sent to Berlin as a secretary working in the headquarters of the American Occupation Forces. Karl had already arrived in March. We were married June 18, 1949, in Berlin—the first marriage of an American woman to a former German POW. We even had a five-piece orchestra. We paid for it and the entire wedding with cigarettes, canned milk, canned meat, and candy.

[Both sides attempted to propagandize their captives; the Allies also attempted to reeducate select POWs; Karl continues his narration.]

At the end of the war the Americans showed us all kinds of propaganda about what had happened in the concentration camps. They showed us exhibits, magazines, newspapers, and films on the atrocities. There were also newsreels of bombed-out German cities. The majority of us just could not believe this had happened. We wondered if we would ever find our parents again. So when we were told we would soon be shipped home, we were a bit reluctant. There just seemed to be nothing left in Germany.

I had taken correspondence courses at Fort Custer through Ohio State University on democracy and other political subjects. The educational officer at Fort Custer told me I had to get away from Nazism and learn about democracy. He told me that the U.S. was the cradle of democracy. So I learned about 1776 and all those other marvelous events of the American past. But when I was shipped to England, I was once again put in a reeducation program where I had to learn about another kind of democracy. When I arrived in Berlin in March of 1948, the Social Democrats were there to greet me. They told me to forget all the democracy I had learned in the U.S. and England because theirs was the only true democracy.

[Like so many POWs held in the States, Hackbarth assumed he would be sent back to Germany at the end of the war; instead, he spent an additional two years in England.]

In April of 1946, our documents labeled us in certain ways. Some of us had "G's" on our papers which we thought meant we were being sent to Germany. What we didn't know was that "G" also stood for Great Britain. So I spent two more years as a POW in England. In the U.S. we had all the food we could want but no freedom; in England it was just the opposite. I was put in a camp in northern England with practically all Africa Corps prisoners. They were still walking around with their Iron and Knight's Crosses on their uniforms. They even greeted us with *Heil Hitler*. The Africa Corps prisoners classified us according to where we were captured. If we had been captured in Italy, we were not worth much. If we came from Normandy, we were worth less than nothing. We wondered if we were back in a Nazi training camp. But by this time the majority of us were convinced there was no future in any of the old politics. So we just ignored the Africa Corps prisoners, especially after we realized they no longer had any power.

2
Captured!

As much as I tried to rationalize my capture by telling myself that I had absolutely no other choice but to surrender, I think the main reason I was trying to forget it is, deep inside myself, I had the feeling I was a coward.

AMERICAN POW

I was so hungry and exhausted. I thought I was going to die. I was in such bad physical and emotional condition. In fact, after he stuck that gun in my back, I thought maybe he would have done me a favor if he had pulled the trigger.

GERMAN POW[1]

A SOLDIER SUFFERED A series of shocks during and immediately after being captured. One moment he was ostensibly an independent force fighting for his country. The next, he was reduced to a helpless object at the mercy of his enemies. As one newly captured American prisoner put it, "You suddenly realize that by passing from the right side of the front to the wrong you have become a nonentity in the huge business of war."[2] Often hungry and sleepless, sometimes feel-

---

[1]Allan Kent Powell, *Splinters of a Nation: German Prisoners of War in Utah* (Salt Lake City, Utah: University of Utah Press), 49.

[2]Powell, *Splinters of a Nation*, 41.

ing an element of shame about the capture itself, and certainly fearing possible execution, the new prisoner faced a most uncertain future. He was also subjected to an interrogation that at times could be brutal. American prisoners also experienced long, humiliating marches, as well as dangerous, debilitating train rides before finally reaching their permanent prison camps.

Allied airmen faced unique dangers. Bailing out of a plane was itself perilous, but landing could be even more hazardous. Revenge-minded citizens, understandably angered by what often appeared to be saturation bombing of non-military targets, sometimes took matters into their own hands, and high-ranking Nazi officials publicly encouraged such actions, especially after the massive air raids of 1944 and '45. Propaganda minister Josef Goebbels editorialized in the May 27, 1944, *Völkischer Beobachter*, "It seems to us hardly possible and tolerable to use German police and soldiers against the German people when they treat murderers of children as they deserve." A few days later, Hitler confidant Martin Bormann admitted that civilians had murdered Allied flyers: "Several instances have occurred where members of the crews of such aircraft, who have bailed out or who have made forced landings, were lynched on the spot immediately after capture by the populace, which was incensed to the highest degree." And Albert Hoffmann, a national defense official in Westphalia, announced, "Fighter-bomber pilots who are shot down are in principle not to be protected against the fury of the people."[3]

Newly captured German prisoners were usually penned in a series of uncomfortable transitional camps, and similarly interrogated, before eventually boarding a ship for an unknown destination. Describing the typical disorientation and vulnerability of these German prisoners, historian Ron Robin writes, "Captivity destroyed all remnants of their predictable routine and hurled the

---

[3]After the deadly fire bombing of Dresden, Josef Goebbels suggested to Hitler that an equal number of Allied POWs be shot to deter future raids. The postwar Nuremberg War Crimes Trials uncovered these proclamations and many other incidents concerning downed airmen; see S. P. MacKenzie, "The Treatment of Prisoners of War in World War II," *The Journal of Modern History* (September 1994), 494–5 and Durand, *Stalag Luft III*, 50.

surrendering troops into a maelstrom of disorder, uncertainty, and disgrace. . . . At every stage of the arduous journey from the temporary stockades in Europe and Africa to POW camps in the United States, the prisoners were systematically deprived of all remaining symbols of their past, pride, and identity."[4]

Popular cultural myths embrace the image of the courageous prisoner whose indomitable spirit remained resolute, whatever the circumstances. In truth, prisoners of all nationalities often broke down and talked. This was certainly true of many enlisted men who were poorly trained, recent inductees or, in the case of German soldiers, after they knew the war was a lost cause. But officers also often told interrogators what they wanted to know. Yet, few of those interviewed for this book admitted volunteering anything but their name, rank, and serial number, as mandated by the 1929 Geneva Convention.

Those doing the interrogating had a considerable initial advantage because newly captured soldiers were often injured, exhausted, and disoriented. Realizing this, the British attempted to separate German prisoners into black, white, or gray groups depending on the intensity of their allegiance to Hitler. The British were tough, successful interrogators. According to one participant, even with hardened Nazis, they often successfully exploited the prisoner's fear of being turned over to the Russians:

A Russian-speaking interpreter, wearing a KGB uniform, would sit in on the interrogation of recalcitrant prisoners. And if his presence failed to frighten the prisoner, the ostentatious stamping of the prisoner's file with "*NR*" usually did. To the prisoner's query as to what "*NR*" meant, the reply was "*Nach Russland*" [to Russia].[5]

According to American intelligence officer Werner Meier, after the Normandy invasion American interrogators also effectively

---

[4]Ron Robin, *The Barbed-Wire College: Reeducating German POWs in the United States During World War II* (Princeton, N.J.: Princeton University Press, 1995), 30, 32.

[5]Colonel A. P. Scotland, *The London Cage* (London: Evans Brothers, 1957), 70.

employed the threat of turning over newly captured prisoners to
the Russians:

> Our job was to deal with the raw meat that was immedi-
> ately sent to us, to interrogate these newly captured sol-
> diers while they were still in battle shock. When a man
> has just been taken in a fire fight, has a gun in his back,
> and doesn't really know if he's going to be shot or not—and
> I assure you some of them were—he's going to talk. I hate
> to admit this, but the difference between a new prisoner
> surviving or not was often the trigger finger of a soldier
> who very possibly considered it an undue burden to move
> his captive safely to the rear lines, especially if he was in
> hostile territory. By the time such a prisoner reached me,
> my job was relatively easy.
>
> Of course, we had an advantage over our German
> counterparts. We were interrogating prisoners toward the
> end of the war, when all but the most fanatic knew the end
> was near. It was much more difficult to break sergeants
> and officers. You sometimes could if you had the time, but
> our technique was to get the enlisted men first. "Hans,
> Fritz, what do you know?" And believe me, sometimes
> they'd tell you even without asking. The men I worked
> with never used force, although we would sometimes
> threaten to turn prisoners over to the Russians if they did-
> n't cooperate. And this threat occasionally even worked on
> officers. I would guess that eighty percent of our German
> prisoners told us what we wanted to know.[6]

German interrogators could employ their own equivalent of
Nach Russland. If an Allied prisoner proved too stubborn, those

---

[6]Personal interview with author. Werner Meier was born near Hamburg,
Germany, but because of harsh economic times he and his parents moved
to the United States in 1928. Drafted into the U.S. Army, Meier eventually was commissioned a lieutenant and trained in intelligence, in part
because of his ability to speak German. He parachuted into Normandy on
D-Day with an Airborne unit and was later wounded in the Battle of the
Bulge where his prime duty was the front-line interrogation of newly
captured German soldiers.

doing the questioning would simply announce, "We'll have to turn you over to the *Gestapo*." This technique apparently worked particularly well on captured airmen who clearly understood the advantages of remaining under the control of the Luftwaffe.[7] And if the American prisoner happened to be Jewish, interrogators sometimes asked him if he understood the status of Jews under the Third Reich.[8]

American and German prisoners experienced vastly different traveling conditions en route to their permanent camps. American captives were either marched on foot or jammed into "40-and-8" railroad box cars. Prisoners were sometimes locked in these cars for days, without food, water, or any kind of sanitary facilities. The result, according to ex-POW Kenneth Simmons, was "a trip that would turn men into swine."[9] Compounding the danger was the "friendly" fire of Allied planes that had no way of knowing who was trapped inside their targets. It is no exaggeration to compare this harrowing experience to the notorious "Middle Passage" endured by captive Africans on their way to slavery in the New World. German prisoners initially suffered similar dangers, but once safely on board ship creature comforts greatly improved, although they did face the possibility of being sunk by their own U-boats. Once they had landed safely in the United States, German prisoners were amazed to discover the comfort of a Pullman car.

This chapter follows the experiences of four American and two German prisoners from the moment of their capture, through

---

[7] For an excellent description of German interrogation techniques used on captured Allied airmen, see Arthur A. Durand, *Stalag Luft III*, 62–67. Psychiatrist Judith Herman, in her *Trauma and Recovery* (New York: Basic Books, 1992), 116, warns that "*complicity* and *cooperation* are terms that apply to situations of free choice. They do not have the same meaning in situations of captivity."

[8] Leonard Winograd, "Double Jeopardy: What an American Army Officer, a Jew, Remembers of Prison Life in Germany," *American Jewish Archives*, Vol. 28 (Cincinnati, 1976), 11.

[9] Kenneth W. Simmons, *Kriege* (New York: Thomas Nelson & Sons, 1960), 210.

their initial interrogation, and on to their eventual arrival in a permanent prison camp. Oskar Schmoling tells what it was like to face the very real possibility of immediate execution; Glenn C. Miller graphically describes the horrors of the "Middle Passage"; Ernst Floeter finds his capture to be a dream fulfilled; Jewish Americans Daniel Abeles and Matthew Radnossky experience vastly different treatment at the hands of their German captors; and Tuskegee airman Alexander Jefferson describes the unique experience of being a black man captured by Hitler's alleged master race.

OSKAR SCHMOLING

Only sixteen years old when captured by the Americans, Oskar Schmoling may well have been the youngest German POW held in the United States when he arrived in July 1944. Immediately after his capture in Normandy, he thought he was going to be executed, an experience so harrowing that he has never before described it to anyone.

I WAS BORN DECEMBER 3, 1927, in Rastenburg, East Prussia, which is now part of Poland. I turned sixteen in December of 1943 and was drafted into the *Arbeitsdienst* which during the war performed all kinds of jobs from building barracks to transporting war materials. I was eventually put into an anti-aircraft unit and sent for six weeks of training to Linz, Austria. Then I was shipped to Normandy to work in an anti-aircraft unit. We were supposed to replace those members who had turned eighteen and were to be transferred into the regular army. We arrived outside of Cherbourg on June 4, just two days before the Normandy invasion. Our officers knew something was going on, so the older boys had to stay because we were not experienced enough to replace them. Initially, we just helped doing little things around the area, but after the Americans landed, we blew up our anti-aircraft guns and fled into Cherbourg. By that time it didn't matter what kind of unit we came from—artillery, infantry, or *Arbeitsdienst*—we all became replacements for those who had been killed or wounded. The youngest of us were put to work carrying wounded soldiers to the rear and transporting ammunition to the front.

It's difficult to say what you feel as a sixteen-year-old boy. I didn't want to be a hero, but I wanted to be strong and do what the others before me had done. Sometimes I felt like a man, but there were also moments when I felt like a child. One of my brothers had already been killed in Italy. I had another brother in

Russia and one in France. My dad had been in World War I, but he was also drafted into the Second World War and served in Poland and Russia. I wanted to be proud, but I could also still feel the child inside of me. I didn't know if I would ever see any of my family again and I even thought I might get killed. But then I would say to myself, "It doesn't matter what happens to us. Let's get them." Your attitude would change back and forth. If you had eaten and slept well, you felt more like fighting. But if you were tired, hungry, and thirsty, you thought, "I wish it was over."

I was captured on June 23, 1944. There were maybe 80 or 100 people around us. We had just delivered some ammunition to the front. When I came back, planes bombed and strafed us. Everybody was running around. Then their artillery opened up. We never knew exactly where the enemy was. Finally, machine guns and every other kind of weapon you can imagine started firing into our position. We expected the Americans to be in front of us, but they had already encircled us and were coming up from the rear. They pushed the German troops in front of them back into us. Our soldiers came in waving white flags and telling us to throw away our weapons. My first thought was, "The war is over. Maybe an armistice has been declared." There was total confusion. Then someone told us to put up our hands. So we threw away our weapons and raised our hands. It all happened so fast.

What happened next I have never told anybody, not even my parents. We were marched three or four miles back to the American rear lines with our hands up. Somehow we felt those guarding us were more frightened than we were. It was hot, and we hadn't had a bath for weeks. We were dirty, hungry, and tired. They put us in a big yard, and we were checked for weapons. Some of us lost our watches. I can remember one American was so proud that he had seven or eight of our watches on his arm. A rumor circulated that Germans had killed some civilians, and this American officer came up and picked out ten of us to be shot for revenge. I was one of the ten. He lined us up and told us to face this stone wall. A command was given, and we heard the ammunition being loaded. We knew they were lining up their machine guns. I could already feel the hot bullet searing my body. At that moment I remembered my religion and murmured a simple prayer: "Lord, I cannot better myself anymore; the end has come.

I pray that my mother will be able to take the news, and I wish they would pull the trigger and get it over with."

To this day I don't know whether they were just trying to scare us or whether some higher-ranking officer ordered them not to kill us. I just don't know. But I do know I can't forget it.

GLENN C. MILLER

Glenn Miller[10] was a nineteen-year-old draftee when the Germans captured him during the first days of the Battle of the Bulge. He was eventually sent to Stalag 4-B at Mühlberg and to nearby work camps at Torgau and Zeitz where conditions were often miserable, although he received good medical treatment for his frostbitten feet and his ear and neck infections. Miller, whose experiences as a POW taught him self-confidence and patience, later became philosophical about his experiences. He also wrote his war memoirs, parts of which are included, although not verbatim, in this remembrance.

WHEN MY DOCTOR FOUND out after the war I had been a prisoner, his first question was, "How did the Germans treat you?" That seemed to be the first question and principal concern of everyone who learned I had been a POW. They must have assumed the Germans treated us like they did the Jews and other political prisoners. In a way, there were two kinds of Germans: One type led the country, launched the Holocaust, and embraced the myth of the master race. Then there were the normal Germans, people like you and me, who were victims of the German belief in order first and results later, and who seldom questioned their national leaders. These included most of the soldiers who fought the frontline war and were civilized enough to follow the Geneva Convention and treat prisoners accordingly. The first type promoted tremendous evil, but even among the second kind, as with people everywhere, there were a few bad apples.

I got to the front lines with the 106th Infantry just in time for

---

[10]Glenn C. Miller entered the service as Glenn C. Potter. After the war he legally changed his name to Miller.

the Battle of the Bulge. When all hell broke loose on December 16, we were kind of a backwater group, and the Germans just bypassed us. But by December 20 they decided to clean up what they had left behind. They fired some artillery rounds into us and then sent an officer carrying a white flag of truce to talk to us. Our officers decided to surrender. We hadn't moved an inch since the battle began, and the Germans were already ten miles past us.

There were probably a thousand of us who surrendered outside the town of Schoenberg. I never even fired a shot, and that was true for most of us. Major General Alan Jones, who was our divisional commander, was blamed, but we were one division trying to cover a twenty-seven-mile front which was ridiculous. I don't blame the general. His son was captured, he suffered a heart attack, and his reputation was ruined.

There's so much luck in combat. I had an 88-mm shell land twenty feet from me, but it was a dud. Another guy had an unexploded 88 shell go between his legs into the side of his foxhole. He went simply mad. They had to haul him out. Chance was everything. But such things are easier to handle when you are only nineteen. At the time, I thought it was all a great, glorious effort. I was very put out that I was captured without ever having fired my rifle. I did have one chance to shoot at a German position, but I only had a carbine, and it was too short range. When I asked my buddy to lend me his rifle, he said, "No, if you shoot at them, they're going to shoot back." It was depressing being on the front and then suddenly being out of the war without ever having done anything. I certainly don't look at it that way now, and that's why I'm not willing to point fingers at those who surrendered us.

Looking back, it seems that the surrender was a wise move to save lives from being wasted on a futile battle. At any rate, we were lined up in columns-of-fours, counted, and then marched down the road towards Germany. It was very cold, and we saw several frozen bodies partially covered with snow. That first night we were bedded down in an old trolley barn with no heat and no glass in the windows. The floor was concrete, and it had a drain about five feet from where I lay down. In the morning I noticed that my blanket was all wet. That drain had become clogged with urine and feces and had backed up underneath my blanket. I was pretty miserable. I shook out the blanket as well as I could, but when I stood up, I had a terrific pain in the back of my right foot.

I took off my shoe and discovered I had a blister on my heel and my socks stuck to the scab. While on patrol a couple of days before I had found these two odd-sized rubber boots that I pulled on over my leather army boots. For my left foot I had a size 12 right-footed boot but at least it was loose. But for my right foot I had jammed a size 10 over my 10½ boot, and that had caused the blister. I had to limp along for about a half hour until the scab pulled loose from my sock; then the heel didn't hurt until the next morning, when I had to go through the same routine. Both of my feet ended up frost-bitten.

On December 24 we were jammed into these railroad box cars. It was so crowded we could not all sit down at once so we took turns standing and sitting. A P–47 strafed us and killed several guys although no one was touched in my car. We could smell those 50-caliber bullets ripping through the sides of those wooden cars. The Germans opened the doors after the airplanes left and rushed around looking for the wounded. They were very concerned. I remember seeing this one guy with his hands across his stomach with stuff oozing out between his fingers. He turned his back to me, and there was a big hole in the middle of his back. One of those 50-caliber bullets had gone right through him. I doubt that he survived. We counted nine guys killed and forty-seven wounded. Local Germans wheeled the wounded on these four-wheeled carts and took them to a nearby town.

I spent Christmas in that boxcar. There was no heat or water. The Germans would not let us out to relieve ourselves so everybody went to the bathroom in their steel helmets. These helmets are round so when the train jerked, they tipped over, and you'd end up sitting in your own crap and urine. Some of the guys tried to sing Christmas carols. They would sing a few words, but then nothing. There was just no spirit to go on. It was a pretty miserable Christmas, but even at my lowest, I never got to the point where I no longer gave a damn. I thought I would make it. Survival is a basic drive that doesn't take any mental skill. So I just reacted as best I could. It also helped that I was only nineteen. You know, there aren't any bullets that can kill a teenager.

They eventually marched us off that train and into a swamp. There was a thin sheet of ice on it, and we kept breaking through. The water was almost up to our knees. Then they formed us into a big *POWUSA*. We looked like a big marching band. I give them a plus for that. We stood there for about three hours. Later that day when we were marching up the road, some P–38s came over, and one of them used his contrails to spell out *POWUSA* in the sky above us. We felt pretty good about that.

We finally came to the town of Koblenz on the Rhine River. We were supposed to stay in Stalag 12-A at Limburg, but the night before it had been bombed by the British so we were put in an old riding stable. We received about a cup of oatmeal that evening. We used our steel helmets to eat out of, the same helmets we had used on the train for a toilet. I remember rubbing the inside of my helmet with straw until I could not see any remains of its previous use.

The next several days we both walked and rode in box cars until we arrived on New Year's Eve at Stalag 4-B at Mühlberg on the Elbe River. We stood in the cold for several hours which was a terrible way to bring in the New Year. We were searched, relieved of our steel helmets and canteens, photographed, registered, and numbered. After that we were given a shower and the chance to see how much thinner we had become. When I put my clothes back on, I discovered I could not get my shoes on because my feet were so swollen. So I wore just my rubber boots instead. We were taken to some large barracks which were already occupied by hundreds of British prisoners who had evidently been there for years. They were neat and clean. They had established an organization, and they received their regular Red Cross parcels. I was sitting in the barracks dirty and depressed when this British prisoner came up, sat down in front of me, and gave me a KLIM [MILK spelled backwards] milk can filled with hot tea with sugar and cream in it. I later realized how much that had cost him. Probably the most expensive part was heating it. He must have noticed what a sad-looking creature I was and decided to do something to cheer me up.

That first night I woke up and realized I had to go. I started to get up, but it was too late. I evacuated everything right in my long-johns. I had zero control. I felt terrible about this. I tried to clean myself up, but I just couldn't, so I just laid back in bed feeling horribly depressed. The next morning the guy below me said, "Hey, you've got to take a bath, and if you don't, we'll do it for you." I got the message. I went out to this little concrete building which contained horse troughs with water running through them. The snow was blowing in through the open windows. It was colder than hell, and I had to strip and clean my long-johns. I can tell you, I didn't know how to face that. This English kid came up and said, "I'll clean your underwear for two cigarettes." I told him, "You've got a deal." He washed them, and I washed myself. We became pretty good friends after that.

ERNST W. FLOETER

While growing up in Stettin, in what is now western Poland, Ernst Floeter was no supporter of Hitler's race-conscious, Aryan nation; in fact, he admits that once the war started, his central objective was to be captured by the Allies and sent to America. He spent most of his POW days picking cotton in Texas and planning how he might become a permanent resident. He eventually succeeded. Today he is a professional photographer living in a small town just west of Lansing, Michigan.

I HAD NO GREAT plans for my future while I was in school; in fact, after the war broke out in 1939, and especially after the Americans entered in 1941, my goal was to become a prisoner and be sent to the United States. We were not Nazis. Our entire family and many others who sent their children to my school did not believe in National Socialism. We had to be careful not to say anything controversial in the *Gymnasium* because our parents could end up in a concentration camp. When the war broke out, my father pointed to the globe and said, "Look at France and England with all their colonies and look at America with all her resources. We'll never win the war." A family friend, who was an army colonel, also told us we were not going to win. When the weather was good, we also listened to radio London, although to be caught meant harsh punishment. The Reverend Dietrich Bonhofer operated not far from Stettin, but I never knew about him. If my father did, he never said anything. When you turned fourteen, you were supposed to join either the Marine, Air Force, Signal Corps, or Motor Branch of the *Hitler Jugend*. But I didn't do anything until I was seventeen years old, when the authorities decreed that every German my age had to report or be severely punished. I had no choice. I had to do it. I joined the *Motor Hitler Jugend*. We had meetings twice a week, but they were a joke. Our superior shouted at us all the time. One day two men came from the *National Socialistik Kraftfahrer Bund* [National Socialist Motor Union], and they were more interesting. They talked to us about how to build a road. A friend and I asked if they could use us. The next week we went to a meeting, and it was completely different. There was no *Heil Hitler*. We simply said *Guten Tag*. We drank our beer and told jokes, but we also learned something.

I was drafted in May into the *Arbeitsdienst*. Our Colonel friend had already urged me to volunteer for a specific army branch because my birth year, which was 1925, was to be drafted into the *SS*. That was certainly the last thing I wanted. The *SS* had already sent me a letter to report to their local headquarters which my mother took to the head of the local *Arbeitsdienst*. He told her not to worry and wrote her a letter to show the *SS*. That saved me; instead, I volunteered for the Signal Corps.

From my induction on I geared everything toward becoming a prisoner of war. That's all I thought about. During my basic training in Danzig for the Signal Corps, I was classified as a bad soldier because I made every possible mistake. So when time came for selection to sergeants' school, only three guys from our company did not qualify, and I, of course, was one of them. Instead, I was sent to Bamholder to the 91st Airlanding Division. On April 20, 1944, which was Hitler's birthday, our major told us we were destined for the decisive mission of the war. He meant, of course, the invasion of England; instead, we became regular infantry and were sent to Normandy.

We were situated in the middle of the Cotentin Peninsula, maybe twenty or thirty miles from Omaha Beach. Nothing really happened at first, and the French people were very nice. Such relations always depended on the German commander. If he was a good person, the French did all right; if he was bad, they suffered. I was a radio operator, and we were supposed to watch at night for paratroopers. I will never forget the night of June 5, 1944. We had been watching every night for the previous couple weeks and had seen very little. Rommel was away in Berlin, and nobody expected an invasion. The weather was so stormy that nobody was really watching the skies. All at once, I was awakened by very low-flying airplanes. Wave after wave of these big planes flew over. At first I thought they were on some big bombing mission over France, but then I realized the invasion had begun.

At the time, I thought the whole D-Day invasion was a perfectly executed American maneuver. Years later, when I was watching an American documentary about D-Day, I realized just how close to a disaster the invasion was. That first night and day we heard very little return fire from our German troops. There was no defense where we were located. Our division commander was killed the first day, so everything was chaos. We were retreating, but the Americans were everywhere. We took mortar fire from morning until night. But on June 13, I met my guardian angel. It was pitch dark, and we were running down a hill. The Americans were shooting at us, and I was wounded by shrapnel. Suddenly I was all alone. Everybody from my unit had moved on. That probably saved me because our regiment was totally destroyed. When I rejoined them, we formed a *Kampfgruppe*—a fighting group—consisting of whoever was still alive.

My personal liberation date was June 18. Our capture was more humorous than anything else. In the middle of the day I had crawled under an apple tree, ate my daily ration, and went promptly to sleep. That evening about seven o'clock someone woke me saying, "Hey, get up. The Americans are here." Americans were everywhere, and they were screaming and hollering. They sounded like a bunch of geese. One of our officers yelled, "Stand up and shoot." Instead, this one guy pulled out a white towel and began waving it. When the first American came up with his machine gun, I threw my rifle on the ground and thought, "Thank God, no more rifle drills."

Almost immediately, Red Cross ambulances drove up and took care of our wounded. The rest of us were standing in a long line with the officers off to the side. We were searched, and they took our knives and notebooks. I had a little good luck piece. I can still see this soldier in front of me. He threw it down on the ground. I said something in French, and he answered in French. So I asked him if I might keep it. He picked it up and gave it back to me, and I still have it.

We had to stand in a ditch with our hands in the air for what seemed like an eternity. Guarding us was an American with a machine gun. My arms got tired and then my glasses started to slip off my face. I thought if I tried to push them back, he would shoot me. When I tried to wiggle them back into place, the guard came up and put them back up on my nose. So my first impression of Americans was positive.

Then we were marched right to Omaha Beach where we were enclosed by a single wire. We stayed there about four days. On the first day we lined up to get K-Rations, and I went through that line three times. That evening somebody said, "If you are looking for good work, go at six in the morning to the gate. They are looking for ten volunteers." I did and ended up working in the mess hall. It was unbelievable. I saw how much food Americans wasted. There was this beautiful soup, and a lot of them just dumped it. The garbage cans were overflowing with food. We had to police up the area, and we found cigarette packages with cigarettes still in them. I pocketed everything I could. The whole thing was like a dream. I was only afraid we would be recaptured by the Germans.

DANIEL S. ABELES

Born of Jewish parents in Philadelphia, Sergeant Daniel Abeles was a radio operator and gunner on a B–17 who was shot down over Emden, Germany, and incarcerated in Stalag 17-B in Krems, Austria. Two of his fellow prisoners were Donald Bevan and Edmund Trzcinski, authors of the popular play and film, *Stalag 17*, which later inspired the even more popular American television series, *Hogan's Heroes*. Although not expressly mistreated because of his religion, Abeles continuously feared he might be.

I WAS SHOT DOWN on my nineteenth mission, but almost as bad was my first mission. I woke up in the morning and had diarrhea. I was scared but I didn't want anybody to know it. I went to breakfast, and afterwards I went to the latrine. Then we had to go to a briefing, after which I had to go to the bathroom again. Then we put on all our gear—our electric underwear and flak jacket and all that stuff. Well, I just got all that on, and I had to take it off to go again. After I got up in the air, I couldn't help myself, and I just let it go in my pants. It was about 45 degrees below zero at the altitude we flew so for the time being it didn't matter. When we landed, I was a mess. I ran right to the showers, and they sent the military police after me. When I told my commander what had happened, he told me I was jeopardizing other people's lives by flying when I wasn't 100 percent. I told him, "I didn't want you to think I was a coward."

After the war people would ask me how many parachuted jumps I made. I'd always tell them, "Two. My first and my last." You never really want to believe you are going to be shot down, but when you returned from a mission and went into the barracks and saw six or seven mattresses rolled up of guys who didn't make it back, that would make you think. I never thought about being killed but about being shot down.

The English bombed at night and we during the day, which was much more dangerous. I can especially remember two daylight raids on Berlin. The flak from Hamburg to Berlin was so thick you could walk on it. It was scary as all hell. The B–17 was supposed to be able to fly over the flak, but that was nonsense. The German fighters could also fly as high as we could. I later heard that more American airmen were killed than were ground soldiers. I was also amazed to find out the average number of missions was only six. If I had known about those averages, I would have run away.

I was shot down on April 19, 1944, over Emden. I was very, very lucky. When we were hit, it knocked out my oxygen and my intercom. I heard nothing at all about bailing out. But I looked through the fuselage and saw that the entire wing was on fire. There was nobody around except one guy who was on his first mission. He sat there frozen, so I pushed him out. Just then the plane dipped a bit but the pilot straightened it out. It takes me twenty times longer to tell this than it actually did to happen. Just three or four seconds after I bailed out, the plane exploded. The pilot and the co-pilot were killed. The pilot was a wonderful guy. We used to call him "Iron Ass" because he was just the opposite. He was a real sweet human being. While I was floating down in my parachute, the pilot of the ME–109 that shot us began circling me. He didn't shoot at me but he tried to dump my chute. He was so close I could see his eyes. He was actually grinning at me so I'm grinning back like, "Hey, this happens every day to me, you son-of-a-bitch." When I landed a bunch of farmers surrounded me and took me and our bombardier to the *Burgermeister*'s house. One of the farmers had hit the bombardier in the face with the butt of a rifle and smashed his nose in. I had a big gash on my hand and blood all over my face from wiping it with my hand. One of the farmers wanted to hit me but another one stopped him. He asked if I had a pistol. I had a little German in high school so I said, "*Kein Pistol.*" A couple of uniformed Germans then arrived and went first to the bombardier because he was a lieutenant. This one officer uttered something and hit him right across his broken nose. He then came up to me, looked at my dog tags, and said, "*Ach, Jude.*" He took out his gun, and I thought he was going to shoot me, but he just whacked me alongside the head. About two and a half hours later two *Gestapo* guys arrived. They must have gone to the same school. They went to the lieutenant first and whacked him right across the nose just like the other guys did. Then they hit me too. The next morning they put us on a train to Frankfurt. The entire railroad yard was a bombed-out mess. As we were marched off the train, the people threw rocks at us. They really thought every one of us was a Chicago gangster because of the propaganda they'd been fed.

We were taken to Dulag Luft at Wetzlar just north of Frankfurt for further interrogation. For three days I was confined to a very hot room containing only a bench. This was supposed to soften me up. During those three days I was repeatedly interrogated by men in *Luftwaffe* uniforms, but I suspected they were *Gestapo*. There wasn't too much physical abuse, but they did threaten me. They'd ask, "You know what is done with Jews here?" They tried to tell me their questions were only for the Red Cross, but that was a crock of shit because they asked me all kinds of military questions. The last day they asked when and where I was captured. Hell, they knew that. They asked me what kinds of bombs we carried. I told them stink bombs. I thought the guy was going to hit me. Only one guy would question me at a time. He had a pack of Camels and started smoking and blowing the smoke toward me. I knew what he was doing, but I didn't even smoke. We were then taken to the train station, put in box cars, and sent to Krems, Austria. The trip took three days and three nights. They'd let us out maybe once or twice a day. We'd get out and piss and shit, and the guards would say to the onlookers, "Look at the barbarians." The fact we had been locked up for eleven or twelve hours without any place to go was never mentioned.

At Stalag 17 they took pictures of us and shaved our heads. On my POW card they put a big red "J" for *Jude*. Later I asked our American chaplain, "Father Kane, I'm very anxious. I know what happened to Jews in Germany after *Kristallnacht*.[11] What

---

[11]On November 7, 1938, a young, disturbed Jew whose parents had been deported to Poland shot a minor official at the German embassy in Paris. When Ernst vom Rath died two days later, German thugs took to the streets and began attacking and burning Jewish businesses, synagogues, and homes. Encouraged by pronouncements from Josef Goebbels and his loyal press, *Kristallnacht*, or the Night of the Broken Glass, quickly spread across Germany. Thirty-six Jews lost their lives, and 814 shops, 171 homes, and 191 synagogues were destroyed.

should I expect?" He said, "It all depends how the war goes. If you were a Gentile and you escaped and were caught, you would be brought back. But if you escaped, nobody would ever hear from you again." There was no segregation of Jews in the Stalag 17, but it was scary. On our forced march at the end of the war, we saw these prisoners with the Star of David on their arms. They were on work gangs and had been sleeping in the fields. Some were dead, and others couldn't get up. The rest could barely walk. The Germans just threw the bodies into these big wagons. When somebody today says that all this never happened, I can tell you I saw it.

MATTHEW RADNOSSKY

Not all American prisoners were as badly treated as was Daniel Abeles; in fact, Matt Radnossky's life was saved by compassionate Catholic nuns and effective medical treatment. Like Abeles, Radnossky was Jewish and also shot down while flying a B–17 bomber. Wounded by flak and suffering an additional wound while parachuting to the ground, he miraculously survived, thanks to the excellent treatment he received in a Catholic civilian hospital. After the war, Radnossky returned to Germany to find those who had saved his life and to this day has retained his German contacts.

I WANTED TO FLY, I wanted to have a clean place to live, and I didn't want to slosh around in the mud. I had been in the cavalry ROTC at the University of Massachusetts, so I joined the air force. I had no romantic view about flying. I actually joined with a group of friends. We all went in together.

I was trained as a navigator and flew on a B–17. Our pilot was Harry Ayielle, our co-pilot was John Murphy, and the bombardier was Chuck Mueller. So we were a real United Nations. We flew some big missions: D-Day, two missions to Saint-Lô, Munich, Augsberg, and Dresden. On the fifteenth mission, Harry Ayielle decided he wanted to fly lead. Because I had considerable training, I was moved to another plane as deputy lead. My old crew suffered a mid-air collision. Everyone was killed except the tail gunner, Hastings Keys, who was the only one able to get out. I watched them go down over the channel.

I flew five or six more missions; then, I was moved to the lead plane. We were shot down over the *Lune Öl Fabrik* on November 21, 1944, on my twenty-sixth mission. It was a synthetic oil factory. We bombed it, and on the way back we were hit by fighters and had to fall back from the formation. We lost an engine and started to lose altitude, and then we got hit by flak. I was wounded in the cockpit; in fact, I was paralyzed. The plane was breaking up, so the bombardier strapped me onto the static line and dumped me out at about 24,000 feet. The only thing that worked during my jump was my parachute. I lost my escape kit and my boots. I was wearing a flak vest and the bullets seemed to go right through it. As I was coming down, I was shot again by a fighter, and a bullet went through my kidney. I wasn't really frightened. I just thought to myself, "If I don't make it what a shame. I won't know how it all ends up." But I made a fairly good landing in a tree and just hung there a couple of feet above the ground. A group of people approached me and one was a priest. He and a soldier carried me to a *Lazaretstadt* (hospital town) called Dechta and put me in a Catholic civilian hospital where I spent the next couple of months.

This hospital was run by nuns, although the head doctor was with the *Luftwaffe*. I had wonderful treatment from everyone. They did not know I was Jewish. I had planned very carefully ahead of time. I had three sets of dog tags. Whenever I flew over northern Germany, I was a Protestant. If we were flying over France, I was a Catholic. Otherwise I wore my regular tags. They operated on me and dressed my wounds. The bullet, by the way, is still in me. I spent Christmas and New Year's there. I was the only non-German in the hospital until they brought in another pilot who had been shot down. He was badly burned, and he also got very good treatment. They even assigned an Italian as our orderly. They called him *ein Gefangener* (a prisoner), I guess because Italy had left the war.

I had studied German in high school, which helped because in the hospital no one spoke English. I had books in the hospital, and I was able to read *Hamlet* and a few other things in German. There was also a Baedeker so I learned all about Germany. Most of the people in the hospital spoke a kind of *Platt Deutsch* which was easy to understand. I became good friends with one of the sisters, Hannalore Knabe. She treated me extremely well. Directly after the war I sent her and the others CARE packages. The head of the operation was Schwester Lucella who was a very old lady at that time. I can remember she packed me a big lunch when I finally left the hospital for a permanent prison camp. Thinking back, the most important thing was that these people were Catholics first and then Germans. Even when I was shot down, I remember local women bending over me and crying as I was lying on the ground. So these were not the evil beasts as they were so often portrayed. In fact, the entire experience had a positive effect on my life, and I look back with no regrets. My only negative flashbacks were of the plane going down. That was dreadful. To this day, I can still see that bursting flak. It always looked like a pair of Dutch pants. It was horrible. You never believed you could fly through it.

ALEXANDER JEFFERSON

Born on the west side of Detroit in 1921, Alexander Jefferson became one of the famous Tuskegee Airmen, those African-American pilots who so distinguished themselves during World War II. Like most of his Tuskegee colleagues, Lieutenant Jefferson sometimes had to fight against two enemies: the Germans, who were trying to shoot him out of the sky, and the racism of his own Army Air Corps. Arguably, the battles he helped fight for equal recognition and human rights on the home front helped prepare him to withstand the rigors of captivity.

IN JULY OF 1942 I joined the enlisted reserve of the Army Air Corps, as it was then called, because I wanted to fly. Later I found out there was a quota of blacks going into the Tuskegee program, and I had to wait until my turn came up. I already had my bachelor's degree from Clark College in Atlanta, so I started work on a master's in chemistry at Howard University. Then in April of 1943 I got my call to report to Tuskegee to begin flight training.

Our preflight and advanced training was exciting and hectic. We were all college graduates, and we were energetic and aggressive. I look back now and realize to be black then and to survive, you had to be that way. I think there were ninety of us who started in my class; at the end of our nine months of training only twenty-five survived. Some were eliminated for flying inadequacies and some for non-military reasons. Years later through the Freedom of Information Act we discovered there had been a quota for how many blacks were allowed to graduate. The phrase used to wash these guys out was "Eliminated while passing for the convenience of the government." Sometimes thirty or so men would go to sleep the night before graduation and then wake up in the morning to find that three or four of them had been eliminated.

That caused a lot of psychological stress among these guys; in fact, some of them are still psychologically wounded because they were washed out. Some had bought their uniforms and their parents and sweethearts were there for graduation. It was a loss of their manhood. I know in my class there were some guys washed out who could fly better than I could. They were certainly better soldiers than I was. Hell, I was a damned civilian, not a soldier.

[The U.S. Armed Forces remained rigidly segregated throughout World War II, and African-American servicemen had to confront the contradiction of fighting and dying for a country that did not grant them full citizenship. Jefferson had just pinned on his wings as a second lieutenant when he was involved in an infamous incident at Selfridge Field outside of Detroit when black officers attempted to integrate the white officers' club.]

We had been clamoring to get into the regular officers' club. If you were black, you were put on the morning report as transient even though you might have been there for two months. If you were white you were immediately classified as permanent personnel. Only permanent personnel had officers' club privileges. We had been paying our six dollars officers' dues just like everybody else so they gave us a room in the barracks—about as large as my present living room—and put a wooden bar in it. This was supposed to serve as our officers' club. Every day we would try to enter the white officers' club, and every day we would be turned away. The NAACP, the *Michigan Chronicle* [a black newspaper], and the Urban League began pressuring the authorities to break down the barriers. Then one day we got an order to report to the post theater. The fifty black officers and all the white officers went inside trying to figure out what was going on. Someone yelled, "Attention!" We popped to. Down the aisle came a two-star general, O. D. Hunter. He told us, "At ease, gentlemen." We sat down. He rambled on for about five or ten minutes and then he said, and I remember his words exactly, "Gentlemen, this is my airfield. As long as I am in command, there will be no socialization between white and colored officers." He paused and then asked, "Are there any questions?" Hell, we were second lieutenants. What could we say? We sat there in shock. Then he said, "If there are any questions, I will deal with that man personally." And he walked out.

We were confined to the post. The gates were locked and we were not allowed to communicate with anyone off base. A couple of days later we were loaded on a train but never told where we were going. We ended up at Walterboro Army Air Base in South Carolina where we were greeted by white soldiers in full battle dress. All this was within the reality of the times. Blacks were still second-class citizens, and especially in the South. The unspoken rule in the army then was if you went counter to the local or state laws, the army would not back you up. You were left on your own. We knew this. It was all part of living so we knew how to deal with it. We tested the system, as best we could, while keeping our noses clean. It was a constant struggle, but our willingness to fight on helped us survive.

[Early in 1944 the Air Corps shipped Alexander overseas as a replacement pilot to the 332nd Fighter Group stationed at Ramitelli Air Base, located in the heel of the Italian boot.]

I flew the P–51 thirty-two missions doing long-range escort flying. We were escorting B–17s and B–24s that were flying from Italy to targets in Greece, Germany, Rumania, France, and Austria. I flew several escort missions over the Ploesti Oil Fields in Rumania. They were the most heavily fortified targets in all of Europe. We would accompany the bombers to their turning point over the target; then we would veer off and wait to see how many flew out of all that flak. Those damn .88s did a tremendous amount of damage. Every time we saw a plane go down, we could chalk off ten men. Even the planes that made it out were all shot up. To stay in the air they would jettison everything aboard except the crew. We tried to protect them as best we could during the long flight back to their base. Over the years I often wondered if any members of those bomber crews ever thought about the black pilots who were at least part of the reason they were able to make it home and enjoy the privileges of this country.

[After being shot down, Jefferson was surprised to discover that his German captors often treated him with more respect and fairness than had some American white officers.]

I got shot down during my first strafing mission. That was August 12, 1944, in southern France. Our objective was to knock out these radar stations. We went in over the coast in four flights of four each. The first three sets of four got through okay. We were the last flight, and as we dived in from 15,000 feet at about 400 knots I saw Robert Daniels flying number two get hit. He was smoking and went on out to sea before we got to the target. The other three of us went right across the top of the target at about 100 feet. We got hits all over the target; then boom. I looked up and there was a hole in the top of my canopy. Then the fire came up through the floor. The other two guys looked back and saw my plane go in, but they didn't see me get out. I jumped at about 800 feet. They reported me killed in action so my mother got a KIA telegram.

At the time things are happening so fast you don't have time to get scared. It's only a couple of days later, when you have time to think about what happened, that it all hits you. I can remember pulling the D-ring and when the chute opened I was already going down through the trees. I hit and rolled over. Intelligence had told us French resistance fighters were in the area. So we were supposed to dig a hole and cover up our parachute and wait for the French to find us. Hell, I hit the ground, rolled over, and a German said, "*Ja, ach so. Ja, Leutnant.*" I had landed right in the middle of the gun crew that had shot me down.

The first things they took were my cigarettes, my Parker pen, and my wristwatch. Then they took me in a car about five or six miles to a house sitting about 100 yards from the Mediterranean on the Riviera. I can still see this guy sitting there in a German uniform. Quite naturally I saluted. He said in perfect English, "Have a seat, lieutenant." He began doing all this talking, and I don't know what's going on. I gave him my name, rank, and serial number, but I'm scared as hell. He asked, "Have you ever been to Denver?" I told him no. "Washington?" Again I said no. He asked about other cities. Then he asked, "Detroit?" When I answered yes, he said, "Then you must know about Paradise Valley?" With all its nightclubs and restaurants Paradise Valley was the black center of Detroit. He then proceeded to describe how to get there and gave me the names of all the people who used to work at Sonny Wilson's bar. It turned out he had graduated from the University of Michigan in 1936. We just talked, without any pressure on me to tell him anything. He even got back my cigarettes. He had returned to Germany, and they had put him in the army. I never saw him again and have no idea what happened to him.

The Germans then moved me to a nearby airfield where I spent the night. I don't remember much about this, but they brought in Robert Daniels. He had put his plane in the water, and the Germans had picked him up. Then they brought in Richard Macon who had also been shot down. His target was Montpelier, about 100 miles down the coast. He was in bad shape. He had two cracked vertebrae in his neck and his eyes were very bloodshot. The three of us traveled up the Rhône Valley in the back of a truck and then on a train. We had two German guards. Naturally, we were a little concerned. We had heard that the Germans considered blacks to be apes and all kinds of other stereotypes. We knew what they thought about Jews. We had encountered some racism in Italy, although we later found out that was mostly because white American soldiers had told the Italians terrible things about blacks. But our two German guards did not treat us this way. They were *Wehrmacht* [regular armed forces] and saw us as officers and almost as celebrities.

We eventually ended up at Dulag Luft at Wetzlar, Germany, where we were again interrogated. The guy who questioned me had a big book about the 332nd Fighter Group. It contained all the photos of my former classmates. He pointed to one and said, "Lieutenant, isn't that you?" It was. He knew my father's social security number and that he worked at Detroit Lubricator. He knew how much money he made and how much in taxes he paid on his house. He had my complete school record and he even knew my sister's grades. He also knew about the inspections we had on our planes. Some of this information was public record, but not the inspection. The Germans had to have had somebody at Ramitelli Air Base or high up the line who was giving them this information. He knew everything about our mission. I couldn't really tell him anything. Maybe he was guessing and maybe some of my answers verified what he was saying, but as a fighter pilot we knew nothing about the reasons for these missions. We would just get up in the morning and be told where to fly. He knew more about all this than I did. We were put in solitary confinement for a couple of days. That was the first time we got some decent food. Quite naturally having a black prisoner was a little odd for the Germans, but I was treated with all the rights and privileges of an American officer; in fact, I had no trouble at all with German authorities because I was black.

The only time I ever became frightened was on the train ride from Frankfurt to Stalag Luft 3. Daniels, Macon, and I were again escorted by two German guards with rifles. The train stopped somewhere, and alongside the track were a group of *Hitler Jugend*, all in their early teens. They were in uniform and were singing these songs and waving Nazi flags. When they saw us on the train, they started ranting and raving and yelling at us. Things got pretty nasty. The two German guards had to threaten to shoot them. We were very happy when the train started again.

I had quite a surprise when I arrived at my permanent camp at Stalag Luft 3 near Sagan, Germany. The camp was already overcrowded so each barracks room had to choose a new roommate. A dyed-in-the-wool cracker with the deepest Southern drawl imaginable walked up to me and said, "Ah think I'll take this 'un." I was naturally very apprehensive, thinking that I had not come all the way from the U.S.A. to be with a bunch of white crackers. When I got to the room I found nine other white guys, all from the South. I soon discovered why these rednecks had chosen me. Their room happened to house all the escape materials, and they wanted to make sure they didn't get a German plant or an American turncoat. They later told me, "We knew we could trust you." I thought it then and have said it many times since, "Ain't that a bitch!" At home black soldiers caught hell from s.o.b.'s just like them. Now five thousand miles from home they can trust a black man because they are scared to death of a strange white face. "Ain't that a bitch!"

3
Life in the Bag

Shedding weight by shitting weight was a time-honored calamity for the Kriegie. It probably was the most common indignity inflicted. The filthy, overcrowded, stinking latrines aided and abetted any such outbreak. Few inmates had the extra clothing to survive such an onslaught with any decency intact. And the general paucity of toilet paper in the Reich added the opposite of "the icing on the cake."

AMERICAN POW[1]

When I was captured I weighed 128 pounds. After two years as an American POW I weighed 185. I had gotten so fat you could no longer see my eyes.

GERMAN POW

MOST AMERICAN PRISONERS of war would agree with Robert Doyle, who in his fine study of POW narratives wrote, "In capture, the individual separates from his primary culture and begins the journey into a world of chaos. The prison landscape is the body of that chaos; it represents a place of evil, a place so horrible that only the most graphic terms can describe it."[2]

---

[1]George J. Davis, *The Hitler Diet as Inflicted on American POWs in World War II* (Los Angeles: Military Literary Guild, 1990), 97.

[2]Doyle, *Voices from Captivity*, 170.

"Life in the bag," as American *Kriegies* called their incarceration, was marked by bitter cold in winter, fleas and mosquitos in summer, and lice, bedbugs, boredom, and unsanitary conditions all year 'round. Above all, they suffered acute hunger. According to the Geneva Convention, "The food ration of prisoners of war shall be equal in quantity and quality to that of troops at base camps of the detaining Power." By 1945, however, food was in such short supply in Germany that no one—soldier, civilian, or prisoner—had enough to eat. Red Cross food parcels were crucial for prisoner survival, but during the war's final months they became very scarce, either because the Allies shut down the German transportation system or because they simply disappeared before reaching the prisoners. In either case, few if any reached the enlisted men's camps. Officers and noncommissioned officers, who in accordance with the Geneva Convention were segregated into their own separate camps, fared slightly better, but by the end of the war they too had little to eat. German prisoners in the United States had no such problems; in fact, most gained weight on a diet that was very similar to that served American soldiers on the home front.

The officers' camps, whether German or American, were more likely to have the kinds of activities that helped mitigate the evils of incarceration. Many had libraries, orchestras, small theater groups, athletic fields, and even opportunities for taking a variety of educational courses, some for college credit. Noncommissioned officers had access to limited educational and recreational activities, but enlisted men had few organized diversions.

Enlisted men could be required to work, and almost all German POWs did so. American enlisted men also worked, but because so many were captured in the final months of the war, when chaos and the fast-closing Allied troops forced their frequent relocation, working outside the camps was not as common. NCOs were to work only in supervisory capacities, although they could volunteer for other duties. Officers were not to work, although a few German officers volunteered their services. The Germans who worked outside the base camps often saw and met normal Americans, and the result was almost always positive. American prisoners who worked outside their permanent camps were seldom so fortunate. In spite of Geneva Convention prohibitions, many were forced to work at hazardous and war-related tasks, and some ended up working alongside slave laborers. Furthermore, German civilians could be most unfriendly.

Living quarters in the permanent camps varied greatly according to rank. Once again the Geneva Convention greatly favored officers: "With regard to dormitories—the total surface, minimum and material of bedding—the conditions shall be the same as for the troops at base camps of the detaining Power." Regular officers' quarters in both armies were superior to those for the noncommissioned officers or the enlisted men, and this continued to be the case in most prison camps.

Regardless of rank, boredom and lethargy were the bane of all prisoners of war, and many had trouble handling their enervating existence. When possible, prisoners tried to fill their empty hours participating in plays and musical groups; studying, painting, carving, reading, daydreaming, sleeping, and walking; playing chess, cards, and sports; and, most often, in endless conversations with fellow prisoners. Some prisoners became devoutly religious, treating their captivity as a kind of spiritual crucible. Others became too depressed to do anything. A few just lay on their bunks, refusing to talk or even eat. Others had to be forcefully restrained from rushing the fence to commit suicide. The more fortunate prisoners learned patience and tolerance, as well as a deeper understanding of self and an appreciation for friendship.

Robert Doyle argues that a prisoner "can passively resist a captor's demands, but more often the survivor neutralizes or numbs the experience completely." Above all, writes Doyle, "The survivor's objective is to live through captivity by avoiding the captor's attention," and to reject "guilt and shame" in order to do so.[3] But such strategies were not easily applied to everyday life in the camps. Enlisted men, who were more likely to experience harsh treatment and debilitating conditions, not surprisingly suffered more incidents of acute depression and neuroses than did NCOs and officers. A lack of training, organization, and leadership were important factors, but so too was the rigid and often condescending class structure that existed in the military and in the prison

---

[3]Doyle, *Voices from Captivity*, 3; see also Terrence Des Pres, *The Survivor: An Anatomy of Life in the Death Camps* (New York: Oxford University Press, 1976), 202.

camps as well. The result was that among the lower ranks dispirited men often exhibited less commitment to discipline and even survival than did the higher ranks.[4]

American-held German prisoners suffered a different kind of stress. Relatively few were overtly mistreated, and acute hunger, cold, and a lack of sanitary facilities were seldom problems in the camps. Nevertheless, they were prisoners, and being incarcerated is an unnatural experience for any human being. They too had to deal with enervating boredom. They also missed and worried about their loved ones back home who lived in constant peril. Finally, because so many of them faced additional years of internment in France, England, and Belgium, the cessation of hostilities did not end their agony.

Regardless of rank, class, nationality, or conditions, it was difficult to predict what kind of individual might best withstand the rigors of imprisonment. Psychiatrist Judith Herman's study of survivors of extreme violence suggests some possibilities: "The capacity to preserve social connection," she writes in her book *Trauma and Recovery*, "even in the face of extremity, seems to protect people to some degree against the later development of post-traumatic syndromes. For example, among survivors of a disaster at sea, the men who had managed to escape by cooperating with others showed relatively little evidence of post-traumatic stress afterward." Herman concludes that those who plunged themselves into impulsive, isolated action and did not affiliate with the others—that is, the *Rambo* types—were more likely to be "highly symptomatic."[5] Her conclusions apply to the majority of POWs, who certainly did much better if they were well organized, had friends, and some kind of support system. But under such extreme conditions, even many of these individuals suffered ter-

---

[4]Because the *Wehrmacht* was so rigidly class conscious, this negative attitude toward enlisted men was especially common in the German prison camps. Arthur A. Durand, in his *Stalag Luft III*, 179, concludes that the Americans in Stalag Luft III suffered comparatively few mental problems, but this was a well organized, *Luftwaffe*-administered Air Corps officers' camp, with a sympathetic German *Kommandant*, where prisoners enjoyed arguably the best conditions of any POW camp in Germany.

[5]Herman, *Trauma and Recovery*, 58–59.

rible stress, and the battle to cope often did not end with liberation.[6]

Not surprisingly, prisoners of war never compare their experiences to those of civilian prison inmates back home. After all, captured soldiers rightly considered themselves innocent of any illegal or criminal act. But the trauma of losing one's self and the illusion of control is very similar, as was the resultant depression and lethargy brought on by what some POWs called "Barbed-Wire Psychosis." A few ex-prisoners compare their experiences to those suffered by the Holocaust victims. And a small number of enlisted men recalled the military indoctrination and discipline of basic training which also reduced them to becoming an object or a number, with an accompanying loss of identity.

The fictional POWs of popular culture, as well as actual prisoners themselves, seldom discussed the question of sex in the camps. Certainly prisoners did dream of their women back home. In fact, they normally so romanticized their loved ones that postwar realities often led to bitter disappointments. But dreaming scarcely satisfies basic urges. It is awkward to ask men what they did to compensate. After all, masturbation was against military regulations and homosexuality was never mentioned. Most of the interviewees insist they were too miserable even to think about sex. Perhaps, but studies of Jewish concentration camp inmates suggest that sexual liaisons existed right to the end.

Paul Fussell's *Wartime*, which is a very provocative study of World War II, concludes that homosexual encounters were not unusual among prisoners. He describes a Japanese camp where such relationships were so common that the camp physician had to act as a kind of "marriage" counselor. However, Fussell concludes that masturbation was much more the norm, although done with considerably more guilt among Americans than among other Allied soldiers.[7]

---

[6]Herman, *Trauma and Recovery*, 87, writes, "Studies of soldiers who had been taken prisoner in the Second World War or the Korean War found that 35–50 years after their release the majority of these men still had nightmares, persistent flashbacks, and extreme reactions to reminders of their POW experiences."

[7]Paul Fussell, *Wartime: Understanding and Behavior in the Second World War* (New York: Oxford University Press, 1989), 109.

Colonel Delmar T. Spivey, who was one of the top-ranking American officers at Stalag Luft 3, admits the men thought constantly about sex, but he denies there was any homosexual activity in his camp:

I had anticipated that . . . homosexual tendencies would appear from time to time. . . . One of the first things I did was to have my squadron commanders keep a special lookout for any queer activities. The long hours of close confinement with overcrowded conditions prevailing nearly all the time offered possibilities for such activities, but they never occurred, or, if they did, they were never brought to the attention of any of my commanders or to me. It is to the everlasting credit of the American officers that they were men and acted in a rational manner concerning sex at all times while POWs.[8]

Many of the prisoners insist that hunger pangs entirely superseded any sexual urges. George J. Davis, who uses humor to describe what food deprivation did to a prisoner's body, graphically describes the process:

The lust in your body will face utter annihilation. . . . The sex organ will become quite *kaputt*. Erotic thoughts, erections and wet dreams will become events of the past. Ten naked beauties could saunter into a room full of *Kriegies*, and if they arrive without snacks, they would go unnoticed.[9]

David Westheimer also presents the conventional view expressed by most interviewees:

We all had sexual dreams but more rarely than would be expected of young men deprived of women. Despite con-

[8]Delmar T. Spivey, *POW Odyssey: Recollections of Center Compound, Stalag Luft III and the Secret German Peace Mission in World War II* (Attleboro, Mass.: Colonial Lithograph, 1984), 74–75.

[9]Davis, *The Hitler Diet*, 3.

siderable sexual tension, cold, hunger, uncertainty, and perhaps subconscious fears shaped our dreams.[10]

A tough American paratrooper describes sleeping with two other men in a very narrow bunk, their arms tightly wrapped around each other. This was, of course, for warmth, but also, one surmises, because it allowed them to touch each other—to still feel part of the human race.

Guards deserve special mention. Although popular images were usually negative, the guards' actual behavior varied greatly. Occasionally a fictional German guard would exhibit an act of kindness, but more commonly American popular culture depicted him as the cruel, humorless *SS* type or, conversely, as a bumbling overweight buffoon such as *Hogan's Heroes'* Sergeant Schultz. Many guards did act badly on both sides of the Atlantic, but when a U.S. Army guard shot and killed several unarmed German prisoners in Utah, Americans recognized the tragedy to be an aberrant act of a mentally deranged man rather than a manifestation of national cruelty.[11]

---

[10]David Westheimer, *Sitting It Out: A World War II POW Memoir* (Houston: Rice University Press, 1992), 62.

[11]On July 8, 1945, two months after the end of the war against Germany, a mentally unbalanced American guard fired 250 rounds from his 30-mm machine gun into the tents of sleeping prisoners at Salina, Utah. Pfc. Clarence V. Bertucci was a sixth-grade dropout who had seen no combat and had been a constant disciplinary problem. Nine of the German prisoners were killed and nineteen wounded. It was the worst such incident to befall German POWs in the United States; see Powell, *Splinters of a Nation*, 1, 77. Powell is very critical of the quality of many of the American guards. He quotes an American soldier at one of the Utah camps who describes the guards being "of low mentality, non-intellectual, (who) could neither understand nor see the reason for the Geneva Convention. Many drank and went AWOL. They read comic books rather than listening to news. They liked to think of themselves as heroes, their one desire being 'to shoot a Kraut'." Powell acknowledges that the quality of the American guards greatly improved toward the end of the war, both because of better training and because some of them had actually been in combat.

Many former POWs do mention a guard or two with whom they had friendly relations. Several German prisoners told of guards who persuaded farmers to give them extra rations when they worked in the fields. On the other hand, prisoners sometimes tried to bribe their guards for special favors, and both American and German prisoners delighted in taunting their guards, although to do so could be dangerous. The American ex-prisoners interviewed for this book spoke of many kind guards as well as a number who were cruel and insensitive. They uniformly disliked guards from the *Hitler Jugend* and the *Gestapo*, but not so battlefield veterans or older guards, who tended to be more understanding. At the end of hostilities, some newly freed American prisoners tried to protect favorite guards from the conquering Russian and American armies. After the war, a few ex-prisoners successfully contacted favorite former guards and invited them to POW reunions.

Many American prisoners thought nothing could be worse than "life in the bag," but they were wrong. During the final weeks of the war, the Germans forced thousands of them to make long, deadly marches to new camps in order to flee the fast-closing Allied forces. Weakened by the bitter cold and their starvation rations, many of these prisoners were simply incapable of keeping up. In some cases, they were allowed to ride on carts, trucks, or trains. Some were shot, and others simply disappeared. Although the number of American prisoners who died in the German camps has been estimated as anywhere from one to four thousand, the actual total was arguably much higher. Many of those who died on these marches were certainly among the 78,773 Americans still listed as missing in action.[12]

The eleven narratives in this chapter reflect not only the sharp differences between German and American camps, but also the differing coping mechanisms prisoners employed to maintain

---

[12]Doyle, in his *Voices from Captivity*, 307–8, puts the death toll for German-held American POWs at 3,822; others state that only one percent died, which would put the figure at less than 1,000. It is possible that only 1,000 died in the camps themselves; the rest died or simply disappeared on the long marches at the end of the war when an accurate accounting was simply impossible.

their mental and spiritual well-being. Americans George J. Davis, Phil Miller, and Ross Calvert sought to protect themselves during their incarceration through the constant use of humor—and still do to this day. On the other hand, William Kalway used his stubborn anger to resist his captors. George Rosie credits his disciplined Airborne training with helping him make the best of a bad situation. No amount of training could have helped Louis Grivetti overcome the horrifying experience of being in Dresden during the fire bombing of February 1944. Clifford Fox had the most positive experiences of any American prisoner interviewed for this book. Henry McKee believed that nothing could really faze him, although his narrative shows that he was affected more than he realized. Miller, McKee, and Calvert were officers, and Miller had the added good fortune to be interned in a *Luftwaffe*-operated camp. German prisoners Eberhard Ladwig, Elmer Beck, and Guenther Oswald had an over-abundance of food, and they suffered no physical deprivations, but their lives, like those of any prisoner, were certainly disrupted and often filled with stress. Especially distressing was learning of the terrible destruction of Germany and not knowing the fate of their loved ones.

Because food plays such a central role in these narratives, this chapter begins with a comparison of the rations Allied and German captives might expect.

THE INTERNATIONAL RED CROSS PARCEL

The following are typical items that a POW in Germany might receive in an International Red Cross Food Parcel. Because these parcels could come from Canada, Australia, or the United States, the contents were not always the same. These parcels were originally intended to serve one man for a week; more often they were shared between two or more men; and all too often they were not available at all.

1 – 12 oz. can of corned beef
1 – 12 oz. can of Spam
1 – 6 oz. can of liver paté
1 – 8 oz. package of cheese
1 – 1 lb. can of Klim dried whole milk
1 – 4 oz. can of instant coffee
1 – 15 oz. package of raisins or prunes
1 – 4 oz. package powdered orange drink
1 – 8 oz. package of sugar cubes
1 – 8 oz. can of "C" ration crackers
2 – 4 oz. bars of "D" ration chocolate
2 – bars of soap
1 – 1 lb. can of margarine
1 – 4 oz. can of instant coffee
5 – books of matches
4 – packages of cigarettes

ROBERT RUTT AND THE HITLER DIET

Detroit-born Robert Rutt was a young second lieutenant when he was captured during the Battle of the Bulge. Rutt kept a diary while a prisoner in Stalag 13-C at Hammelburg. Included was the following official weekly German food issue; however, Rutt notes that many of the items were not always available or served in the listed quantities. Ten grams is equal to 0.3527 ounces.

meat (& bone)	250 grams	= 8.8 oz
oleo or butter	150 grams	= 5.3 oz
cooking oleo	68 grams	= 2.4 oz
barley or peas	150 grams	= 5.3 oz
cheese	62 1/2 grams	= 2.2 oz
potatoes	3,350 grams	= 7.4 lb
sugar	175 grams	= 6.2 oz
coffee	17 1/2 grams	= 0.6 oz
tea	7 grams	= 0.3 oz
bread	1,850 grams	= 4.1 lb
flour	59 grams	= 2.1 oz
dehydrated turnips	90 grams	= 3.2 oz
sauerkraut	175 grams	= 6.2 oz
green tops	30 grams	= 1.1 oz
salt	70 grams	= 2.5 oz
brown flour	25 grams	= 0.9 oz
soup fat	30 grams	= 1.1 oz

JOSEF KRUMBACHNER AND DINING AT SEA

Josef Krumbachner, whose full story appears in Chapter Four, recorded what he and his fellow German prisoners were served on the ship coming over to the United States. Although actual prison camp food was not nearly so elegant, the ship's menu for July 24, 1944, reprinted below, affords an interesting contrast with Robert Rutt's weekly fare

BREAKFAST
Stewed Fruit
Rolled Oats with Milk
Assorted Dry Cereals
Smoked Haddock, Butter Sauce
Eggs – Boiled, Fried or Scrambled
Broiled Breakfast Bacon
Sliced Minced Beef on Toast
Hashed Brown Potatoes
Breakfast Rolls with Preserves and Marmalade
Tea or Coffee

DINNER
Pickled Lamb's Tongue, Vinaigrette
Green Olives
Potage Jackson aux Croutons
Broiled Fresh Fish with Lemon Butter
Potted Round Steak, Esterhazy
Buttered Spaghetti, Parmesan
Buttered Kernel Corn
Baked Potatoes
Mixed Green Salad with Thousand Island Dressing
Mocha Layer Cake and Fruit Jello Macedoine
Cheese and Crackers
Fresh Fruit
Bread and Butter
Coffee

GEORGE J. DAVIS

Pfc. George J. Davis, who joined the army immediately after his high school graduation in Hyde Park, New York, went into battle in southern France with the Seventh Army's 103rd Infantry Division. He was captured on December 5, 1944, near Colmar, Alsace. After a brief time in Stalag 12-A at Limburg, Germany, Davis was shipped to Stalag 4-B at Mühlberg and then on to an *Arbeitskommando* (work camp) in Czechoslovakia just north of Prague. After the war, Davis, who also served as a First Lieutenant in the Korean War before becoming a high school history teacher, wrote a short, witty book entitled *The Hitler Diet*, excerpts from which are included in the narrative below.[13] Behind the humor, however, emerges a dreary picture of what physical hardships and acute hunger could do to a prisoner's personal well-being.

FOR EVERY CAPTIVE, AS Alvin Lamb, a cell mate of mine, recalls, "It was a humbling experience." Perhaps doubly so, as we were detained by the losers. Individually and collectively, we were humbled by our loss of freedom, our inability to influence events in our daily lives, and by our ignorance of events that were determining the outcome of the war. This deprivation included the inability to communicate with family and loved ones. Not hearing from home was a major burden for all prisoners. By daydreaming, by chatting endlessly with all within earshot, and in the Stalags by sleeping as much as possible, each inmate worked at blotting out the ugly present. Each guy created a fantasy world that would leap to life once the endless war ended.

---

[13]The first four paragraphs are from Davis, *The Hitler Diet*, 93–4.

The realities of K.G.[14] life were oppressive. Lines for food, lines for the smelly latrines, lines for washing, lines for water, lines for cooking, lines for *Appell* (roll call), lines for everything of importance, it seemed. The chance for solitude was non-existent; opportunities for comfort and satisfaction fell into the same void. No matter where one experienced it, the *Kriegie* experience was a shitty one. And in the most literal sense as the "GIs" *[diarrhea]* hit everyone, sooner and later both.

When not standing in line, working, sleeping, or actively engaged with something edible, the unhappy prisoner could pick at the lice and vermin occupying his foul garments and attacking his emaciated body. Periodically, when deemed necessary, one shaved his armpits and had a dependable friend shave his crotch. Clothing and bedding were aired only after the arrival of warmer weather. Bony bodies sought the salubrious effects of the springtime sun.

For those who doubt the severity of the prisoner's plight, ponder the condition of Hurve Cress upon his liberation. U.S. Army doctors diagnosed Cress as suffering from seriously infected ulcerated lice sores, scabies, yellow jaundice, dysentery, and acute malnutrition. All this took only three months of captivity under our not so generous hosts. Maybe they were trying to make us feel like genuine *Untermensch*[15] to reconcile their tottering image as a nation of supermen.

I received one Red Cross food package while I was in Stalag 4-B at Mühlberg. Two of us had to share it. After that it was rather piecemeal. The Germans would give them to us item by item. The cans would already be punctured so we couldn't hoard them in an escape kit. Altogether my buddy and I received maybe two and a half packages during our almost five months of captivity. We did have the chance to either steal or bargain for food while we were on work details, and we sometimes saw things outside our base camp that made us feel a little better. We'd occasionally see boxcars filled with wounded German soldiers coming back from the front, which made us realize they were suffering heavy losses. We

---

[14]Short for *Kriegsgefangener* or prisoner of war.

[15]Undesirable people, something less than human.

also noticed that train schedules were no longer being maintained, and we saw lots of refugees fleeing the front lines. We also picked up rumors about the fighting from the slave laborers with whom we often worked, but the worst rumor we encountered circulated among our fellow prisoners. I don't know how it started, but we heard that all of us would be court martialed after the war for allowing ourselves to be captured. We constantly discussed this topic in our work camp. We thought we were losing our home support, and quite naturally, a lot of us felt terribly depressed that something like this might happen. After all, we had almost been killed in battle, after which we had to suffer those long months as guests of the Germans. Certainly we didn't choose to become prisoners. I can remember after the war attending a POW reunion and walking behind two air force couples. The one woman said to her husband, "I can understand how you could become a prisoner if you were a flier, but how could you ever be captured if you were on the ground?" I thought to myself, "Madam, buy me a beer or two, and I might explain it to you."

Decent treatment from the guards occasionally alleviated the constant pain of being a POW. I became friends with one of the guards on our work detail. My buddy and I were such goof-offs that the Germans finally would just assign us to a specific job with one guard to watch over us. That's how I got to know this guard. We were always bitching and moaning about the damn war going on forever, and one day he said, "Don't worry, Patton is in Bavaria and the war will soon be over." He had been wounded on the Russian front, which was true of many of our guards. They had been in combat, and they knew they were losing. When I suffered an acute case of diarrhea, this guard gave me some small potatoes which had been burned black, and they helped. On my final day in captivity, we exchanged addresses. After the war I sent a letter to him in care of his father. At the time he was being held prisoner in the British Zone, so his father took the letter and rode his bike some fifty miles to where his son was incarcerated. He showed the letter to the appropriate British officers who then freed his son. In the ensuing years we visited him several times in Germany before he died in the early 1980s.

PHILIP B. MILLER

Phil Miller spent 405 days in a German prison camp without ever losing his sense of humor. Drafted into the army as a private just forty days after Pearl Harbor, Miller soon became an Army Air Corps cadet. Unfortunately, he washed out of pilot training for watching cloud formations rather than his instruments and, as he put it, for a variety of other original flying techniques. His flight instructor suggested his failure might well have saved his life and those who might have flown with him. Miller thought his failure so reprehensible that he invited his wife to divorce him, but she refused. Miller became a bombardier on a B–24 and was shot down on April 1, 1944.

ON APRIL 1, 1944 we flew a mission over Ludwigshafen, Germany, near the border of Switzerland to bomb a chemical plant. We used to say the flak was thick enough to walk on, and it was that day. We were doing saturation bombing so the ground forces responded with saturation flak. They would figure out where we were going to release our bombs and just fire a barrage at that point, and we would all have to fly into it. They could change the barrage area a lot faster than the formation could change course. There was a certain fascination in watching the ships ahead of you going into this dense area of smoke and exploding shells, except for the sobering thought that in a very short time you would be experiencing the same thing. I could see a few black columns of black smoke reaching all the way to the ground marking the paths of the luckless burning ships. Anybody having the misfortune to bail out over hostile territory also had the problem of facing ill-tempered and hostile civilians when he hit the ground. One bomber crew even had the poor judgment to name their ship *Murder, Inc.* and the additional poor judgment to have this name painted on the backs of their jackets. They then compounded their mistakes by getting shot down and captured.

Everybody's version of what happened to our plane over Ludwigshafen differed from mine. From my viewpoint in the nose I could only look directly ahead, but I could see that one engine was stopped completely and another was faltering. We lost about fifty knots of speed and quickly fell behind the formation. That was a real lonely feeling. We had set a course for home when suddenly we found ourselves being escorted by two beautiful P–51s. They stayed with us as long as they could, but we knew their gas was getting low and eventually they had to leave. Our altitude kept dropping. When we reached 5,000 feet, our pilot, William Lafferty, rang the bail-out bell indicating it was his intention to jump. I figured if he was leaving, the rest of us should certainly follow. The navigator, Harold Garman, and I opened the nose wheel door. I motioned him to go, and he motioned for me to do the honors. Frankly, neither of us was enthusiastic about jumping into that open air. When I jumped everything suddenly became quiet. I pulled the rip cord, but nothing happened. I began pulling the cloth out with my hands, but it remained tangled in the center and began to billow out on both sides of the tangled pack. The shroud lines were twisted, and I rotated myself and jerked on the lines to get as much air in the chute as possible. I was so busy looking up, I never looked at the ground. I hit with a severe jolt which dazed me and knocked my breath out. I tried to breathe but couldn't. Finally I quit trying and immediately felt better. I was in the middle of a plowed field, and for a few seconds I couldn't remember how I came to be there. Things cleared up, and I ran to the edge of the field and hid my parachute under some bushes. I looked around and saw German soldiers with rifles coming toward me in a small car. I watched until they came near and then raised my hands in the air to indicate there was no need for them to start shooting on my account. They motioned me to get into the car, and we drove to a nearby small French town. Our copilot Rufe Reed and radioman Herman Schmidt were already there. The Germans took my escape kit which contained $300 in money, water purifying pills, a compass, maps, some chocolate, and a few other escape aids. They also cut the cord off my electric suit because I suppose they considered this a weapon. We were then taken outside and marched through the gathering crowd of French people, all of whom were openly sympathetic. The women were crying and shouting in French which was clearly meant to encourage us. We did not feel very jovial, but we managed a couple of faint smiles. We were taken to another house where we were guarded by three German soldiers who jumped up and clicked their heels whenever one of their officers came in. They offered us some cold coffee and dark bread, but we declined to take it. Bread later became our most important food, and I never again turned any down.

[Because they were under the control of the Luftwaffe, Air Corps personnel were normally better treated than were other prisoners of war, but this was not always true during interrogations.]

We were next sent to Dulag Luft which was a transition and interrogation center for Air Corps prisoners. Our superiors told us while we were still in England that if captured our interrogation would begin with simple harmless questions, which we were not to answer. They also told us about the bad guy/good guy technique. The first interrogator would threaten us with execution if we did not give him all the information he wanted. Then the nice guy would tell us he could save us from execution if we would cooperate. After that we were supposed to be left alone with a beautiful woman who would give us the friendship treatment, including the offer of her personal favors in exchange for a few simple facts. Everybody said how they would lead her on and make her perform, and then tell her nothing but lies.

My first interrogator had me pretty well convinced that in spite of my forewarning he was going to execute me. He went into a towering rage. He called me a spy and saboteur and told me execution was what I deserved. I decided that when I got in front of the firing squad, I would begin talking my head off but not before they pointed their rifles at me. The second man was as friendly as predicted. He told me all about himself, how he had worked in the U.S. as a traveling salesman in Tennessee and so forth. He said it was true that I was suspected of being a saboteur with a false serial number and rank, and that they needed additional information to verify my true identification. I told him if I had been going to assume a false rank, I would have picked one higher than a second lieutenant. He ignored my reply and asked where I lived in the U.S., my mother's name, and what schools I had attended. I told him that none of these things had the remotest connection to the war. He agreed, but said they would speed up the identification process and that might save me. He then sent me back to solitary confinement to think it over.

During this time I spent about ten hours a day sending messages home by mental telepathy. I tried all the channels, but none of them worked. My folks did not know I was missing until much later. One day the door to my cell opened and a young girl was standing there with the guard. I anticipated treatment number three was about to begin. But she only stood outside staring and did not come in. She must have been a friend of the guard who only wanted to see what one of the *Terrorflieger* looked like.

After three or four more sessions, the friendly interrogator said our visits were over, but that first he would tell me a few things. He then read off the names of our crew members. It was the original crew to which we had been assigned in the U.S. and included one man who had grounded himself. It also included two other men who had the good judgment to stay in bed the morning of April 1. But he also told me some things I didn't know. He informed me that Major Jimmy Stewart had been promoted to Colonel and no longer commanded the 703rd Squadron, having been succeeded by Captain Casey. My surprise must have been evident to him, but he sent me back to a large barracks where I was reunited with Rufe and Smitty. If the Germans didn't have concealed microphones in that barracks, they were not as smart as we thought they were. All of us who had been in solitary confinement were finally back with our friends, and we began chattering like magpies, including stories about all the information we had kept from our interrogators.

[Although he still attends therapy sessions at a nearby VA hospital, Miller insists his treatment as a POW was not that bad considering the deteriorating conditions for Germans generally.]

Germany was under the rule of an insane man who murdered millions of people. Germany was also fighting a total war on two fronts and was losing on both. All the country's production and transportation systems were trying to support an all-out war effort, and the Allied air forces were bombing these systems and the civilian populations day and night. Hundreds of thousands of civilians were being killed in these bombing raids, and the ones who survived were increasingly living at near subsistence levels.

Under such circumstances there was no way that a captured Allied airman was going to receive exemplary treatment, but I believe the treatment I received was as good as could be expected. The German prisoners held in the U.S. may have lived better, but so did the American civilians.

I spent most of my imprisonment in Stalag Luft 1 at Barth, Germany, directly north of Berlin on the Baltic Sea. I was given German identification tag number 4216 which I believe was the count for prisoners coming into that camp. Smitty was sent to another camp, but Rufe and I were put in a room with fourteen other men and eight double bunks. Each bunk had a wooden bottom covered by an excelsior-filled mattress. We received food packages from the Red Cross that were wrapped in cardboard with metal bands around them. We strung these bands between the sides of our bunks and laid the cardboard on top of them, which was much better than the wooden boards. We used the boards for many other things, including chairs and benches. They were so comfortable that we vowed to make the same kind when we got home. Of course, we never did.

The food varied in proportion to the weather and the bombing raids on Germany's transportation system. We began getting three meals a day, but soon that dropped to two with two loaves of bread for each room. During the Battle of the Bulge we dropped to one loaf of bread at noon and one meal in the mess hall at night. There were approximately 1,200 men in our section of the North Compound, and breakfast, when we got it, consisted of six sacks of barley soaked overnight and heated early in the morning. This barley inevitably had a few grubs and insects boiled in, but we soon discovered they couldn't harm us. The noon bread ration was divided into sixteen parts and laid out on a table. A playing card was put on each piece of bread. Then the men drew matching cards from another deck to see who got which piece of bread. This bread was baked with sawdust as a partial filling and wood chips were sometimes found in the loaves. It was absolutely delicious, and many of us agreed we'd never had such bread before. Supper consisted of potatoes and some kind of gravy. Sometimes animals killed in the war were cut up and mixed in the gravy. Occasionally we had pudding made of bread and chocolate with some prunes or raisins. This was always a real treat. The prunes and raisins were soaked in barrels, and the juice was then saved and put into kegs to ferment. There always seemed to be an adequate supply of fermented juice for the kitchen staff and some of the higher ranking officers.

The best food came in our ten-pound Red Cross package. Each of us was supposed to get one package per week. Each package also contained five packages of cigarettes and some Vitamin C pills. I didn't smoke so I always traded my cigarettes for bread. The guys often threw away their ascorbic acid pills, but I collected them, and they helped me maintain better health during the winter when pneumonia was always a threat.

Cigarettes were the medium of exchange, and commodity prices were listed on a bulletin board. Supply naturally determined whether the price was going up or down. Bread would vary from sixteen to sixty cigarettes. Chocolate bars ranged from 200 to 500 because they were so scarce. When packages came from home all sorts of new items would be listed, and trading would become more active.

Many men had decks of cards and bridge became very popular. There were always games going on, and arguments and debates would go long into the night. No domestic friction was ever more spirited than those conversations in the dark about the bridge games.

There were other endless arguments that went on and on. One was about the type of aerial maneuver performed by a fly when landing on the ceiling. That went on all summer. A fly apparently flew with his feet below him but had to land with them above him. You couldn't answer the question by watching him do it. They flew around and around in circles, and when they decided to land they did it so suddenly there was no way to observe their method. We watched flies for months and never resolved anything.

Every room had a chess game. We made some sets out of pieces of wood and others we got by trading cigarettes with the guards. I even brought one of these sets home with me. After we learned the game and played everyone a few times, we would settle down to play only at our own level. This was also true of the bridge games. You wanted to play against those who were considered as good as you.

We also had a daily camp newspaper. One of its staff was Lowell Bennett, a captured war correspondent. Some of the news came from recently arriving prisoners, but there was also a radio. On Sunday there was even a comic strip featuring Klim Kriegie, who was always trying to escape, but never with any luck

There were constant escape attempts in our camp, but none was ever successful. A few of the guys got out but were quickly recaptured. Everybody considered building a tunnel. One barracks had so much dirt dug away on the side toward the fence that it leaned over in that direction. Every night the guards crawled around under the buildings looking for new tunnels. One night some men poured water on one of these tunnel hunters. He took out his pistol and began shooting up through the floor. The men went charging over to the Colonel the next day to protest that the guard had violated their rights under the Geneva Convention.

The YMCA sent in some garden seeds, and the Germans allowed us to plant these along the warning wire. I planted a few carrots. Two men had made some wire cutters from a couple of stove handles, and they were pretending to be working in the garden, but actually they were cutting the bottom wires of the fence. The tower guards were watching the whole thing, so when these two guys started crawling under the fence, they just sent a couple of other guards to pick them up. A short time later a German officer came in with a detail of men and began stamping all over my carrots. I protested, but he told me to save my breath.

There was this major who worked on escape plans all the time. He noticed this old trash wagon which was left inside the compound until it was filled with ashes and cans. Then a man would come in with an old horse and a couple of guards, haul it out, dump the trash, and return the wagon for a new load. The major took one of his blankets, sewed tin cans and trash all over it, and covered it with ashes. When the trash cart was almost full, he had some of his friends wrap him in his blanket and put him on the wagon with the rest of the trash. He stayed in that wagon for a couple of days, and each morning his buddies would take him a little bread and water. The tower guards, of course, were watching his friends when they came to converse with the trash wagon. So they let the wagon stand in the sun a couple of extra days. When the wagon was ready to move out of the compound, the guards took pains to probe the ashes very thoroughly, so all the major got for his trouble was ten days in solitary confinement.

[Tormenting the guards was a constant source of amusement on both sides of the Atlantic, although a prisoner had to know exactly how far to push someone who was holding a gun.]

The entrance to the compound had two gates with an enclosure between, and one gate was always closed before the other was opened. New prisoners were coming in every few days, and the whole compound would gather at the entrance to see their arrival. This always involved a long wait and the only entertainment was watching the guard march back and forth to let people in and out. We drove this one guard practically mad. He marched very stiffly so the prisoners began to count cadence: "Hup, two, three, four." And just as he reached the gate everyone would holler, "Halt!" He tolerated this for awhile but began growing noticeably more angry. He tried speeding up his steps, but the count speeded up with him. He slowed down, but so did the count. He stopped and faced the crowd, and the count stopped. He started up again, and the count went right along with him. He finally whirled, leveled his rifle at the crowd, and started shouting in German. Those in the back shouted, "Don't let the son of a bitch bluff you." Those in the front didn't say anything, but a few of them tried to get back into the rear rank where all the brave people were. When the guard started to move again, the front rank remained silent, but the courageous rear bravely took up the count. When the guard again leveled his rifle, the rear rank had to keep tightly closed to prevent those cowards in front from breaking ranks. The tower guards had been watching all this, and they called the orderly room to relieve this poor guy before all hell broke loose. His replacement had a good sense of humor and just laughed and counted cadence with the prisoners. We never saw our tormented victim again.

[Of course, sometimes the guards and their watchdogs won these games of wits.]

There was no freedom, no girls, insufficient food, poor clothing, poor quarters, no pay, dirt, loneliness, and endless monotony. But we still were able to laugh; in fact, there was more laughter in that dreary camp, even in the depths of winter, than back at our training camps in the U.S. where we had plenty of sunshine and more food than we could eat. We didn't laugh from gaiety, but because we wanted to retain our sanity. And we would especially laugh when one of our buddies would do something stupid.

One night Tony Tavernit and Jack Armitoski tried to get a little more fresh air in our room. Every night the guards would close our shutters but only with a hook and staple so it was not difficult to slide an object between the shutters and lift the hook. Jack and Tony were working away on this one night when Jack saw the toe of a boot at the bottom of the shutter. He didn't say anything about his discovery but just went quickly to bed with all his clothes on. Tony didn't notice Jack's sudden departure and kept working away. He finally got the hook loose, but when he swung open the shutter, he found himself looking into the muzzle of the guard's pistol. The guard yelled, "*'Raus mit dir. 'Raus!*" Tony was taken completely by surprise and said, "Who, me?" The guard repeated, "*'Raus!*"

Tony began to retreat, but the guard reached in, took him by the shirt, and dragged him through the window. It was below zero, Tony had no coat, and the snow crunched under their feet as they marched away. Tony was well liked, but he was not the brightest guy in the world and things like this always seemed to happen to him. We knew that solitary confinement was the standard penalty for such behavior so we had no cause to protest. We got back in bed and somebody said, "I just knew it would be Tony." This started everybody laughing, and when Jack told us about seeing the boot and not telling Tony, we all started laughing harder. About the time we would quiet down, somebody would yell, "*'Raus mit dir!*" Somebody else would say, "Who, me?" And we would all start laughing again.

The guards also used police dogs at night to make sure we stayed in our barracks. They would run and jump against a shutter that might be partially opened. They would snarl and bark and seemed to enjoy their work. The dogs would often jump without warning, so the first you knew was when their weight hit the shutter. But in the winter, when the snow was packed down or it was icy, we would hear their claws scratching as they tried to get up speed to make their jump.

One night we tried to outwit this big police dog. We opened the shutter just a little and waited for him to jump against it. We then waited awhile and opened it again, and the dog responded. The guard was somewhere standing out of the wind letting the dog do all the work. Pete Belitsos took a stick with a tin can on the end and said, "I'm going to open that shutter, and when that dog jumps, he'll get this tin can jammed down his throat." About five men stood well behind Pete as noninvolved observers. When he heard the claws scratching on the ice, Pete opened the shutters, but then his resolve began to waver. That dog came hurtling through the window, and there was a stampede of men jumping for their beds. You never heard such growling and snarling. It sounded like a bunch of wolves were loose in the room. I was well satisfied to be snug in my top bunk. Everybody thought that several of the guys must have had their legs chewed off. When all of us were in our beds, the dog jumped back out the window. We all started asking, "Who got bit?" To our surprise not a single person had even been nipped. That dog had faked us all out with pure bluff.

[In fictional accounts, and especially in the movies, it is always the weak who break down in the face of adversity. In reality, most POWs agree it was difficult to predict who would have problems coping.]

A couple of guys in our room broke down mentally. Frank R. suffered a complete nervous breakdown. He told us when his ship was shot down, he had neglected to open the bomb bay doors which he thought caused two men to be trapped inside. In reality, those doors could be opened in several ways. There was a lever right in the bomb bay that would do it, or you could knock them open by just jumping on them. We told him this, but he insisted he had caused the death of these men. He brooded a lot. He once spent the entire day trying to write a letter to his parents. At the end of the day he had written only six words: "I am fine. Your son, Frank." He showed it to us and said, "It's not much of a letter is it." He got steadily worse. He told us he did a lot of things wrong when he was a boy in New York, such as going down by the East River and playing with himself. Glen Zentz tried to reassure him by saying, "Why hell, Frank, that ain't anything. Look at Rufe there. That's his favorite sport. When was the last time Rufe?" Rufe answered, "Last night."

Frank wouldn't be consoled and repeatedly told us we should give him what he deserved. Then he began to stay awake all night. You would constantly see a cigarette glowing in his hand.

This made us all uneasy because those excelsior mattresses were flammable. We tried to get him to stop, but apparently he couldn't. He refused to go to the mess hall at the proper times, but went over when it was closed and locked and banged on the door. Finally he tried to climb the barbed-wire fences in broad daylight in full view of the tower guards. The Germans had made it very clear that such an action would bring on a burst of rifle fire, but they obviously recognized him as disturbed and did not shoot. They just came over and took him away. They may well have repatriated him.

Rob M. was withdrawn and quiet. One day he cut his throat and wrists with a razor blade and lost enough blood to paint a house. There was an excellent British doctor who stitched him up, and he was returned to the compound. He only came back to our room once, and that was to apologize to us. No one felt he was owed any apology, but Glen Zentz said we probably owed Rob one because "we must have driven him around the bend."

We did drive one major out of our room. He was temporarily assigned to our room after arriving in camp. It was dark when he came in, and he only got a brief look around. He had come straight to our camp without going through Dulag Luft, which meant a couple of days earlier he had been eating steak and eggs back in England. The next morning he was the first man up. The shock was a little too much for his system. We had always commented about how everybody's room stank but ours. Those closed and locked shutters at night meant the ventilation was considerably less than adequate. That morning the rest of us noticed a look of complete disbelief and disgust on the major's face. He left immediately and never returned, having used his rank to obtain a place where there were fewer men to a room.

[Shortly before ending his own life, Hitler allegedly ordered the execution of all prisoners. Fortunately, this final command was never implemented. A mixture of relief, anxiety, and chaos marked the final days for Miller and most American POWs.]

In April of 1945, we could hear the Russian artillery closing in. We also had been watching our 8th Air Corps pass over on its way to bomb Berlin. This was a tremendous show. You could hear them coming long before they came into sight. Then they passed overhead in a gigantic, relentless mass. We would jump up and down, wave our arms, and yell our heads off. I believe those were our most exciting days. Had they not been our own ships, I can well understand the hatred and terror they must have inspired.

The end was getting near. One day we got up, and there were no guards in the towers. The officers had departed, leaving instructions for the enlisted men to stay on duty. They stayed just long enough for the camp to get good and dark, and then they left. We were now in charge. We turned on the water and the lights, tore down the fences, and the P.A. system was tuned to the BBC. I can still remember the song of the day was "Don't Fence Me In."

The Germans had some warehouses that contained shoes, clothing, and Red Cross packages. During our few remaining days in camp, we simply helped ourselves. I discovered a room filled with shoes and found two that fit well enough to keep my toes out of the cold air. Rufe took three fur hats and a couple of ski poles.

About eight in the evening of May 1, we heard a tremendous roar in the South Compound. It sounded like the crowd at a football game. The advance elements of the Russian Army had arrived. The next day they were there in full force. The Germans had described them as "the Mongol hordes of Ghengis Khan," and they pretty well looked the part. They had been fighting and living outdoors all winter and were a tough-looking bunch. They had moved across the German countryside like Sherman's army across Georgia. They drove about 150 cattle into our camp and presented them to us as a gift. This was the first fresh meat we had since arriving in Germany, and all those cattle disappeared in one day.

After a few days, the 8th Air Corps arranged to move out the entire camp in one day. We marched out in a long column. The P.A. system was blasting "You Gotta Accentuate the Positive." The B–17s came in one minute apart. Fifty men were loaded in about twenty seconds and took off. We landed at Rheims, France, and I have never been on a plane since.

EBERHARD LADWIG

Eberhard Ladwig, whom the British captured in North Africa and subsequently turned over to the Americans, is a multilingual botanist who took advantage of his imprisonment to improve both his language and professional skills. Ladwig's POW experiences also altered the way he felt about Jews and life in the Third Reich. Now a retired teacher, Ladwig lives in Mühlhausen, Germany, where he cultivates a garden filled with exotic fruits, vegetables, and flowers.

I WAS BORN IN Erfurt in 1923 which is now the capital of Thuringia but at age two we moved to a little village about forty kilometers away where my father was a teacher. Like all youngsters I was in the *Hitler Jugend* and then the *Arbeitsdienst* where I dug ditches and did some landscaping in Polish territory near the Weizel River. After passing my high school *Abitur* [graduation exam] in 1941, I was drafted into the army. I applied to go to the Medical Corps, but, against my wishes, I was put in the infantry. A friend and I applied to the *Afrikakorps*, and we were the only two from the whole company who were accepted. The rest went to the Russian front.

There were many wild rumors from soldiers on leave about what to expect if the Allies took you prisoner. During my final summer vacation from school in 1940, I had happily worked on a family farm in a neighboring village where I became acquainted with a Flemish POW from Belgium. To a certain extent we could converse in a kind of French dialect. Although it was forbidden, he was invited to eat his meals with us. At the same time every evening, he had to leave and return to the prisoners' quarters in the village. Because he was so well treated, I thought that perhaps at least among the Western Allies a German prisoner might receive the same kind of treatment.

I expected something quite different from the Russians. We

had heard the savage accounts and crude jokes told by our Eastern Front soldiers about how they treated Russian prisoners. Only later did I discover the full extent of the cruelty and even extermination suffered by Russian POWs, but I already knew that I didn't want to be captured by Soviet troops.

We were replacement troops in North Africa which meant we were sent wherever they needed us. Mostly we were shot at by artillery in North Africa. When you were awake it was awful. But when you were asleep you wouldn't even hear it. I figured one of two things would happen to me: I would be shot and killed or I would be wounded and not killed. In the latter scenario, I would recover but spend the rest of my life as part of an occupying army, and that idea was even more untenable than the former. We were constantly moving around, and that's why we were captured. We were in an unfamiliar place, and during the night our lieutenant led us to the top of a hill. The next morning we discovered we were right in the middle of the British. I don't know quite how that happened, but on April 29, 1943, we became prisoners of war.

We were first put in a temporary tent camp which may have been near Constantine, Algeria, close to the Tunisian border. We were put in an enclosure where normally one might keep animals. They picked two of us to act as translators which is what I did for most of my time in captivity.

We were transported to Oran by train. The Americans placed food packages in the cars, but we had French guards, and they never let us off the car to relieve ourselves. This was very bad. When we reached the railroad station at Oran we couldn't help ourselves; we just had to urinate. This French officer became so angry he shouted, "You people are totally uncultured." I answered him in French and told him we had been two days without getting out of the railroad car so we couldn't really help ourselves and what we had done had nothing to do with our culture. I was afraid he might hit me, but he calmed down.

I have some very bad memories of that prison camp in Oran. It was very dirty and wet, and we were forced to sleep on the ground in the mud. It was a relief to be taken down to the harbor and loaded on a civilian ship of the New York/Puerto Rico Line. The guards asked who among us could speak English. I again volunteered. My job was to transmit any complaints from the prisoners to the American officers.

We were quite comfortable on board. The food was wonderful, but I was disgusted when some of our men ate everything they could get their hands on. Not even a wolf eats more than he can digest. One of our guys bragged that he had eaten thirty-six sausages at one meal. That's terrible. Many of them naturally became seasick, although the seas were not rough.

That voyage fundamentally changed my life. I found a book on board entitled *Jewish Thought*. It was a brief philosophical treatment of Jewish thinking which I discovered contained many similarities to Christian thought. I had heard so many bad things about Jews, but this book profoundly changed me

[Tears begin to well up in Ladwig's eyes.]

The German race laws had been introduced in 1935 and *Kristallnacht* was in 1938, but all I really knew about such things was what I read in the papers. After reading this book, I consciously rejected any and all aspects of anti-Semitism. Nor did I ever have any bad experiences with Jews. At Camp Albany, Georgia, I even became friends with the American camp interpreter who was a Jew from Prague who had emigrated to the U.S. in 1936.

As one of the company interpreters, I helped with the morning roll call and with the selection of the men for work details. Each day I also had to keep a record of the hours worked for each member of our company so they could receive their canteen credits at the end of the month. I also thought I could help everyone get along with each other. I tried to get justice for everybody because as an interpreter I could make things better or worse. I attempted to satisfy both sides, although that was not easy. For example, I would often tone down what the Germans said before I would translate it for the Americans. I could not say to an American, "He says you are a *Rindvieh*" [blockhead] anymore than I could tell a German prisoner, "The American officer just called you a son-of-a-bitch."

Being an interpreter also gave me the opportunity occasionally to accompany the work details. This allowed me to come in contact with nature in the surrounding forests and farms. At Camp Opelika, Alabama, there was a forest in which I could identify various plants and butterflies. I made sketches of them, but unfortunately I was unable to take most of them back to Germany.

Some of my comrades wanted to do nothing but eat, play, and sleep. Others were more into intellectual matters—to find something of a higher calling in life than just existence. So I learned much about human nature and different ways of thinking about things. The Austrians, for example, greatly influenced my political thinking. Of course, I already had certain ideas. I even had the nickname "Democrat." But the Austrians had a different perspective on things than did we Germans. Most Germans applied Wilhelm Busch's words to the Austrians—*da bin ich aber wirklich froh, denn Gott sei dank ich bin nicht so* ["I am so overjoyed that thank God Almighty I have never sunk so low"]—but I learned differently. For example, I had only learned bad things about the Dollfuss government, but I discovered the Austrians had a better democratic tradition than did we Germans.

I had a good Austrian friend in the work camp at Albany, Georgia. Every day we argued. He would defend Catholicism and I would argue for Protestantism. He defended Austria and I tried to defend Germany. We had long conversations while walking around the camp enclosure and in the barracks at night. We thought and talked about everything including what would happen after the war. We studied the daily news reports, and we were both convinced that Germany would not win.

We received the *New York Times* daily. We interpreters took it upon ourselves to examine the paper for relevant news. We translated and condensed the war news into two or three typed pages and tacked them up on a board outside our tent for everyone to read. We included commentaries from the British, French, and American armies and sometimes the *Wehrmachts Bericht*.[16] We also included reports from the camp authorities. So we knew about the final Battle of Stalingrad, the fall of North Africa, and the Normandy invasion. We even learned about the liberation of the Maidanek concentration camp, which for me and several others was a great shock. We already sensed and feared that Germany had committed terrible atrocities, but this went far beyond anything we could have imagined; in fact, many of the prisoners refused to believe such reports.

---

[16]A German military newspaper.

WILLIAM KALWAY

Born in Buffalo, New York, William Kalway volunteered for the U.S. Army in 1940 and was with the Twenty-Sixth Infantry when captured on February 19, 1943, during the Battle of Kasserine Pass in Tunisia. As a prisoner, the Germans considered Sgt. Kalway a troublemaker, primarily because he refused to work. But in spite of his feisty nature, quick intelligence, and considerable courage, the horrible conditions and harsh treatment eventually took their toll on Kalway and many of his fellow prisoners. Since the war Kalway has suffered several nervous breakdowns and is presently on 100 percent disability. During his final months in captivity, Kalway kept a diary, which he later turned into a very detailed account of the "two years, two months, three days, and fourteen and one-half hours" he spent as a prisoner of war. Part of what follows is based on this memoir.

FOR A LONG TIME I just tried to forget my experiences as a POW. In spite of trying to rationalize my capture by telling myself I had absolutely no other choice, deep inside I considered myself a coward. Then in 1970 I wrote the Office of the Adjutant General to inquire as to what medals and ribbons I was entitled. I learned that in addition to the usual "Fruit Salad," I had earned the Bronze Star and the Combat Infantryman's Badge, and that my battalion had earned the French *Croix de Guerre* for the Battle of Kasserine Pass. Learning this made me change my mind about calling myself a coward.

[Kalway was incarcerated in two Italian and eight German POW camps, including two labor camps, where he was forced to work because the Italians had confiscated his AGO card which would have certified his NCO status. Stalag 3-B at Fürstenburg was Kalway's fifth German POW camp.]

Stalag 3-B was a very large camp, containing prisoners of every nationality who were separated into compounds according to nationality. The American compound was for all ground force NCOs. It was here that I first heard the term "Confidence Man" in reference to a fellow POW who had our confidence to represent our interests with the Germans. If we had a legitimate grievance, this man was supposed to be able to speak to the *Kommandant*, who presumably would then attempt to iron out any difficulties. This was fine in theory, but more than once I heard the Germans say, "*Scheisse am Schweitz*," which literally translates into "Shit on Switzerland." They were referring, of course, to the Geneva Convention, which stipulated that all prisoners had a right to representation.

Around September 1, 1944, the *Gestapo* pulled a surprise raid on our compound, looking for contraband articles. They ordered us out of the barracks into the open compound while they searched everywhere in the barracks. They even inspected rolls of toilet paper, looking for escape maps. They found a huge cache of food and cigarettes, which we had been hoarding in case the war ended suddenly. They even found a large American flag which we planned to fly over the camp to identify us when the Russians arrived. When we returned to our barracks after the raid, we discovered that many of our American uniforms were missing. When we complained, the *Kommandant* told our Confidence Man that we were only allowed to have one complete uniform, with no extra items. Since we were already dressed while the barracks were being searched, they declared the extra clothing to be contraband.

When I found out after the war that during the Battle of the Bulge many of the attacking Germans wore American uniforms, I wondered if those uniforms were not the ones which were stolen from us during that raid. If so, the Germans were certainly doing some long-range planning.

One day, a buddy and I were sitting at the edge of the trash pit when we saw a German major and a sergeant walking along outside our compound, inspecting the fence and grounds. We turned our backs and pretended that we hadn't seen them. The officer came closer and shouted at us. We just turned and looked at him. He began to rant and rave about why we hadn't stood and saluted when an officer spoke to us. Although we understood perfectly, we just said, "*Nix versteh*," which was an insulting slang way of saying, "I don't understand." He got so mad that he couldn't even draw his pistol. I had taken German in high school, my father often spoke German around the house, and I had worked with civilians in Munich, so I had a pretty fair command of the language. However, I had learned that the less you let the enemy know about you, the better off you were.

I was in Stalag 3-B only about six weeks when I was transferred to *Arbeitskommando #1* at Trattendorf bei Spremberg which was a work camp. The Germans were building a huge power plant, and our job was to carry the construction materials to the civilian workers so they could do the actual building. We also shoveled the sand, gravel, and cement into a huge mixer. Through some sort of pressure system, this concrete was forced through pipes to the upper levels of the building under construction. The work was hard and, as usual, the food was bad. If it were not for the Red Cross food parcels, we would have starved to death.

We were mostly NCOs, but we were treated like enlisted men and made to work. The Germans told us they had no papers on us, but we had earlier heard about a list of NCO names at Stalag Luft 3 where several of us had been sent to serve as orderlies for Air Corps officers. That list confirmed us as NCOs so we decided it was our right to refuse to work. When we fell out for work formation the next morning, only about ten of us stood by our resolution. The rest went off to work. The *Kommandant*, speaking through an interpreter, ordered the rest of us to go to work immediately. We all stood fast. Then the *Kommandant* ordered the guards to load their rifles. One guard was standing right next to me, and when I saw that brass cartridge going into the chamber, I knew that we had better move, even before the interpreter translated the orders. When we started moving towards the gate, one of the guards deliberately kicked one of our men in the small of the back, and he dropped unconscious to the ground. We later heard that he was paralyzed from the waist down, but I can't verify this. We never did see him again.

After we arrived at work, the interpreter came over and called me a troublemaker and referred to the work strike I had earlier been involved in *Arbeitskommando 3342/46* in Munich. This was my first experience with this type of German thoroughness. Up until then, I didn't know they kept a dossier on prisoners of war.

The interpreter asked me why I did such things and if I was trying to get myself killed. I will be forever proud of the answer I
gave, because I did not think that I had the guts. I told him that
I was an American soldier and that as long as I was wearing the
American uniform, it was my duty to cause as much trouble for
the enemy as I could. I don't know why I said this. Maybe it was
a subconscious desire for death.

By this time I was becoming inured to all abuse, discomfort,
filth, and everything else. In fact, I was becoming quite apathetic
about life itself. I didn't give a damn if I lived or died. After almost
two years, when all you can see in the morning when you get up
is that goddam barbed wire and with no future but more barbed
wire, you begin to wonder whether life is worth living. After I
finally got home, I often wondered how the prisoners of the
Japanese lasted out the war. I would surely have gone psychotic
instead of just neurotic.

*[After Trattendorf, Kalway was returned to Stalag 3-B at
Fürstenburg but not for long. The advancing Russian troops
forced the Germans to move literally thousands of Allied prisoners. Kalway and his group were marched westward to Stalag 3-A
at Luckenwalde.]*

On January 31, 1945, we were given orders to pack whatever
we could carry and the next morning we moved out. We didn't
know where we were going but it was to be on foot. It is difficult
for me to remember everything about this march because this was
the worst time of all. I don't know how many thousands of prisoners there were, but it seemed as though the whole countryside
was one moving mass of men. After a few hours, most of us were
so tired that we got rid of everything except our blanket and mess
kit. During my stay at Stalag Luft 3 I had started a diary into
which I had managed to insert several political cartoons from the
Völkischer Beobachter, which was the official newspaper of the
Nazi Party. These cartoons were extremely vicious caricatures of
the Allied leaders.

That first night we had to sleep in open fields. It was bitter
cold, so two of us would double up so we'd have two blankets over
us. The Germans fed us absolutely nothing for the first two days,
and the only water we had was from scooping up snow. There
were also many civilians fleeing, but they were forced to move

through the fields. Only POWs and military traffic were allowed on the roads. About the third day, we received one loaf of black bread for eight men and one half kilo of cheese for five men. For the rest of the eight-day march, we received nothing more. We saw many bodies lying alongside the roads. One time we heard an SS officer telling the officer in charge of our section that if we didn't move fast enough, he should order the guards to shoot us. Several times we had to step over the bodies of Americans who had been shot. At least one of our men who had stopped to urinate was also shot.

We arrived at Stalag 3-A at Luckenwalde on the afternoon of February 8. This was by far the worst camp I had been in. I later read about Andersonville, the Civil War Confederate prison, but I believe Stalag 3-A was equally bad. We lived under unspeakable conditions. A lot of the men were assigned to open areas with no protection. We were so crowded that it was absolutely impossible to maintain even the rudimentary conditions of cleanliness. We were about 3,000 men and there were absolutely no sanitary facilities and only one water tap. Every man became infested with lice. We would take our undershirts off and hang them on a line and try to burn off the lice with matches. This would work for a few hours, but it was impossible to get rid of them for good. It was here that I first met men who were from the 106th Division who had been taken prisoner during the Battle of the Bulge. Many of them had been brutally treated, and some had wounds for which they had received no treatment.

The mental condition of the men began to deteriorate rapidly. This deterioration took many forms. Mostly, the men would just sit and stare into space. If you asked a question, you received a blank stare for about a minute before the person realized you had asked him something. Then his answer was so disjointed, you wondered if he really understood the question. Some men refused to speak at all, and several times individuals had to be forcefully restrained from rushing the fence to commit suicide.

There were Russian prisoners in the next compound. They were evidently better conditioned for this kind of life because I didn't see any of the mental conditions so prevalent in the American compound. However, they were dropping like flies from typhus while not one American suffered from this disease even though we were all being bitten by the same lice. This was good proof that the American army inoculations were very effective.

On Hitler's birthday we all stood in the open and watched one of those thousand-plane raids on Berlin. What a birthday present! It seemed as though there was a solid stream of bombers coming in from the west. We could see the lead plane in each formation drop a smoke bomb, and then the other planes in that formation would drop their loads on the smoke target. We could feel the concussion, even though we were some forty kilometers to the south.

There was a kindly sergeant in charge of our compound. He had been in a Panzer outfit, but had been wounded so badly that his right arm had been amputated at the shoulder. When we received news of Roosevelt's death, he allowed a bugler to go into a patch of woods just outside the camp and blow Taps while the rest of the Americans stood at attention and saluted. By the way, the headline in the *Völkischer Beobachter* that day read, *"Rosenfeld, der grosste Kriegskriminal aller Zeit, ist tod"* ["Rosenfeld, the biggest war criminal of all time, is dead"].

CLIFFORD FOX

Captured in Tunisia on March 26, 1943, Pfc. Clifford Fox was soon shipped to Germany where he was interned in Stalag 7-A, just north of Munich, and in Stalag 2-A at Hammerstein near the present-day Polish city of Szczecinek. Fox eventually had the good fortune to work on a farm; in fact, his story is very similar to that of many German POWs who worked in agriculture in the United States. Less fortunate were the female Russian and Polish slave laborers who also worked on the farm, a photo of whom appears in this book. Fox was one of the few American prisoners who decided to learn German, which, along with his natural curiosity and the good working conditions he experienced, makes his POW story much more positive than those told by most American prisoners.

AN UNFORGETTABLE THING HAPPENED right after we were liberated by the Second Armor just north of Hanover. The Germans had marched us all the way from Schneidemühl in what is now northwest Poland, a distance of about 250 miles. The American officer in charge said we could go out in the countryside and help ourselves to food or drink, but not to hurt or abuse anybody. We went down to the railroad station in this little nearby village, and I'll never forget the sight of a bunch of German troops returning from the front. These were just young kids, and many seemed shellshocked. I know they weren't much older than sixteen or seventeen. Some were frightened and would try to hide in the boxcars. They had been through some terrible times on the Eastern Front fighting the Russians, and they just didn't know what was now going to happen to them. They appeared to have no idea where they were. They just sat there dazed. I really felt sorry for them. I told my companion, "I can't stand to watch this. We've got to leave." I suppose it reminded me of my own capture.

I was in the 34th Infantry Division that landed in North Africa in November of 1942. A few months later, on March 26, 1943, my squad was out on point. Our purpose was to draw fire so our main force would know where the Germans were. Once we drew fire, we were supposed to retreat. I was dodging back through some olive trees, and all of a sudden I ran into three Germans pointing their guns at me. So there I was all alone and a prisoner of the Germans. It was a horrible feeling. It felt like my life had fallen completely apart. But I was soon joined by several others who had also been captured, and we were moved to the rear lines. I was interrogated, but I didn't know anything. Finally, this German came in who spoke beautiful English. He told me all he wanted to know was if I were hungry. I had only eaten a can of crackers and sardines at noon so I told him I was. One of the soldiers brought in a thin piece of chocolate and gave it to me. I later learned that a single piece of thin chocolate was a two-week ration for him. I don't know if I would have done the same thing for a German prisoner. Later this same soldier brought me some potato soup. He told me not to worry about being badly treated because the next day he might be in my shoes on the other side of the line.

They flew us to Naples on those old tri-motor planes, and I was praying that our air force wasn't in the air that day. The German authorities in Naples offered to send a message to our families. Some of the guys thought this was a trick, but I gave them my name and address, and it worked. My folks found out I was a POW. It wasn't until a month later that they received the official notice from our government.

From Naples we were loaded onto these old boxcars and moved to Munich. Most of the guys just sat on the floor moaning and groaning, but I had a different attitude. I wanted to see everything so I looked out these little barred windows in the boxcar and watched the scenery go by. In fact, I stood almost the entire way. I thought, "Well, I'm here, and there's nothing I can do about it, so I might as well make the best of it." I think I had learned this attitude during the Depression. We had learned simply to accept things and make do with what we had, and that's how I figured I would act as a prisoner. I just accepted my lot, and if I didn't get home, I had at least made the effort to get along as best I could. Of course, I was lucky to end up on a farm. So many of the guys in the regular POW camps spent their waking moments just walking the barbed-wire fence like caged animals. I couldn't have done that.

It was at my first permanent camp in Moosberg just north of Munich that I decided to learn German. We would be sent out on these work details, and one of the French workers gave me a German-English dictionary. I then began asking the German guards, "*Was ist der Name das?*" Of course, that made no sense. But I finally learned to ask, "*Wie heisst das?*" Then they would tell me. Then I learned the basic names I needed for daily living. It took me a long time to realize you couldn't translate literally. It was broken German, but I really began to enjoy learning the language. I eventually got so I could have conversations, and that greatly helped me when I worked on the farm.

It was also in Stalag 7-A that I learned the futility of causing too much trouble. We were treated quite decently, but you know how Americans are. From time to time we would refuse to do something and threaten to go on strike. A German officer would then threaten us with the *Gestapo* if we didn't behave properly. He'd say, "Now boys, I don't want to get the *SS* troops in here, but that will be my only recourse. And if those guys come in here, they will crack heads." Well, that stopped any nonsense.

I even tried to escape in Moosberg. I was on a work detail in Munich. One of my buddies was an Italian-American, and he told me if we could get to the mountains on the Italian side of the Alps we could get along because he spoke Italian. I thought it was worth a shot. We started saving foodstuff. We would take it with us and hide it on the job. Finally, one day during our noon lunch break we took off right through town. There were a lot of French workers walking the streets so we thought we'd blend in. We got quite a ways before we met one of the officers from our guard company. He asked us what we were doing. We didn't have a satisfactory answer so he took us back with him. We got five days in the guardhouse on bread and water. One of the German guards asked us, "What were you guys going to do? Swim back to New York?" I told him getting out was the most important thing.

In the fall of 1943 the Germans shipped us to Stalag 2-B at Hammerstein which was located about halfway up the old Danzig Corridor. About ten of us were assigned to this farm outside of Resko which was owned by a large landowner. He also owned several other farms in the area. At the time he was serving as a colonel in the army so these farms were being run by ordinary

German families. Emma and Karl Schulz were in charge of the farm on which I worked, and I stayed with them for almost a year.

Karl Schulz had belonged to the Communist Party in the early 1930s and had been some kind of local official. But when Hitler took over, the Nazis locked him up for six months. He later told me the Nazis would come into the concentration camp every day and say, "*Heil Hitler!*" When he refused to respond, they beat the daylights out of him. After a few such beatings he figured this made no sense. So one morning, he answered with his own "Heil Hitler." After another month or so they turned him loose. He was put on parole and had to check in with the new town officials.

I got to know Emma and Karl very well. They were wonderful people. They insisted that I *duzen* them [use the familiar form of address] although I was properly supposed to use the more formal *Sie*. What really amazed me was how they took to me rather than to anybody else in the group. Perhaps it was because their son was tall and so was I. Emma told me, "You write your mother that I will be your mother while you're here." She knitted me socks and gloves. When I was alone with Karl, he would talk to me about Hitler. The same was true of his brother Eric, but neither would say anything if the other was around. Emma also talked to me by the hour about the war. She was so afraid the Americans would come in and rip everything apart, but I assured her they wouldn't.

We slept in a garage on the farm which originally had been for the owner's three or four cars. This was not like being in a regular POW camp. The door was never locked until eleven o'clock at night. We had a guard named Hans. He was a wounded veteran from the Russian front. He had a bad limp and one of his eyes had been badly injured. We all got to know each other, and it was a far different relationship than could ever have existed in the Stalag. He would even come into the barracks, lay his gun on the bed, and play cards with us.

Potatoes were our main staple on the farm. We took our meat out of our Red Cross parcels. On Sunday we occasionally had horse meat if a horse had died which, along with our canned meat, really made a pretty decent Sunday meal. We never had any fresh vegetables. Sometimes Emma would make some *Kuchen*, you know pastry. When I was liberated I weighed about 190 pounds which was about fifteen pounds less than when I was captured.

The only time in my life I got drunk was while I was a prisoner of war. We had a distillery on the farm. The workers would harvest potatoes and grain, and Karl would then dump some of them into these seven large vats that kept bubbling away in the basement of the house where he and Emma lived. After all this fermented, Karl would distill it. He would then take some of the distilled liquor and trade it in the town, but the rest was for drinking. This one Sunday we went up to the house for our weekly hot bath, and Karl invited us to try his brew. I tasted it, but I couldn't stand it. So he mixed in something or other that was probably honey, and then it didn't taste so bad. I drank it, and I swear to goodness I had no idea what happened. Everything turned into spots. The guys later told me I went over to the door and was beating on it. Well, finally I just keeled over. It's ironic that the only time I ever got drunk was when I was a prisoner of war. I had never been drunk before and never since. I just don't care for it, but I sure did that day.

Our meals were prepared by Polish and Russian women. The Germans had simply brought them back with them from the Eastern Front as slave laborers, and put them to work on the farm. Each day two of them were assigned to work for the colonel's wife who still lived in the main house. They would do the housework and prepare the meals while the others worked in the fields. In the evening we'd go up to the kitchen and get our big kettle of food and bring it back. Two of these women were Polish and the others were Russian. One of them was named Maria, and she had been a nurse in the Ukraine, but on the farm she was assigned to clean the barn. She would clean out the manure, load it on a skid, and then take it out to the fields. I never saw any mistreatment of these women sexually, although sometimes they were abused in other ways. One day one of them did something wrong when assigned to the big house where they all hated to work. The old colonel's wife was a high-and-mighty type, and I'm sure she was never satisfied with their work. One of the girls was ordered to substitute for another one who was sick, but she refused. A constable from the village was called in, and he beat her up right in front of us and then marched her right up to the house. That was really hard for us to watch and be unable to do anything. When I think back on what happened, in many ways they had it worse than we did.

GUENTHER OSWALD

Born in Boizenburg some 45 miles east of Hamburg, Guenther Oswald was a *Luftwaffe* lieutenant in an anti-aircraft artillery unit when captured shortly after the Normandy invasion. He was incarcerated in Camp Trinidad, Colorado, where he was one of the few German officers who willingly worked outside the camp. It proved a good decision. Oswald came in contact with normal Americans and their way of life, and this affected his postwar decision to emigrate to the United States. In 1952, Oswald settled in Austin, Texas, where he is still a renowned cabinetmaker, as well as an amateur paleontologist.

Although American authorities introduced elaborate reeducation programs for select German prisoners, being well treated and having the opportunity to mix with people outside the normal POW camp clearly proved a much more effective way to introduce German captives to the American way of life.

GROWING UP UNDER THE Nazis we were brainwashed. We considered it perfectly all right to sacrifice ourselves—even our lives—for the fatherland. I began to change my attitude toward Hitler and National Socialism when I went out on labor details from Camp Trinidad, Colorado, and met the common American people. They were friendly and open and didn't hesitate to express themselves. They were not filled with hatred toward us. We were somehow just a bunch of boys who got caught. In Nazi Germany, we would never have been allowed to talk and act the way Americans did. Our parents couldn't educate us in the right way because it was too dangerous for them. So what I saw in American civilian society made me think about German society, and what I wanted to do with my life.

After I graduated from *Gymnasium* with my *Abitur*, I was

drafted into the *Arbeitsdienst*. Then, when war broke out, I was drafted into the military where for one and a half years I served as an enlisted man before being sent to an officers' training school. The military checked your academic record and your general behavior and attitude. We were also given a kind of psychological test. For example, those doing the questioning asked one of my school friends, who was a brilliant student, but who had taken a couple of years off from his studies to help his parents, what he would do if he went on furlough to his parents' farm, and they asked him to shovel manure. He quite naturally answered that he would help his parents. He was rejected for officers' training because no officer would do such a thing. If you considered it more important to help your parents get the manure on the fields than conducting yourself like an officer, the military didn't consider you officer material.

After I received my commission, I served in a *Luftwaffe* anti-aircraft artillery unit. I was wounded for the first time in Russia. I had a piece of shrapnel go in my ear and cut a nerve. Fortunately, they shipped me out and that night our unit was completely cut off and destroyed. Sometimes what looks like a disaster can be a blessing. After I recovered, I was still not fit for Russia so they sent me to France. I was wounded again when an airplane was shot down and hit the house next to us. I was on the roof and was blown off and fell two stories.

After five years of fighting, my morale was still okay. Even at the time of the Normandy invasion, many of us still thought Germany might win. What did bother me personally was having to adopt the Nazi salute. We were military and we were supposed to salute like the military and not get involved in politics.

After the Normandy invasion our unit was decimated, and we had orders to withdraw. Our commanding officer, a corporal, and I went from gun to gun to destroy them so the Allies couldn't use them. By the time we finished, our unit was gone. So we were on our own. We tried to reach our lines marching at night, but on the third night we got caught. We fought our way out but we lost the corporal. I don't know whether he made it or not. The next night we were wet, hungry, and exhausted, when we went to sleep in a barn. We woke up hearing gun shots. The barn was surrounded by French civilians who were shooting at us. One bullet hit my backbone. I was partially paralyzed, so there was no way to get out. I was carried to a French doctor who treated my wounds. There was no interrogation, probably because I was wounded. Two or three days later I could walk again.

The French turned us over to the British who shipped us to England from where we were sent on to the United States. We landed in Boston and took the train to Camp Trinidad which was a camp for officers below the rank of general. The generals had their own camp somewhere else. We were treated very well at first. The American commander seemed almost proud of us. We had so much food that we finally even refused to eat mutton because we had too much of it. So it was burned to make it disappear. On some rare occasions even beer was available. We could sometimes leave camp if we gave our word of honor we would be back at a certain time. We could not go to town, but we could wander out on the hills and the open prairie for nature studies. There was also the opportunity to take classes which the universities of Denver and Colorado sponsored, and many of us did so. I enrolled in the first classes for becoming a medical doctor which was then my goal. The teachers were German physicians who were prisoners in the camp. There were also church services but I didn't participate in them.

Evidently it became known that our American camp commander liked the Germans too well, and we heard he was supposed to be arrested and replaced. But one of his assistants later told me the commander had some connections so he was not punished but simply transferred to another kind of duty. I think this was during the fall of 1944. The next commander hated Germans. He wouldn't even talk to the highest-ranking German officer even though he was much higher in rank than the commander. He supposedly said that even his adjutant was too good to talk to Germans. He took away all our special privileges. Food also got short. We didn't starve but we were hungry.

One prisoner at Trinidad did get special treatment. He was the only one I know of who was allowed to remain in the States without going home after the war. He was a rocket scientist, and the Americans wanted him. They transferred him from one camp to the other and somewhere along the line he got "lost." I knew him slightly in the camp, but I've since forgotten his name.

[According to the Geneva Convention officers could not be required to work. Although Oswald does not remember volunteer-

ing to work, such must have been the case. Working outside the
camp provided a welcome diversion from the boredom of the
daily routine, and it also allowed the prisoners to come in contact
with non-military people.]

We worked in the sugar beet harvest. The farmers would sometimes feed us extra rations and give us cigarettes as well. So we were happy to cooperate with them because we got something in exchange for our labor. One exception was a farmer of Danish descent. He didn't like us, and the feeling was mutual. His sugar beets were of such poor quality they should have been plowed under. But since he got cheap labor he wanted them harvested. We slept in an old school building, and the water main cut through his property. When we refused to harvest his sugar beets, he cut off the water. This got him in trouble with the American authorities, and the water was turned back on. But this was our only negative experience.

A much more pleasant farmer promised to take us to his home if we would sing some German songs for his grandmother. They were Germans who had emigrated to Russia—what we call *Volgadeutsche*—and then later had fled Russia to come to the United States. We sang, the old lady cried, and we got lots of food and cigarettes.

When we worked outside the base camp, we also had civilian clothes, and we would tell the guards, "Turn around for a minute. We're going for a little walk, but we'll be back by 10:00 o'clock." And we were. No one I know took advantage of this freedom to escape. Several had earlier tried to escape but never under those circumstances. We had given our word and under our code of honor that was that.

HENRY H. "MAC" McKEE

Supremely disciplined and confident, Henry "Mac" McKee is a retired colonel who refuses to admit to any lasting effects from his imprisonment. However, to this day he is still angry at his superior for surrendering his men during the Battle of the Bulge. McKee, who was incarcerated in Stalag 12-A at Limburg and Stalag 13-C at Hammelburg, is also critical of those few fellow officers who as prisoners did not always comport themselves in a military manner. McKee's prison diary makes it clear that although conditions were bad—he once was forced to go sixty-six days without changing his underwear or brushing his teeth—as an officer he certainly suffered less than the enlisted men. The availability of Red Cross packages, as well as rations from some friendly Serbian officers in the next compound, helped McKee and his fellow officers endure their captivity. Excerpts from McKee's prison diary appear in this remembrance.

JUST A FEW DAYS before we got to Stalag 12-A at Limburg, Germany, the British mistakenly bombed the camp killing about sixty Americans. It is terrible to be bombed by friendly forces. We had spent over thirty-six hours in Frankfurt in a boxcar, and I lost more perspiration during that time than during an entire summer in Texas. The Germans were supposed to mark the boxcars with a Red Cross insignia, but they never did ours.

The Germans transported us to Limburg in trucks. On the way we stopped at this ammo dump, and the guards told us to start loading ammo onto these other trucks. I told the guard in charge, "Can't do it. Geneva Convention and all that rubbish." He insisted, so I told him again, "We're not allowed to do it because it's a violation of the Geneva Convention. We cannot do anything that will help the war effort." He and one of his men grabbed a couple of my guys, took them aside, and pointed these automatic weapons at them. Then he said, "I'll ask you one more time. Load the ammo or you're going to lose your men, two at a time." I told the guys, "Load ammo."

From Limburg we were moved to Stalag 13-C at Hammelburg. There were a lot of Serbians in the compound next to ours. These were upper-class, loyalist officers who were very well educated. They had American Red Cross packages; in fact, they had a warehouse full of these parcels. But when we got into camp there were no parcels for us. Our senior officer got together with a Serb general and pointed to the American labels on those packages. He worked out a deal where we could draw some of his parcels out of this warehouse which we would pay back after ours began arriving. The Serb general didn't want to do it. Finally, as the front started to move toward us and you could hear the artillery, we threatened to turn him over to the American authorities. So, he put us on the same deal as his men.

I became friends with several of the Serbs, and they were great. At night I would climb under the compound fence and visit them. They gave us all kinds of things. One gave me a real neat coffee cup and a pan for heating water, both of which were made from jam cans. I got a hat from another Serb. I have never in my life seen such a spirit of giving. When we first got to Hammelburg we had no cigarettes, and the Serbs were getting twenty-five a week. So they donated ten to each of us. That was a particularly good deal for me, because I didn't smoke, and I could trade them for food. You could get anything for cigarettes. For example, I traded for sugar, chocolate bars, a pen, gloves, and always extra bread.

The Serbs even had an orchestra containing two violins, a bass fiddle, a clarinet, and an accordion. I remember one particular night our chaplain, another captain, and I visited my Serb friends. They served us hot coffee that was very strong and sweet. Then they brought in a big bowl of what we called Stalag pudding. On the top was a layer of raspberry jam and the rest was a very sweet custard made from sugar, barley, flour, raisins, and powdered milk. The Serbs made the three of us eat all of it. It was the best thing I had tasted since my capture.

Another favorite dish of mine was Stalag Prune-Bread Pudding. I still know the recipe. You begin with an empty milk can and put eight prunes in it which you have soaked for several hours. Bring the prunes to a boil, and then mash them up with a spoon. Add four large lumps of sugar which you have dissolved in one-eighth cup of water. Cook for ten minutes, then stir in pieces of bread crusts cut off from our daily ration. Stir constantly and cook for another fifteen minutes. Delicious!

Many things were tough, but I have to say I can't spell "cope" or "psychoanalysis" or "psychology." It was not fun being hungry and having no toothbrush or a change of underwear for weeks at a time. But one manages. I had no lasting problems with imprisonment. I mean I didn't like it and I wouldn't want to go through it again, but it didn't really affect me. When I was in the service or in a POW camp, I was in, and when I was out, I was out. I was surprised at a few things I did, and after the war when I thought about them, I thought I was nuts. But you react to the spur of the moment, and you just act instinctively.

[McKee's prison diary does describe the tremendous deprivations and stress he and his fellow prisoners suffered. At least three-quarters of his diary deals exclusively with food. It is also clear that toward the end of his imprisonment, when food became very scarce, McKee spent much of his time in bed. Religion also played an increasingly important role for him. Several times he described how much church and prayer meant to him, especially when feeling lonely and despondent because of his prolonged separation from his wife and young son. McKee's notations for March 21, 1945, are especially revealing when, in the same paragraph, he describes an officer being killed because he was outside the barracks during an air raid, the arrival of several Red Cross trucks, the day's menu, and the first day of spring:

"Today the Germans killed another one of our officers! They announced that during an overhead alert, we could go to the latrine singly. Formerly we could not go at all and the Germans would shoot anyone caught outside his building. Today Lieutenant Weeks of our Division went out during an alert, and a guard, evidently not knowing the new orders, shot him in the back. From thirty yards [the guard] leaned his rifle on a fence and shot him! He died instantly, his hands still in his pockets. His funeral was today about six hours after he was killed. The whole camp turned

out. There are several Red Cross trucks in camp. We do not know
whether they contain food or not but hope so. Today [we ate] barley
and potatoes and turnips. Today was first day of spring and was a
real sunny day but windy and a bit chilly."]

I saw a lot of despondency and the loss of morale in the prison
camps. Much more than I was happy about. There was a considerable let-down in discipline. And this was in an officers' camp. A
lot depends on the individual and his background. Although I
agree it is difficult to anticipate beforehand just who will break
down, once inside the camps, I think you could predict who was
likely to do so. They wouldn't keep themselves clean, and they
began to look like tramps. Certain guys would try to talk to them
and remind them that they were American army officers.
Sometimes it helped, but not with most of them. These guys
would just let themselves go. We couldn't really wash our clothes
in winter. We didn't have much soap, but cold water and a little
rubbing helped. We did have some razors. The blades got pretty
bad but you could scrape some of your beard off.

I saw Russians in a compound next to ours in Limburg who
were in terrible shape. It was a death camp for them. The
Germans fed them nothing but some kind of soup. We also ate
plenty of this soup; in fact, you got so much liquid in your system,
and your kidneys were so weak, that at night you constantly had
to urinate. You had to keep a bottle right by your bed because you
couldn't walk to the latrine for fear the guards would shoot you.
But about half the time you didn't reach the bottle. You just had
so much liquid in you, and your system was so debilitated, that
you just couldn't hold it.

I can tell you, if we had stayed in the camps long enough, we
all would have starved to death. Even so some of the guys traded
their food for cigarettes. I've had men who were literally starving
to death approach me because I didn't smoke and offer to trade
their food for my cigarettes. That's when I realized what an addiction nicotine is.

Friendship or a buddy system in the camps made a hell of a
difference. You also have to bring religion into it. The closer one
gets to trouble, the closer everyone seems to get to God. I watched
a lot of people who hadn't prayed in years get down on their knees
and begin praying like mad.

ROSS H. CALVERT

Cynical and bemused by most of his experiences, Nashville-born Ross Calvert tells a very disjointed, sometimes humorous story, which is often difficult to follow. Captured as a young lieutenant near the city of Colmar, France, he was sent to Stalag 13-C at Hammelburg, Germany, where even the officers had little to eat. Calvert also almost died from pneumonia in Hammelburg and still suffers problems with his lungs. A career officer, Calvert retired from the U.S. Army in 1973 as a lieutenant colonel.

AFTER WE WERE CAPTURED, the officers were segregated in Stuttgart and put into jail cells, two or three to a cell. Then someone came up to our cell and said, "Calvert? Come on. An *SS* officer wants to talk to you." I figured, "Hell, this is not a good thing." I went down to this small room and was told to sit. The interrogator had a ledger, and he read from it: "Your name is Calvert and you are an intelligence officer with your regiment." He had a roster of everyone which one of our guys must have illegally had with him. He asked, "Third Division?" I didn't say anything. So he reached over and ripped the camouflage netting off my helmet so he could see the insignia. I said, "Okay, Third Division." He asked quite a few other questions, but nothing seemed to need an answer so he sent me back. That was it.

They then moved us to Stalag 13-C at Hammelburg. We lived in brick buildings. The doors closed and fit well enough that we were snug but horribly crowded. We had one small, wood-burning stove in our room and three sets of four-high bunks and three tables. We had wooden planks for springs, and we filled our mattress covers with straw which helped keep in a little warmth. We had eight pieces of coal a day for our stove. Each chunk was about the size of a fist, which didn't afford us much heat. Sometimes we'd save two or three days allotment and burn them all at once to really get the room warm.

We had an ongoing war with the camp personnel—especially the guards who were very, very German. They were enlisted men and were supposed to treat us as officers, but there was some question in their minds how this was supposed to work. We had one American lieutenant who could bawl out German enlisted men so convincingly they just wanted to cry. He would make them stand at attention when they talked to him. He'd just give them hell. I don't know why the guards didn't just butt-strike him and leave, but he got away with it.

We would also try to foul up the guards during roll call. After the German sergeant counted off the front rank, our guys would jump in the second or third row. Then there would be too many of us. Finally, this old German stood behind us to make sure we didn't do this anymore.

We stole everything we could get our hands on. We even stole coal from the camp *Kommandant*. He was a pitiful fellow—short and fat—not a soldier at all. Someone had just put a uniform on him and told him he was *Kommandant* of our camp. He would tell us, "Gentlemen, just think. In a few weeks the war will be over and you can go home—but I have to stay."

That was about the time Hitler gave the order to kill all prisoners, but no one was interested in doing that. This *Kommandant* had a very elegant fat cat. A really good-looking animal. A few of us got to thinking about a nice "rabbit" stew. All we had to do was catch that cat, but he was the smartest feline in the world. He never walked alongside a building. He would only walk in the middle of the street, and when he got to an intersection, he would turn and stay right in the middle.

Food was of considerable interest to us. We were given a loaf of bread for seven men. It was guaranteed not to have been more that twenty-five percent sawdust, but it did not always meet that standard. It looked like regular German bread, but it didn't taste like much of anything. We divided it very carefully. That was our ration for the day. Some people would wolf down their piece immediately, while others would just nibble on it. Nobody ever knew which was the better approach. We never knew whether our breakfast beverage was coffee or shaving water. It came out about the same. It was not even decent ersatz coffee; it was just barely colored. We had that and whatever bread we possessed. Lunch was supposed to be the heavy meal of the day, although it was really pretty light. It was mostly a dehydrated vegetable—I can't think of the name—just dried-up leaves which, of course, added to our dietary problems. Once a week we had a real "beef" stew. Mostly it was made from a carcass which never had any flesh on it. It also contained rice and maybe a bit of potato. The rice had eyes, which I tried never to look at. Somehow it was too disgusting when you realized the rice was really maggots. The evening meal was usually a repeat of breakfast: coffee and whatever bread you might have saved. Occasionally they would bring us something else but not often. The Red Cross parcels were a very sore point. None was issued to us. They were issued on a regular basis to the Serb prisoners in the next compound. During World War II, unlike today, the Serbs were the good guys, and they shared with us. It wasn't a whole lot of food, but it was different. And it had taste.

We had very poor experiences with the Red Cross. A representative came to visit us occasionally and explained in great detail how our captors were doing all they could to keep us comfortable and that we shouldn't be complaining because it made the Germans nervous. Well, 900 calories a day made us nervous. We saw some Germans who obviously had quite a bit more. The Red Cross packages came in from Switzerland. When we asked why we weren't getting any, although the Serbs were, the Red Cross officials just changed the subject. I never did get a good feeling about the Red Cross. After I was released I wanted to see a bit of Paris. I went to the Red Cross and asked if I could borrow money to buy some clothes. I was wearing my old uniform that I had in the prison camp, and it was embarrassing. About all that was left were my lieutenant bars. They asked to see my identification card. Of course, I didn't have one. They asked why not. I told them the Germans preferred I didn't. I think I got ten dollars from them which even then wouldn't buy a uniform.

We only had one man die in prison camp. He crossed the first trip wire and got shot. The Serbs provided us with a very nice funeral for him that even included a casket. They passed it over the wire, and we dug a grave and gave him a proper burial. The Serbs were very good on ceremony. On George Washington's birthday, they had a big party. They even made a small cake. They sang something like "America the Beautiful," and presented us with this cake.

There was one case where a lieutenant stole somebody's rations, but he was caught right quick. I'm not sure what they did to him, but he was pretty subdued from then on and did very little socializing.

One subject seldom talked about in the prison camps was sex. Normally, young soldiers spend a good portion of their waking moments reflecting enthusiastically on this subject. But among the thirty-plus men who shared my room in the prison barracks, I cannot recall sex ever being discussed. At times it would appear in such comments as "I know this blonde in Nashville who can fry chicken better than you could ever imagine." I remember one night we were fighting boredom by planning a series of lectures on subjects we thought we possessed some expertise. One acceptable suggestion concerned the breeding of prize-winning cattle. When one of the guys who had been a medical doctor suggested a two-part lecture on sex, he was turned down without a vote. Our hunger drive was so strong that it displaced all sexual urges.

Every prisoner I knew had some kind of stomach problem—diarrhea usually. After a week or so diarrhea ceased, but then one's urination went out of control. Mostly we were drinking rather than eating. I know that anytime you had to take a leak at night, you got up and ran like hell—and sometimes you even made it to the latrine. You had to be careful where you walked, particularly at night. In the beginning, diarrhea was certainly uncontrollable. I remember one time when someone almost got to the latrine, but dropped everything right in the doorway. Our senior lieutenant colonel just raised hell about it the next morning. He had everybody assembled. He asked the medical officer if it were possible that the men could not control themselves. The medical officer said, "Colonel, any man can control his bowels. It takes a little effort, but they can be controlled." The next morning it was the same thing. The colonel demanded, "Who did this? Who's the guilty party?" But this time the medical officer answered, "I was wrong, sir. You really can't always control your bowels."

ELMER BECK

Born in 1915 in Baden Baden in the Black Forest, Elmer Beck
was drafted into the German army in 1937. Two years later he
was part of the invasion of Poland. After that quick victory, he
fought against the French before returning east for the invasion
of Russia. In late 1942, he fought in North Africa where on May
12, 1943, he was captured by the British, who turned him over to
the Americans. He ended up in Fort Custer, Michigan, where he
worked in the mess hall and the PX. Although fraternization was
strictly forbidden, the opportunity to meet ordinary Americans
outside the prison camp fundamentally changed Beck's attitude
toward German society.

I RAN THE PX for the POWs for most of my time at Fort Custer. As
a result I had pretty good relations with one of the sergeants, and
he sometimes took me outside the camp. Fraternization with outside civilians was strictly forbidden, but this allowed me to see
something of normal American life, and I liked what I saw. It was
a very different life than I was accustomed to growing up in
Germany. I had been in the *Hitler Jugend,* and we only had one
way of thinking about anything. Everything was laid out, and
that's the way it was. Germany also had a much more rigid class
structure. Once you were born into it, you had few opportunities
to change your position. I could see that the American society was
much more open, and I liked that. I liked it so well that when I
came home in 1946, I said to my wife, "If we get a chance to go to
the U.S., we should try it."

The anti-fraternization regulation was very foolish. The
Americans considered all of us Nazis, although most of us were
not political—only soldiers. Toward the end, the Americans also
wanted us to think a certain way—to reject our traditional way of

life and especially National Socialism. But no one likes to be pro-pagandized. The Americans should have realized they would have gained more by introducing us to normal, everyday life than by telling us how much better things were in the U.S. than in Germany.

That's why I disliked *der Ruf*.[17] It was a very disturbing paper for many of us. I know it was written by Germans, but it was filled with lots of propaganda. We knew the war was coming to an end, and we were worried about our families back home. We naturally thought of our wives and sweethearts and of the American sol-diers who would soon be overrunning our country. We had no newspaper of our own in Fort Custer to give us a different view.

I kept myself in reasonably good mental shape because I had good relations with those around me. Many of us were Swäbisch, from the southern part of Germany, and we understood each other. We played cards, chess, and soccer together. We had evening class-es at Fort Custer, so I started studying English. The teachers were fellow prisoners. We also had a library where we could get reading materials, and we had occasional movies in the mess hall. There were also Sunday morning church services. I was married with two children and had a good relationship with my wife. When I would get letters from her that she and the kids were all right, I naturally felt much better. Of course, my daughter was born in 1939, and I didn't see her until she was six years old.

We had good food and general treatment until the war ended. But when the Americans learned about the concentration camps, the treatment and the food got worse. That was also about the time many of the Austrians asked to be separated from us. But we Germans had no political conflicts among ourselves, although the atmosphere in the prison camps changed when prisoners started arriving after the Normandy invasion. We Africa Corps soldiers were mostly guys who had been drafted in the army during peace-time, and we were different.

---

[17]An elitist paper put out by German prisoners at Fort Kearney, *der Ruf* circulated to the other camps as part of an ambitious reeducation pro-gram to introduce prisoners to American-style democracy in preparation for their return to postwar Germany.

We believed—at least until 1945—that Germany would be victorious. I first began to suspect we would not win when the Allies crossed the Rhine. Most of our information came from *der Ruf.* Sometimes those who could read English would tell us what was in the American newspapers. There was a radio in my PX, but it played mostly music. When I learned the Allies had crossed the Rhine, I knew that the war was pretty much over. What we felt was simple. We just wanted to go home. That was the most important thing. We wanted to see for ourselves what was going on. Toward the end there was no mail coming in. I had received one or two letters a month, but then they stopped coming. So we didn't know for a long time what was going on with our families.

LOUIS G. GRIVETTI

For years Louis Grivetti felt embarrassed about having been a POW; in fact, only in the past few years has he begun talking about his experiences. Grivetti, who was only nineteen when he was captured in the Battle of the Bulge, was with novelist Kurt Vonnegut during the catastrophic fire bombing of Dresden, after which he had to climb down into bomb shelters and drag out German bodies. He was also in Stalag 12-A at Limburg on the night of December 23, 1944, when the British accidently bombed one of the barracks, killing sixty American officers. Both events left their mark on him. Like so many of his fellow prisoners, Grivetti has had a difficult time getting help from the Veterans Administration. Finally, in 1991 he began receiving thirty percent disability payments for post-traumatic stress disorder (PTSD).

KURT VONNEGUT AND I were together in Dresden, but I really don't remember him that well. When I came back to the States I just tried to forget everything about being a POW. It's only been the last few years that I can recollect many of the things that went on. I have written a brief memoir, and little things keep coming back. But for years, like a lot of other guys, I just tried to wipe out my memory of the war and my imprisonment in Dresden.

It was wrong, but I know one reason why I did this. We had one guy die in our prison camp. His name was Edward "Joe" Crone and he slept close to me. He had been an Eagle Scout and had attended college so you'd think he'd know how to survive, but he lost his will to live and gave up. He would just sit there, not talking, and then he was gone. After the war I got a letter from his parents asking what had happened to their son, but at that time I just could not talk about such things, and I never did answer them. It was a bad thing to do, but I just couldn't help myself. Years later Kurt Vonnegut changed Joe Crone's name to Billy Pilgrim and made him the leading character in his novel *Slaughterhouse-Five*.[18]

Just as Vonnegut wrote in his novel, our work camp in Dresden was *Schlachthof Fünf*, and it really was a slaughterhouse. Vonnegut knew some German and served as the interpreter for us prisoners. But I really can't remember too much about him. We would go out on work details each day, cleaning the streets of Dresden. As the official interpreter, Kurt did not have to go with us. One day a German guard was pushing around this guy who was left behind to clean the barracks. Kurt called him a *Schweinehund* under his breath. The guard heard it and turned him in. After that Kurt had to go out with us on work details. We had a teenage German guard we called Junior. He would go after Kurt every day. I guess he was going to show Kurt that you didn't insult German soldiers. He would prod Kurt with his bayonet to try and provoke him to do something so he could really stick him. But Kurt pretty well stuck it out.

The Germans had converted Building Five from an actual slaughterhouse into a barracks. They had cleaned it up and put in two or three high tiers of bunks, all very close to one another. At supper time we'd get our one daily meal—a small can filled with soup. For breakfast we got a cup of ersatz coffee. Every morning Junior would take two prisoners to another building to get our coffee. As they marched the two guys would sort of separate. It was always dark, and Junior would get real nervous and cock his gun and tell them to come back together. They would do this day after day to scare him. Then one day Junior was gone. We asked one of the other guards what had happened to him. He said he'd probably been sent to the Russian front.

The fire bombing of Dresden occurred on February 13 and 14, 1945. When the fires started, the guards noticed we were losing oxygen, so they took us out of the air-raid shelters. That's how we survived. The slaughterhouse complex was in the old town of Dresden so it wasn't right in the main part of the city which was totally destroyed by the fires. After it was over, we had to go to the

---

[18]For an interesting account of Crone/Pilgrim see the Rochester, New York, *Democrat and Chronicle*, May 3, 1995.

most devastated sections of the city and drag all the bodies out of the shelters.

In Vonnegut's novel, one of the Americans got drunk while cleaning up the city and was wheeled back in a wheelbarrow. What really happened was we were dragging these bodies out of a shelter, but before we did we would always check their backpacks for food and possibly wine or schnapps. Most of us, however, were just looking for food. Well, this one guy kept drinking all the booze, and he got completely drunk. We told the guards that he had been overcome by the fumes in the shelter, and that was why we had to wheel him back to camp in a wheelbarrow. If the Germans had known he had taken anything from the bodies, they would probably have shot him.

Whenever someone would have to go to the bathroom on these work details, he would say, *"Ich muss geh scheisse."*[19] The guards would tell us to go into these cellars. We wanted to get down there because we knew we would find food. If we found any, we'd take some and tell the others where to find it. Then they'd go down in the cellar. One of the guys brought his food back up with him and hid it, but when he kept checking to see that his food was still there, these SS troops spotted him and found the food. There was a trial of sorts, and then they shot him. The Germans selected some of his close friends for the burial detail, to show the rest of us what would happen if we took any more food. Vonnegut knew the guy who was shot, but in his novel he calls him Edgar Derby, the high school history teacher, and has him shot for picking up a Dresden china teapot. I guess that sounds more ironic than being shot for just picking up a jar of food.[20]

We were afraid when we went out in the streets after the bombing. Our guards were real rough on us because many of their homes had been destroyed. We had to be very careful for a few days. We had to watch for civilians who would throw rocks at us. This one time I asked to go down into one of these cellars, and when I came back up my work detail had disappeared. Oh, I was

---

[19]In very literal and incorrect German this meant "I must go shit."

[20]The name of the prisoner who was actually executed was Michael Palaia.

scared. I knew this other work detail was just around the corner. I went over to them and told the guard that I was down in the cellar doing my business and my group left without me. Of course, we taught the Germans some nice G.I. English so this one guard says, "Oh, you was whipping off." So I just fell in with his detail, and when we got back to camp I simply rejoined my group.

We knew at the time that many people had been killed, but we didn't know there were tens of thousands. The dead were just piled up in the bomb shelters where they had been asphyxiated. We had to wear rags around our face because of the fumes and the stench. We would simply tie a rope around their ankles and drag them out to this open area where we stacked them, and the Germans eventually burned them.

It was a terrible job. We had to do it for several days. There were other prisoners of different nationalities who also were on this detail. When we were doing this, one of the guards told me, "You are the cause of all this." I told him, "Nix versteh." Well, he hit me in the back with his rifle butt and knocked me down. I'm still trying to get some disability for that. I've even got letters from one of my fellow prisoners who saw it happen. I now have chronic back problems, and my feet, which were badly frost-bitten, also give me considerable trouble. But I just can't get anything out of the Veterans Administration for my physical infirmities.

GEORGE ROSIE

George Rosie was a rough, tough, yet sensitive American para-trooper who jumped into Normandy on D-Day and was captured just hours later. Although his initial fifty days and final three months as a prisoner were especially challenging, Rosie insists the Airborne's rigid training and iron discipline helped him survive. Shortly after his capture, the Germans marched Rosie and several hundred other American prisoners through the streets of Paris, and then photographed the humiliating event for its propaganda value. Rosie also was on one of the deadly forced marches near the end of the war when the Germans moved thousands of prisoners away from the collapsing Eastern Front. Rosie, who admits he was ashamed of being captured but proud of how he conducted himself as a prisoner of war, is a past president of the 101st Airborne Division Association and has written extensively on his war experiences, excerpts from which appear below.[21]

WHEN THE GERMANS MARCHED us through the streets of Paris, they had loudspeakers mounted on trucks announcing we were murderers and rapists let out of prison to fight in the war. Men and women would hit and spit on us as we marched by. I can remember seeing a Frenchman just walking up and smacking one of our soldiers alongside the head. That made my blood run cold. One woman was running alongside of us, spitting in our faces. She got to my buddy Jim Bradley, and as she started to spit, he spit right in her face. I thought, "Boy, we're going to catch hell now," but the

---

[21]For help in writing his memoirs, George Rosie acknowledges his debt to fellow prisoner Tom Gintjee who after the war sent him his unpublished 148-page diary.

guard just pushed her back into the crowd and we moved on.

We were marched down to the railroad yards to be shipped to Stalag 12-A in Limburg, Germany. While we were waiting in the yard, some of the German guards lit up cigarettes, took a couple of puffs, and threw them on the ground. Smokers like myself wanted a smoke in the worst way. It had probably been two weeks since I had had a cigarette. The Germans had cameras, and they were taking pictures of all this. Every time a guard threw his cigarette on the ground, three or four of our guys scrambled for it. Jim Bradley, who was guts personified, and I got pissed off that some of our Airborne buddies would do such a thing. So whenever a guard threw away his cigarette, Jim or I immediately stepped on it, as well as on any grasping fingers that might try to grab it. We got cursed by our own men, but we ended that humiliating show.

[After being transported in a badly overcrowded boxcar under typically horrifying conditions, Rosie arrived at his first base camp.]

About five o'clock the next morning we unloaded at Limburg and marched through the gates of Stalag 12-A. The guards moving us had huge police dogs that constantly circled our columns. We were individually searched and marched to the showers. This was my first bath in fifty days. I could have stayed in there for a week. Our clothes were sprayed for fleas and lice. We ended up in three, circuslike tents with straw on the ground. We had stone latrines with running water. The next day we received our first Red Cross parcels. During my eleven months as a POW we didn't get them every week, but most of the time we got one box for two men, although sometimes it was one box for four. I am convinced these Red Cross boxes made the difference for a lot of people when it came to surviving. With good management we could have oatmeal for breakfast, a German issue of bread and soup for lunch, and perhaps Spam, cheese, and crackers for dinner. After fifty days of bread and soup the chocolate bars, cheese, and Spam proved too rich. Most of us ate too much and had diarrhea which was a real problem in POW camps; in fact, it killed some of the prisoners.

We stayed in Limburg only briefly before we were shipped to Stalag 4-B at Mühlberg. All told, I was in four prison camps and

Stalag 4-B was by far the best run. The Brits were there first, and they had everything organized; in fact, they ran it like it was just another British colony. Their Sergeant Major was in charge of the barracks, and he let you know it in no uncertain terms. The camp Confidence Man was Jack Meyers, a Canadian flight lieutenant. He was supposed to represent us to the Germans and to any possible visiting International Red Cross inspection teams. He was also in charge of our records. We played basketball together, so he changed my rank. I was a private first class, but he changed it to corporal. This meant I could not be required to go out on work details. I was probably the only American promoted while in a POW camp.

We had a regular barter system based on cigarettes. Everything had a price in cigarettes, but they became especially valuable when trading for Red Cross parcels. Pat Bogie, Jim Bradley, and I became the closest of buddies. We only kept some of our cigarettes and traded the rest for food. Some of the duplicate items from our Red Cross boxes we traded for additional food. We also bet cigarettes on our basketball games, and because we won most of the time, we got even more cigarettes. More smokes meant more food. I guess that made us professional athletes.

In November it turned really cold. We had no heat in the barracks. Bogie, Bradley, and I were sleeping in a double bunk with six blankets. Each of us took turns sleeping in the middle—we called it the warm spot—until we discovered I was the only one who didn't have to get up in the middle of the night to go pee. From then on I had the warm spot.

In early January of 1945 prisoners taken during the Battle of the Bulge began coming into camp. Some of them were Airborne, and a lot were from the 106th Division which was a very green outfit that the Germans had just chewed up. On January 6 we were taken down to the railroad station, put in German army boxcars which had a small stove in them and a small supply of coal plus three days of rations. We three old experienced Kriegies volunteered to tend the stove so we could be closer to the heat. We were again packed in like sardines and that also helped keep us warm. Everything was all right until some of the new POWs started getting sick—what we called a sour stomach—and started throwing up and getting diarrhea. One of the poor guys was crawling to get to the other end of the car to the latrine bucket. It was dark, people were lying everywhere, and he couldn't see where he was going. He was pleading with people to help him so he wouldn't mess his pants. Men were kicking and swearing at him. We'd all been through that kind of pain, so I got up and opened the stove door for some light and started toward the bucket, kicking heads or feet or whatever was in my way until I made room for him to get to the bucket. I came back to the stove and Bogie says to me, "You could have gotten the hell kicked out of you, you dumb shit." I told him anybody who is lousy enough not to want to help somebody in that condition, I wasn't too worried about him putting any lumps on me.

In a few days we arrived at Stalag 3-B at Fürstenburg/Oder. We were issued twenty French cigarettes that evening but no food. The next day we got a hot shower, clean underwear, which was a minor miracle, and one American Red Cross parcel between two men. The rations the Germans gave us there were probably the best I received. Fürstenburg was an American NCO stalag. There were Americans there who had been captured in Africa in 1942, and they could really deal with the Krauts. Trading with the guards was normal. You could go out to the fence with a package of cigarettes. They'd make sure they weren't being watched by any of the officers, and then go over to the guardhouse and come back with a loaf of bread or whatever.

[As they did with so many American prisoners, the Germans forced Rosie to spend his final weeks as a POW on a long and often deadly march in an unsuccessful attempt to escape the fast-closing Allied troops.]

Things were normal for a couple of weeks at Stalag 3-B, but with the Russians moving closer, the orders came once more to move out. On January 31, more than four thousand American NCOs started on a six-day march. The Germans gave us some old overcoats which were indeed a blessing, but no one had hats, gloves, or boots. And it was cold! I mean to tell you it was down around zero. The guards kept us moving all afternoon and all night, with three short breaks. We were carrying everything we could, but it was getting so tough people just started pitching things. We stopped by some barns about five o'clock the next afternoon. One POW walked over to an old German woman standing by her fence and tried to trade a bar of soap for some food. One of the guards walked up behind him and smacked him in the back of the head with his rifle butt. He dropped like a sack of potatoes. As we were marched into the barn, we walked by him but there was no sign of life. The back of his head was smashed in and he was bleeding profusely.

That night we slept on hay. In the morning everyone was cold and stiff as hell. It felt like you were ninety years old. There was no food. Out on the road German civilians with carts were evacuating along with us. We took an afternoon break near a Jewish concentration camp.[22] This was my first look at so-called political prisoners. They had these ridiculous-looking black-and-white uniforms hanging on them, and they were nothing but skin and bones. They looked like walking skeletons. We saw a guard beat them with clubs. As we moved back on the road, one guy yelled out, "You lousy, goddam Krauts. God will get even with you some day. He will! He will! He will!" That started others hollering and swearing at the guards. It's a wonder we didn't all get ourselves shot, but they really didn't pay much attention to us. Further on down the road we saw Jews digging gun emplacements and trenches. As we walked by we saw a guard pull a revolver and shoot one of the Jews who dropped into the ditch. It was a day I'll never forget. To this day when I see a photo or film about those concentration camps, I get sick all over again.

Later that day we took another break, and as the guards were getting us back on the road we heard a shot. Apparently at the head of the column one of the Airborne guys didn't get up quickly enough to suit one of the guards, so he shot him right in the forehead. As we walked by, he was lying on his back by the side of the road.

That night we slept in barns, again without food or water. Some of us ate handfuls of snow which really didn't help much. The next morning we were back on the road, but moving very slowly. Now it no longer mattered how much the Germans yelled at us. We were just too damn weak from hunger and cold to move any faster. That evening we stopped in a small farm community. About thirty of us were put in this one barn. After awhile the old

---

[22]This was probably one of the branch slave labor camps of Sachsenhausen.

farm woman came in with what she called her slave laborer who was a young Russian girl. They gave us a few potatoes and some soup.

The next day we crossed over the eight-lane, Berlin Ring Highway which was probably the biggest highway I had seen in my life. But it was completely empty. Not a car in sight. That night we were split up and again stayed in small barns. The Germans distributed small cans of cheese, which was the first food they had given us since we hit the road. The next morning we met another column of POWs heading for Stalag 3-A. We received a can of cheese for nine men and a loaf of bread for five. That night we stayed in a mock village which the Germans had used to train troops. The wooden buildings were all shot to hell. We were issued some soup that night. The next morning we got up early and were given a loaf of bread for four men. The following day we reached Luckenwalde. They marched us through the city, but there were very few civilians, and the ones who were there just looked quietly at us. We were a sad-looking group. About three kilometers on the other side of Luckenwalde we arrived in Stalag 3-A. I was told that of the 4,000 men who had left Stalag 3-B only some 2,800 made it to 3-A.

We were herded into compounds with seven huge circus tents. There were about 700 men in each of these tents which had straw floors. There was just about enough room to stretch out and lie down on your side. We slept very well that night. The next morning we were given showers and our clothes were deloused. We were told there were no Red Cross parcels in camp. We were issued a loaf of bread to be divided among five people. Prisoners were coming into 3-A from all over. Evidently thousands of prisoners had been on the road either fleeing from the Russians on the Eastern Front or from the American and British troops in the West. To the left of our tents were two water spigots, but you never knew when the water would be turned on. Sometimes someone would discover they were on in the middle of the night. He would then come back and inform the people in his tent. Someone would get buckets and go out and stand in line to get the water.

The guards at Stalag 3-A were mostly in their fifties and sixties. There was one small guard, probably five feet, two inches, heavyset, and in his sixties. Every other morning he was on duty in the tower just to the left of where the water spigots were. We used to sit there in the morning and watch this little guy with a rifle slung over his shoulder climb up the ladder to the tower. He had just one hell of a time. The rifle would keep slipping off his shoulder, and he'd have to reach down for it. We'd just sit there and laugh at this poor, little guy, but we also felt some compassion for him. There was a guard in our tent who didn't have a mean bone in his body. He was doing a job because he had to. He would come in the barracks every morning, and you could hear his voice echo all over the tent: *"raus mit Euch!* Roll Call. *Aufstehen!* Get up!"* Then the guys in the tent would start mimicking him.

Whenever a new guard came into the compound the guys would check him out. Somebody would stand behind him and say something very threatening, and the guys in front of him would watch his eyes to see if he understood English. If he flinched or looked startled, you knew he understood English. Most of the older guards did not. We had one guard who read the morning roll call. He was not too bright. He would call off, "Bradley, James . . . Rosie, George," and so on down the line. After about a week of this, instead of answering "Here" or "Present" someone began answering, "Here, you dumb shit" or "Here, Pisshead" or "Here, you stupid S.O.B." We would stand there roaring with laughter while the poor guard would stand there scratching his head trying to figure out why we were laughing, which, of course, he never did.

Stalag 3-A was about twenty-five miles south of Berlin. For the last thirty days or so before we were liberated, around noon each day hundreds and hundreds of American bombers flying very high would turn just as they passed the camp and head for Berlin. A short time later we could hear the sounds of exploding bombs. The guards would point up to the sky and say, *"Luftwaffe, Luftwaffe."* Our response was, "Your ass."

We could hear artillery in the distance, but we also heard that Roosevelt had died. That news certainly did not make any of us feel very good. On April 23 somebody in our tent was up early, probably to check on the water tap. When he went out he discovered there were no guards, not even on the main gate. He came back to the tent hollering. Everybody ran out to look around. About 9:00 A.M. a Russian Sherman tank outfit came driving in. The tanks knocked the main gate down and then flattened the barbed-wire fences. One of the tank commanders was a big husky woman, I'd say about thirty-five years old. At one point she jumped off the tank and ran over to one of the little, half-starved Russian prisoners, picked him up and hugged him. We later heard he was her brother who she thought had been killed. There were also female soldiers carrying rifles and tommy guns. The Russians in the POW camp were given rifles and put back in the army. They were half starved but nevertheless they were back fighting. I've often thought that I would have hated like hell to have been any Kraut that got in their way as they marched on to Berlin.

4
Escape!

Why did I always try to escape? I've never been asked that question before. It was my duty, and, besides, nobody has the right to hold me against my will. I never liked regimentation and I still don't. I want my independence.

AMERICAN POW

Some of us thought it foolish to escape from a place where we were enjoying relative freedom and good care to return to a Germany where death, hunger, and other dangers were still the rule of the day.

GERMAN POW

I never tried to escape because I knew I wouldn't make it home alive. I knew I would be let go if I kept quiet and obeyed orders. My advice to any POW is to behave yourself and don't make your life miserable worrying about things you can't do anything about. Keep faith in the Lord. He's always there. You might not know it or think it but He's always there.

AMERICAN POW

SUCCESSFUL ESCAPES TOOK PLACE much more frequently in popular culture than they did in reality. Novels, plays, and films such as *Stalag 17*, *Bridge on the River Kwai*, and *The Great Escape* featured highly romanticized and successful Allied escapes, but in truth these were few; in fact, in spite of the 1929 Geneva Convention's provision that prisoners had the right to escape, few actually attempted to do so.[1]

An attendant myth suggested that escapees greatly helped the war effort by keeping the enemy occupied. In the United States, less than one percent of the German prisoners attempted to escape.[2] The percentage of escapees was approximately the same in the German-run camps, and was certainly lower in those run by the Japanese. Roger Bushell, one of the Englishmen executed after the so-called Great Escape from Germany's Stalag Luft 3, was posthumously quoted as saying, "The only reason that God allowed us this extra ration of life is so we can make life hell for the Hun."[3] In reality, escapes made it tougher on everyone. The rest of the prisoners suffered increased security, the loss of privi-

---

[1]Robert C. Doyle, in his *Voices from Captivity*, 222, writes that 7,498 Americans in the European Theater "either escaped from prison camps or evaded capture in World War II." "Evaded capture" is an elusive phrase that might explain these inflated numbers. Between one and two percent actually tried to escape. Of the more than 150 American POWs interviewed for this book, only three said they had tried to escape.

[2]Krammer, *Nazi Prisoners of War In America*, 115. Powell, *Splinters of a Nation*, 147, puts the number of German escapees at 2,222, which would be almost two percent. His discrepancy with Krammer's figures is undoubtedly because he included those escaping in the year following the end of hostilities. According to Powell, sixty percent were recaptured within one day or less and eighty-five percent within three days. As of 1947, 17 were still at large, the last of whom, Georg Gaertner, surrendered to Krammer in 1985. Krammer chronicled Gaertner's story in his *Hitler's Last Soldier in America* (New York: Stein & Day, 1985).

[3]Quoted in Alan Burgess, *The Longest Tunnel: The True Story of World War II's Great Escape* (New York: Grove Weidenfeld, 1990), 13. As was the case with Bushell, Burgess includes many long quotes from men he would have had no opportunity to have interviewed before their deaths.

leges, and harsher treatment. Nor is there any evidence that such escapes hurt the Axis war effort any more than German escapes hurt the United States.[4]

David Westheimer, who wrote *Von Ryan's Express*, a novel about a POW escape from Italy that was turned into a successful movie, was himself a prisoner. In his autobiography, *Sitting It Out*, which is much more factual than his novel or the film, Westheimer describes what he calls "POW inertia" which left the men so passive they had neither the energy nor inclination to escape.[5] Such an admission contrasts sharply with the popular image of freedom-loving Americans and British constantly scheming to escape and making life generally miserable for their captors. Before his ill-fated escape, Bushell allegedly said, "At this moment there are about 850 officer POWs in this camp. Half of the buggers intend to lie on their backs, dreaming of the past, improving their education, and writing nice little letters home to Mom, or their girl friend, and waiting until the war ends."[6] Interviews with ex-POWs indicate that such behavior was the sane thing to do. Westheimer put it best when he explained in his memoirs why a real escape was so out of the question, in spite of the fact that his sleeping guard's rifle had just fallen into his lap:

> Grumpily I leaned it back in place and dozed off. It fell on me again. This time it occurred to me we could easily disarm our guards and escape. I didn't even consider it. Like most veteran prisoners, I'd have loved to escape if it were handed to me on a platter but when it came to planning one I found the obstacles daunting. . . . I didn't know where I was except that it was deep in enemy territory with no underground to help me, it was too cold to exist for

---

[4]Arthur A. Durand, in his *Stalag Luft III*, 80–87; 254–255, argues that escapes did indeed hurt Germany by tying up "thousands of police, troops, and civilian volunteers," but more convincing is his observation that the *planning* of escapes was good for prisoner morale.

[5]David Westheimer, *Sitting It Out: A World War II POW Memoir* (Houston, Tex.: Rice University Press, 1992), 118.

[6]Burgess, *The Longest Tunnel*, 15.

long in open country, I was in the wrong uniform, and my German would never fool anyone. Maybe most important, when I was picked up, as I certainly would be, I'd have lost all the food and clothing I'd accumulated so painstakingly over the long months.[7]

Such rational comments contrast starkly with Westheimer's novel and subsequent film, both of which featured a daring escape, a thrilling train ride across enemy territory, and many heroic deaths.

The chances for a successful escape were slim on both sides of the Atlantic. Extreme distances, language barriers, unpleasant consequences when caught, and possible retaliation against those left behind discouraged all but the most determined prisoners. To be sure, the men talked of escaping, and there were escape committees, but inertia kept most prisoners securely impounded in their barbed-wire enclosures. Even as the end of hostilities approached in Germany, and the guards left the prisoners unattended, most remained where they were.

The overwhelming majority of German prisoners also preferred to sit out their captivity. Josef Krumbachner, who in this chapter describes several ill-fated German attempts to escape from Camp Como, Mississippi, thought it foolish to leave a situation that he considered much more secure and healthy than anything that existed in Nazi Germany or on the front lines with the *Wehrmacht*.

Any attempt to escape was fraught with peril. According to U.S. War Department statistics, fifty-six Germans were shot to death while trying to escape. Usually those doing the shooting were guards, but when three German prisoners escaped from Camp Crossville, Tennessee, and tried to get water from a pump next to a remote mountain cabin, an angry mountain woman shot and killed one of them. When informed that she had killed a German POW, she was most upset: "Why, I thought they wuz Yankees."[8]

---

[7]Westheimer, *Sitting It Out*, 161.

[8]John Hammond Moore, *The Faustball Tunnel: German POWs in America and Their Great Escape* (New York: Random House, 1978), 65.

There was nothing humorous about the most famous Allied escape. On the cold, snowy night of March 25, 1944, seventy-eight prisoners escaped from Stalag Luft 3 at Sagan, some 105 miles southeast of Berlin. Only three made it safely out of Germany. The rest were quickly rounded up, and fifty of them were summarily executed. General Wilhelm von Keitel praised these executions as a good lesson for the other prisoners:

> As an intimidating example, the names of those shot are to be posted in camp so that everyone can see them. The urns are to be in camp so that everyone can see them. . . . I forbid that anything be recorded in writing concerning the shootings . . . I hope, however, that prisoners of war will get such a shock that in future they will not attempt to escape.[9]

The escape from Sagan had severe repercussions for Allied prisoners. On October 1, 1944, Heinrich Himmler took complete charge of all POW affairs, in part because he and other high-ranking German officials felt the prisoners had been treated too well. The result was withdrawal of privileges, longer and more frequent roll calls, and *Aktion Kugel*, an order to shoot any escapees on sight.

But what of those few who did make serious—even successful—attempts? What motivates a man to defy all odds? According to historian Allan Kent Powell, the desire to escape boredom was the chief motivation given by German prisoners.[10] Others felt it was their duty to escape, and some were determined to get back to Germany and their families. And a few simply wanted to see

---

[9]As quoted in Alan Burgess, *The Longest Tunnel*, 154. Burgess' book, like the film *The Great Escape*, leads the reader to believe it was primarily a British and American venture; in reality, several other nationalities were more involved in the actual escape than were Americans. For example, of the three men who made it safely back to Allied territory, two were Norwegians and one was Dutch.

[10]Powell, *Splinters of a Nation*, 148.

the country.[11] Similar motivation applied to Americans who tried to escape, some of whom did insist that their escaping would hurt the German war effort by tying up much-needed soldiers. In most fictional accounts, there were numerous incidents of escaped prisoners sabotaging enemy installations, but in reality there is no evidence that either German or American escapees ever did so. Finally, there were those whose psychological makeup forced them into repeated escape attempts, no matter how bad the odds. The high-strung, Texas-born Ernest de los Santos was such an individual, whereas Joseph Beyrle possessed the kind of heroic nature that would have stimulated the creative juices of Hollywood's most flamboyant movie-makers.

---

[11]The most famous escape in the United States occurred on December 23, 1944, when twenty-five German prisoners crawled through a 178-foot tunnel they had dug under the Papago Park Camp, just outside of Scottsdale, Arizona. Most of the prisoners were quickly rounded up, although their leader, U-Boat Commander Jürgen Wattenberg, lasted thirty-six days. In addition to John Hammond Moore's *The Faustball Tunnel*, the escape also inspired Glendon Swarthout's novel, *The Eagle and the Iron Cross* (New York: New American Library, 1966).

ERNEST DE LOS SANTOS

Sergeant Ernest de los Santos was a top turret gunner on a B–17 when he was shot down over France in 1943. Born and raised in Eastland, Texas, of Hispanic parents, de los Santos was anxious for combat and equally anxious to escape once he was captured. Nervous, emotional, and ill-at-ease, de los Santos clearly has never been at peace with himself, a fact that helps explain his need to escape.

THERE ARE A LOT of criminals you just can't keep in prison. They'd rather be dead than spend their lives behind bars. I can understand that. I was always trying to escape. I'm not sure why. Even before I went in the service, I just couldn't stay put. I used to hitchhike everywhere. We lived out on a farm outside of Eastland, Texas, about 100 miles southwest of Dallas. We had no close contact with anybody. All we knew was what our family knew. We didn't have any city experiences. We went to town occasionally, but we didn't mix much. White society at that time was pretty much against Mexican-Americans, and many of the whites in town discriminated against us. We were not allowed in certain places. Maybe that's why I never could stand being locked up.

I escaped from Stalag 7-A at Moosberg three times. The first time I was by myself. I watched the way the guards were spaced. About ten feet away from the main fence was a wire and beyond that was the death area. They would shoot you without question if you were caught in this no-man's-land. That night I stripped down to my shorts and rolled my shirt and trousers real tight and carried them over my shoulder with a strap I had made. I sneaked out of the barracks and crawled out to the warning area and watched how the tower light worked. Then I made a dash for it. There were double fences, about ten feet apart with a lot of barbed-wire entanglements. I went over the first fence with no trouble and jumped down. I started for the next fence, but my shoe string got tangled up in the barbed wire, and I couldn't get it loose. The guards had tied tin cans to the fence, and when I pulled on my shoe lace, the wire rattled. When this guard came over to see what the noise was, he found me. He was supposed to shoot me, but he started yelling instead. I guess he was just so proud he had caught someone trying to escape. The tower guard put his light on me and asked the guard why he hadn't shot me. He couldn't because his gun was not loaded. When I heard him put a shell in the chamber, I looked right at him and thought, "Well, this is it." I just stood there staring at him. The tower guard kept yelling at him to shoot, but he didn't. He let me crawl back over the fence and took me to the officer in charge who put me in solitary confinement.

Some of the camps had escape committees, and that was all well and good, but someone planning to escape was not going to talk to anybody. A lot of us who escaped were loners, and a loner keeps things to himself. After I had escaped the second time and got caught, somebody—I suppose it was the escape committee— set up a meeting for all escapees to talk among themselves and to compare notes. They said maybe this would help those planning future escapes. Several of us went, but a funny thing happened. Each of us sat by himself, getting as far away from everybody else as he could. We weren't about to sit next to anybody, and we weren't planning on talking to anyone either.

I just had to try and break out. The other prisoners wouldn't even try. I don't know why. If you don't try, you'll never do it. I just wasn't going to sit in the barracks. I didn't really have any friends, so I'd go out for a walk and start looking around to see how I could get out—and I'd find a way. Each day I'd think about it a little more, and then I'd decide to take a chance. You knew you were going to get caught, but you just chose to go anyway. If you are determined, there's a way out. You just have to see your chance and take it. Evidently, nobody else was trying to escape because after I made it out the third time, the escape committee wondered how I did it. I told them, once you make up your mind, nobody's going to hold you.

The second time I escaped I went with a buddy. He stuck right on my coat tail. He wasn't about to let me out of his sight. I couldn't shake him, and we got caught the first night out. The next time he went with me again. Red Cross parcels had arrived on a four-wheel wagon, and I sneaked under it. There was a metal band hanging below the wagon bed, and I was able to crawl up and rest on it. Several of the prisoners saw me do it, including my buddy who decided he had to tag along. So here he comes. He crawled up and laid on top of the back axle. We stayed there from about three o'clock in the afternoon until dark when they came for the wagon. The guard at the front gate waved us out, and we had two or three nights of very cold, rainy weather. We human beings can't stay out in the weather too long. My buddy talked me into walking in the daylight. If I had been by myself, I would have holed up in the daytime and walked at night. But he insisted we walk in the daylight. We were heading for Switzerland. The first day we got away with it. The soldiers didn't pay any attention to us. But kids and women were suspicious as hell. The second day they turned us in. A constable came after us with a gun and took us back to Moosberg.

I just never wanted anybody to have control of my life. In fact, I'm having trouble with that now. I receive a ten percent disability for my back. The VA doctors say I have arthritis. I'm having all kinds of problems, but I have the same kind of trouble with hospitals I did in the POW camps. I just can't stay in them. Twice I just walked out. All the doctors do is talk to me and give me pills that haven't helped me at all. Sometimes the doctors say, "We've done all we can do for you." Then they want to give me another appointment. So why give me another appointment if they can't do anything for me?

JOSEPH R. BEYRLE

Sergeant Joe Beyrle's extraordinary war experiences will stretch the reader's credulity. He was one of 2,094 paratroopers of the 101st Airborne known as the "Screaming Eagles" who jumped behind Utah Beach during the early hours of D-Day. Thirty-six hours later he was captured and later became part of the infamous march of American prisoners through the streets of Paris. He was badly beaten during an interrogation, lost sixty pounds as a prisoner, and three times attempted to escape. The third time he made it and joined the advancing Russians troops with whom he fought and was wounded. His parents, who had been notified their son had been killed in action, held a funeral mass for him on September 17, 1944. In 1979, the U.S.S.R. honored him for his heroic service. President Boris Yeltsin also paid tribute to Beyrle in a White House Rose Garden ceremony during a 1994 State visit to Washington, D.C., and the following year invited him to Moscow for the Russian VE-Day celebration.

I HAD NO IDEA what being a paratrooper was all about. I knew they were elite troops, I had read about German paratroopers, and I knew Max Schmeling was a paratrooper. I had also seen newsreels of German paratroopers invading Holland and Crete. But I certainly had no idea what it meant to jump out of a plane in combat. But by the time we finished jump school, we were so highly trained and motivated that we would have jumped out of a plane without a parachute. In fact, if the parachute hadn't opened the first two or three times I jumped, I don't even think I would have noticed. Part of it was the training and part was the peer pressure which made you believe you could do anything anybody else could do. We were young, fine-tuned, robust Americans who were ready for anything.

Our objective on D-Day was to take two wooden bridges. We flew in across France, circled back, but then jumped about five seconds too soon. Normally the plane would throttle down from 220 or 230 knots to 160 or 180, but the pilot didn't, and we jumped at somewhere between 400 and 700 feet. About the same time my chute opened, I landed on a church roof at Saint Come Du Mont. I couldn't see much, but I scrambled off the church as quickly as I could. The Germans had an observation group in the church steeple, and they were shooting at me, but with all the paratroopers and gliders landing there was mass confusion, and I was able to make my way safely through the surrounding cemetery. I took out my compass and oriented myself, and took off in what I thought was the right direction. But after one or two hours, I realized I was wrong. So I had to turn around and go back to the church and start over again. I ran into a small electric generating plant and blew it up with a couple of quarter-pounders. I was working my way along a hedgerow, when I heard a bunch of Germans standing in the middle of the road talking. I lobbed a grenade into them and took off. Hours later, I stuck my head through another hedgerow and everything looked real good. I went through the opening and ran immediately into three German machine guns and a mortar crew. I was carrying a Thompson submachine gun, and by the time I recovered and realized where I was, they grabbed me. They didn't shoot me because they were as startled as I was. They were *Fallschirmjäger*, German paratroopers, and they immediately spotted my boots and the .45 I was carrying. They asked if I were an officer. I told them I was a sergeant. They wanted to know why I was carrying a .45, which was not standard issue. They were very confused. They didn't think the invasion was coming in Normandy. They took me to an underground headquarters in an orchard where a major interrogated me. Basically name, rank, and serial number. From there I was moved to another headquarters underground and interrogated again. Strangely enough, the second interrogation team included a woman who knew me. Just three weeks before she had danced with some of the men where we were stationed in Ramsbury, England. I had not danced with her, but she had evidently noticed me. I don't know whether she was German or British or both, but she was a German spy. At the interrogation, she told me, "Sergeant, you're from I-Company. You trained

at Ramsbury. Colonel Wolverton is your Third Battalion commander." I told her and the officer who was there that according to the
Geneva Convention I only had to give them my name, rank, and
serial number. He agreed, but they just wanted me to verify what
they already knew. They asked what our objective was. I told
them I didn't know, that we were supposed to get our orders when
we got on the ground.

Later, the Germans moved about 100 of us down the road
towards Carentan. All of a sudden, an American ship started lob-
bing shells around us. The second or third round hit right in our
midst. I was blown into the ditch, and I got hit in the butt with a
piece of shrapnel, but it was nothing serious. Some Germans were
killed, and two guys I knew lost legs and another buddy lost a
hand. They were in shock. A captain, another man, and I applied
tourniquets and pulled them up on the side of the road and told
them to yell, "I am wounded, I am wounded. Please help me."
Then we took off. I found out later a German patrol did pick them
up and took them to an aid station. One of them later died in a
hospital in Rheims, but the other fellow made it. In 1971, I was
attending a Memorial Day ceremony in Washington, D.C., and a
mutual friend, who also had been a POW, brought the two of us
together. He had heard both our stories and figured out I was one
of the soldiers who had put the tourniquet on the trooper's stump.
They tell me it was quite an emotional scene, and it's still very difficult for me to talk about it.

After our escape, we started moving back toward our objec-
tives. The captain was company commander of H-Company, and
their objective was some locks about a quarter of a mile away. I
somehow became separated from them and started taking fire.
When that happens, you just lie there, listen, and hope you are
going to hear an American voice, but you don't. After awhile, I
once more started moving toward the bridge area, and once again
I got captured almost the same way I did the first time. I stumbled onto a position I didn't know was there. The guy put a rifle
on me and said, "*Hände hoch.*" These Germans were naturally
surprised I didn't have any weapons. I told them I had been
already captured. They took me into Carentan where I was held
overnight in a barn with some other prisoners. We were then
moved by truck to Saint-Lô. Just as we were driving down the hill
into Saint-Lô, we were strafed. Some of the prisoners who were

not ambulatory and couldn't jump into the ditch were wounded or killed.

They kept us in a horse stable in Saint-Lô, and that was the night the Allies bombed the city. The only thing that didn't get hit was the church across the street and our stable. The next morning they marched us to a monastery outside the small village of Tessy-sur-Mur which we called "Starvation Hill." I was singled out and removed to a very professional interrogation center for three days of intensive questioning. They used the hard guy/soft guy approach. They insulted me; then they offered me food if I would answer this or that. They knew everything. Some of the questions were more psychological than military. They were attempting to get into my mind to try and figure out what Americans were all about. They asked why a German like myself was fighting "for the Jews Roosevelt and Morgenthau" and against my own people. At one point, I called the German officer "a son-of-a-bitch." A guard hit me in the head with his rifle butt. I was out for several days and ended up in a German hospital. I was then sent to Chartres and kept in a warehouse seven or eight days. I don't know exactly how long. It's all pretty hazy. I know those of us who were kept there got good and dirty and then were put in that march through the streets of Paris. People threw things at us, and some of the French women spit on us when we marched by.

In late July we were put on a train for Stalag 12-A at Limburg. With fifty men in a boxcar that was designed to hold 40 men or 8 horses, we were in pretty close quarters. It took us seven days and seven nights, and those cars were never opened. On the second day, we were strafed, so we had wounded and dead in the car for five days. We also had no food or water. If you had anything left in you to eliminate, there was a bucket.

My mental state at the end of that week was as low as at any time during my imprisonment. First of all, you feel guilty about being captured; then there are the effects of the harsh treatment and the radical changes in your life. I've thought back on all that, and I have to quote my good friend and fellow POW, George Rosie, who said, "I've never been real proud of being captured, but I'm very proud of how I conducted myself after I was captured."[12]

---

[12]George Rosie's story is in Chapter Three.

When we got to a permanent camp, we formed our own groups, either of paratroopers or people we knew and respected, and this helped. We had to retain a measure of pride in ourselves, and the rigorous discipline of our Airborne training helped, as did the marvelous physical shape we were in. Put simply, we considered ourselves to be elite troops. Before we were segregated, I can remember the disgust I felt watching a colonel and an enlisted man fight over a bone. I'm talking about really fighting. Each wanted the bone to suck the marrow out of it. I've also watched both officers and enlisted men fight over cigarettes. They'd do anything to get a smoke, even puff on dried grass. The Germans were very contemptuous of such behavior. Most of the prisoners comported themselves very well, but we were ashamed of a few of them.

We were registered as prisoners of war in Stalag 12-A in Limburg, Germany, but we only stayed there for a few days before we were moved to Mühlberg. Stalag 4-B was a British camp, although the top-ranking prisoner was a Canadian. It was the first POW camp in Germany; in fact, the first British flier shot down in 1939 was still there when we arrived. Everything was very well organized. As in the other camps, cigarettes were the currency. You could buy anything with them, even your way to Switzerland. For the right price, the German *Kommandant* would let you escape. I am not quite sure how it worked because I was not there long enough to get into the inner circle. On September 17, we were put on another train and sent to Stalag 3-C which was on the Oder River just outside Altdrewitz, about forty-five miles east of Berlin.

There were already French and Russian POWs in the camp, including some 200–300 Russian females; in fact, I later helped Russian troops liberate the camp. There were maybe one or two thousand of us, and we were the first American prisoners. The senior NCO ran things and handled all the dealings with the Germans. He had his own executive committee which in turn set up separate committees for procurement, information, and escape.

I was on the escape and information committees, in part because I knew some German from my early family training. Even if you wanted to buy your way out, you first had to get permission from the escape committee. You would present your plan to the committee members who would then make a decision. We were so well organized in part because we had so much time on our hands.

Winning a lot of cigarettes helped me escape the first time from Stalag 3-C. We had received Red Cross parcels, and as GIs were wont to do, we had a crap game. The payoff was in cigarettes, and I won sixty packs. I decided to try and buy off one of the older guards. We used to talk to some of the guards and occasionally throw them cigarettes. I approached this guard and asked him if he would like 200 cigarettes. He said, "What do you mean?" I told him I would give him 200 cigarettes if he would let me cut the wire and escape. He said, "I can't do that. It would cost me my life." I told him I would cut the wire on his watch but not escape until his replacement was on duty so no one would suspect him. He told me he would have to think about it. About two or three weeks went by, and I was concerned. He could easily have set me up. He could just let me escape and then he or somebody else would simply shoot me as I was going through the wire. I talked to him again and told him to think what he could do for his family. With 200 cigarettes he would be a rich man. Finally, he said he would do it. I told him he wouldn't get the cigarettes until the three of us had escaped. I also told him Americans could be trusted.

We got out and hopped a freight train that ran behind the camp at approximately the same time every night. We thought it was going toward Poland, but we discovered it hit a junction and went in almost the opposite direction. So we ended up in a Berlin railroad yard that was being bombed by the British at night and by the Americans during the day. From the escape and information committees we knew the anti-Nazi underground would hide us and help us get back to the Allied lines. All the large cities had such an underground. You just had to make the right contact. On the first day we stayed in the empty boxcar and watched. The second day we started to move early in the morning. We watched this old German checking the bearings on the railroad cars, and I finally approached him. I spoke to him in broken English and German and told him we had escaped from a POW camp and were trying to make our way back to the American lines. I asked if he could help us. He was very fearful at first. I thanked him and left. We watched him as much as we could. About two hours later I went back and asked him again. He said he was going to leave work that afternoon and would try to make a contact for us and be back. He came back a couple of hours later and said he had a friend in a Safe House who could get us food and transportation. We decided to take a chance. We thought we had nothing to lose and a lot to gain. Unfortunately, we lost.

He had gone to the *Gestapo*. They kept us for about ten days. They really worked us over. They didn't bother with the good guy/bad guy routine. They wanted to humiliate us. If we fell asleep while they were questioning us, they knocked us off our stool. We were kicked, knocked around, walked on, hung up by our arms backwards, and hit with whips, clubs, and rifle butts. I can still see their sadistic faces. When you thought they could do no more, they would think of new ways to torture you. When you would slip into semiconsciousness, they would start again. This went on for days, and then they would dump you into a cold, dark cell, with no sanitary facilities and still dirty from the previous occupant.

The politics of war probably saved us. Word got out that the *Gestapo* had us, and the *Wehrmacht* moved in to claim us. That was about the time the *Gestapo*, in clear violation of the Geneva Convention, had executed fifty of the prisoners who were part of the so-called Great Escape from Stalag Luft 3 at Sagan. This upset many decent *Wehrmacht* officers who didn't much care for the *Gestapo* anyway. I was only semiconscious, but I can remember the *Hauptmann* telling the *Gestapo* officers that we were their property because we were military prisoners and as such came under the Geneva Convention. Fortunately, the *Wehrmacht* prevailed. I am convinced the *Gestapo* would have executed us.

We were then sent to Luft 3 which was an air force camp. There was always a question in which camp we belonged. German paratroopers belonged to the air force but we belonged to the army. We were there for seven days and the ranking American prisoners kept us in isolation. New POWs were greeted with a degree of suspicion about whether or not they really were Americans. They separated the three of us, and kept an American with us at all times to test us for slip-ups. It was very frustrating but I understood why. When you moved in a mass of men, there was not much you could do. But the moving in of only one or two guys was suspicious. They wondered why the Germans had put us into their compound which was supposedly full.

Earlier, we had found a German in Stalag 3-C who was posing as an American POW. He crossed himself up, and somebody discovered it. I sat on the court-martial and we executed him. The evidence was conclusive. He claimed to have lived in Cleveland, Ohio. We brought up expert witnesses who proved he had never lived in Cleveland. I don't know exactly how he was executed, but he was cut up and the body parts were then thrown into the latrine. In fact, I took a small part of his body and dumped it. This was done very quietly. It was not public knowledge in the camp. As far as I know, there was a record of this court-martial which was given to different people to take back to the American authorities after the war. It should be some place in Washington. The Germans must have discovered what had happened, but they never acknowledged it. If we had found an American traitor it would have been our duty to have executed him for betraying us. So I can also understand the German POWs in the U.S. who killed some of their own men for collaborating with the American authorities.

After our week at Luft 3, we were returned to 3-C. After a couple of weeks of being kept in a kind of metal cage and fed only bread and water, I was released and went back on the escape committee. The last time I escaped was kind of a fluke. We were out on the exercise field, and one of our guys pretended to pass out. We told the guard he had suffered a seizure and we had to get him to the hospital. Somebody brought a stretcher. I got on one end of it and someone else on the other. Our guard took us to the gate of our compound where another guard was supposed to pick us up. But a fight broke out close to the gate, and when the second guard went to break it up, we kept right on going through the gate and hid behind some of buildings. We spotted a German who every day brought several barrels of potatoes into the camp on his wagon. Each of us climbed into a barrel. The driver must have known we were in there, but he never turned around. We got out the camp gate and down the hill, but at the bottom the wagon slipped on a patch of ice, and all three barrels rolled off into a ditch. We jumped out and started running toward the woods. When we popped out of those barrels, one of the guards spotted us. He was as surprised as we were, but he opened fire. I made it; the other two did not.

I hit a small stream and followed it downstream in what I figured was an easterly direction. The guards cut the dogs loose, but they couldn't track me. I followed that stream for maybe half an hour. It was very cold, and I was pretty much exhausted when I got out of the water. I rested until dark, and then started walking. I could hear artillery, so I figured the Russians were not that far away.

The next day I stopped at a farmhouse and asked for something hot to drink. I told the old man and his wife who I was. They gave me some coffee or schnapps, I don't remember which, but they would not let me in the house. They said if I was found there the Germans would shoot them. They knew the Russians were close, and they were also afraid of them. They told me I could hide in the barn and to burrow down in the straw to keep warm. I did, and I fell asleep. Why I didn't freeze to death I don't know. The next morning a Russian armored outfit came through but didn't stop. I stayed in the barn. The couple brought me some bread, sausage, and something to drink. That night the Russians came back and brought some wounded into the house. They killed that German couple and fed them to the pigs, and the next day they butchered the pigs. In the meantime, I had come out of the barn and identified myself in broken Polish and English that I was an American escaped POW and that I wanted to join them and go to Berlin and defeat Hitler. I had what was left of my American uniform on. The Russian military commander accepted me, but not the Russian commissar who traveled with them. He remained suspicious.

The Russians wanted to send me back behind the lines, but I insisted that I was a soldier and wanted to fight with them against the Germans. I stayed with that Russian armor outfit for about a month. They were driving Sherman lend-lease tanks. They gave me one of those submachine guns with the drum on it and put me with a tank crew that was commanded by a woman. So there I was, an escaped American Airborne sergeant fighting in a Sherman tank against Nazi Germany as a member of a Russian tank unit commanded by a woman. I regret very much that I never wrote down any names or addresses. Those Russians came to treat me as one of their own. At night we would drink toasts to Stalin, Roosevelt, Churchill, and to the American-made Studebaker truck they also had.

About two or three days after I joined them we were advancing west on a two-track road when the lead tanks opened fire. I learned later they had fired on a column of U.S. POWs being marched from Stalag 3-C which was, of course, my old camp. Several scout cars and other vehicles were at the head of the column, and many Germans were killed but so were two or three American POWs, and others were wounded. The next day we entered 3-C. After a small fire fight with the guards, I was asked to come to the *Kommandant*'s office. The Russians had some quarter-pound blocks of American-made explosives, but they didn't know how to set them off. I blew open the big safe in the office. The Russians were interested in the cameras, watches, rings, and any Russian rubles. I was able to liberate most of the U.S. dollars and invasion currency as well as Canadian dollars, British pounds, and French francs. I had a satchel as big as a three-suiter filled with currency which I tied on the back of our tank. I was also able to get my POW record and the POW photo the Germans had taken of me. *[See photograph.]*

We left the camp and headed west. Over the next week or two we advanced each day but were sometimes held up by tanks or artillery. Early one morning our tank column was attacked from the rear by Stuka dive bombers, and I got hit by fragments of an anti-personnel bomb. Some Russian medics took me to a field hospital which was so primitive you would have to go back to our Civil War to find something similar. Most of the doctors were women. They had very few medical supplies and were forced to operate without anesthetics. I was close enough to the room where they were operating that I could hear the screams. It's hard to describe. I was wounded in the groin, and it had become infected. About all they were doing was putting a fresh bandage on it.

I met Marshal Zhukov, the great Russian general, while I was in that field hospital. Through an interpreter he asked how I got wounded and how I happened to be there. I told him I had asked to fight with our Soviet comrades in order to defeat the Germans. I guess I said the right thing because he asked if there was anything he could do for me. I told him I did not have any identification to prove I was an American. The next day I received a piece of paper in Russian stating that I was an American. About two days later I left the hospital because I was afraid that if I stayed there much longer, they were going to cut off my leg.

I got to Warsaw, but the American embassy was a pile of rubble. I then made my way to Moscow. Fortunately that piece of paper from Zhukov got me on a hospital train, then a military convoy, and finally on a regular train going east. Traveling through Poland and Russia forced me to see what war had brought the people. Since our Civil War, we Americans have never experienced what it's like to have war on our own land. The memory of that devastation convinced me during the Cold War that the Russians did not want to fight us. Certainly the people did not want war. What they fought so hard to win the politicians on both sides lost.

Those thoughts were still with me when I returned to the Soviet Union in 1979 when a Soviet veterans' organization held a special dinner to honor me. I made a brief speech. Among other things, I told them, "All veterans who have lived through war are united in the striving for peace. We must meet more often and strengthen our friendship. Veterans are not politicians. If they get into politics, it should be only to do everything so there may be no more wars. We are a peaceful people, and the war took us away from peaceful work, from normal human life. We were young, wanted to marry and start a family; instead, we had to put on military uniforms and take up arms."

JOSEF KRUMBACHNER

Josef Krumbachner was a divinity student when drafted into the Germany army where he eventually became an artillery officer. He was clearly a good soldier but deeply distrustful of National Socialist fanatics and their antireligious bigotry. Krumbachner also recognized the futility and even stupidity of trying to escape from a prison camp where he was secure and reasonably well treated to attempt a perilous journey of thousands of miles to fight again for a regime he despised. After the war Krumbachner returned to his divinity studies and subsequently became a Catholic priest. In 1988 he wrote *Das Kriegsgefangenenlager Como – Mississippi USA*, a brief remembrance about his POW experiences in the United States. Excerpts from this memoir are included in his narrative.

MY GREATEST WISH, AS well as that of several of my comrades, was to be captured by the Americans. For several reasons we considered this to be a genuine liberation: we would be freed from a war which we considered to be criminal; we would no longer have to worry about life and limb; and, most of all, we would no longer be under the spiritual and mental bondage of the Third Reich. Naturally, such thoughts made our disillusionment all the worse when we discovered that on American soil we would still have to fight against Nazi terror.

In the summer of 1941, some six weeks after the beginning of the Russian campaign, my commander, Lt. Colonel K., quite unexpectedly sent me back to Germany to the weapons' school at Jüterbog where in February 1942 I received my commission. When I returned to my unit on the Russian front, Colonel K., who had since been promoted to a full colonel, pulled me aside and said, "Herr Krumbachner, you can now make the military your permanent career, but only if you put aside your previous beliefs."

At that moment I realized why he had sent me to become an officer. My *Soldbuch*[13] stated that I was a theological student in civilian life, and Colonel K. had undoubtedly noticed this. He was one of the so-called *alter Kämpfer* who already in 1923 had marched with Hitler and who thus proudly wore his *Blutorden*.[14] I told him, "Colonel, I am sorry, but I continue to believe as I always have." I can still remember how upset I was, not only about the colonel's fascist way of thinking, which I fully understood, but about the stupefying suggestion of using such a war to make one's career. After I was captured during the Normandy invasion, I frequently encountered fellow officers who exhibited the same kind of entrenched and naive fanaticism. Many of these men came from the upper levels of society and so deeply believed their anti-Christian ideology that they had lost any sense of reality.

Camp Como, Mississippi, contained approximately 2,000 German prisoners, including 200 *SS* officers. Some of these men were unbelievable craftsmen. For example, one of them crafted a miniature violin using wooden matches, razor blades, glue and other materials purchased from the canteen, and then used fingernail polish to put a finish on it. Some of the men created other tiny works of art such as miniature dollhouse furniture which were only centimeters high. One talented prisoner who made such furniture took tremendous pleasure in anticipating the children's excitement when they received his creations. He had been a prosecuting attorney and judge back in Germany who could also dispassionately describe the death sentences he had meted out to deserters whom the state considered to be war criminals. Many of us were simply appalled by this contradiction.

The POWs were so inventive that one American newspaper suggested that if you gave a German prisoner a stovepipe, he would soon turn it into a cannon. We had a symphony orchestra;

---

[13]Every German soldier carried his *Soldbuch* ["Soldier's Book"] which contained basic information about himself and his military career.

[14]Literally translated, *alter Kämpfer* means "old fighter" or "warrior," but here it refers to those who were with Hitler during his ill-fated November 8, 1923, Munich beer-hall putsch. *Blutorden* refers to the *Order of the Blood*, which honored those early followers of the *Führer*.

there were reading circles in which fine literature was read and discussed; and there was a camp university with high standards. Professors Walter Hallstein and Albert Mirgeler were two of the more important lecturers, but there were many others. Dr. Hallstein, who after the war became part of the Adenauer administration, was targeted by the camp fascists because they suspected him of receiving books from his Jewish-American academic colleagues. Fortunately, these same individuals were not bright enough to recognize how contrary Dr. Mirgeler's lectures were to National Socialist ideology. One of Dr. Mirgeler's students was a young *SS* officer named Werner Schlepper, who, in his youthful enthusiasm, had no idea how the Nazi criminal element had taken over the *Waffen SS*. Because he was so impressed with Dr. Mirgeler, who was a Catholic, Schlepper even converted to Catholicism. One day he warned us that some of his fellow *SS* officers were planning to attack Dr. Mirgeler that night. We armed ourselves with clubs, but the attack never came.

Dr. Poppelbaum, who taught philosophy in the camp, was also attacked by the Nazi leadership. He had allegedly said, "Himmler is the most odious man in Germany." With considerable ceremony, the leaders set up an "official" war crimes trial. They designated one of the barracks to be the courtroom and even appointed a prosecuting attorney and judge. The judge wore a simulated uniform of a German war tribunal. These sympathetic officers had used their twenty-dollar-a-month pay to employ an American tailor, whom the American commander allowed to work for us, to make this uniform. The color was a bit off but everything else was a good reproduction. These same officers then marched into the "courtroom" bedecked in all their military finery. The judge sentenced Dr. Poppelbaum to be completely ostracized. No one was to speak to him. The judge also announced that after Germany's final victory all the trial documents would be turned over to the proper authorities for further criminal proceedings. And this was late 1944 or early 1945! After the sentence, I rushed over to Dr. Poppelbaum's barracks—I was also one of his students—but he had already sought protective custody from the American authorities—imagine, protective custody from your own people.

The Nazi fanatics terrorized everyone in the camp. They were already well established at Como before we Western Front prisoners arrived. They were mostly Africa Corps officers who were taken prisoner at a time when the German military was at its strongest. Even after it became apparent the war was obviously lost, they stubbornly and foolishly continued to hold onto their National Socialist convictions and their belief in final victory.

One of their leaders was Heinz H., who had been a prosecuting attorney in Berlin. We new prisoners thought we had been thrown into an insane asylum when Heinz H., who was also the official spokesman for the prisoners, greeted us in a very shrill voice: "You are in a German officers' prison camp. Only National Socialist thought is allowed here. Anyone who disagrees should understand that in many camps traitors have already been removed from their barracks in the middle of the night and hanged from a post."

We were also told that those of us attending church services would be duly noted in order to register us as traitors after the final victory, but whether this was actually done I cannot say. The Nazis also organized Sunday celebrations to counter our church services. Strangely enough one of the camp leaders, who was too dim-witted to recognize the contradiction, participated in both services.

One way to prove your undying allegiance to the Führer was to attempt an escape. We were expected to break out of camp, make our way back to Germany, and once again fight for the Third Reich. Of course, some of us thought it foolish to escape from a place where we were enjoying relative freedom and good care to return to a Germany where death, hunger, and other dangers were still the rule of the day.

There were all kinds of crazy escape schemes. Usually, only two men would actually try to escape, but the rest of us were expected to help. At least two days' rations had to be smuggled out of the mess hall for them. In one such escape those whose barracks were near the barbed wire built fires out of wet brushwood so that thick clouds of smoke hid the two men crawling along the fence. Using homemade pliers they cut through the wire and made their escape. They almost reached New York before they were recaptured.

Another pair tried to make a folding boat out of some kind of waterproof material, which was probably an old raincoat. It was then disassembled and smuggled out of the camp with the garbage. They planned to float down the Mississippi and then, if

I remember correctly, stow away on a freighter bound for Europe. They were captured after two days—very possibly betrayed by fellow prisoners, which was, of course, a very dangerous practice for those doing the informing.

Two others used cigarettes to bribe American guards to leave the motor pool gate open and the keys in the ignition of a vehicle. Using our monthly allowance, we could buy cigarettes even more cheaply than could the American soldiers. I think we paid only thirteen cents a pack for them. They then drove their vehicle out the gate wearing stolen American uniforms. When they were recaptured, they were charged with stealing an automobile and sentenced to a couple of years in prison.

A couple of escapees got on a ferryboat, but when they sat down in the section reserved for blacks, the white Americans on board knew something was wrong. Another escapee, looking for information and not knowing the local customs, politely greeted a group of blacks which, of course, aroused suspicion. Someone else even attempted unsuccessfully to build a catapult to hurl himself over the fence.

When someone escaped, the rest of us were expected to cover for them at the daily roll calls. Sometimes a full-sized doll was constructed to look like one of us. Two other prisoners would then hold the doll between them during the daily roll call. The German camp leader would report to the American officer, "Everyone present and accounted for." Then the doll would be sneaked back into the barracks. One time they even held the doll in a way to look like it was a prisoner who had drunk too much.

Another method was for a couple of the prisoners in the first rank to sneak to the rear after they had been counted so they would be counted again. I remember one time when the count revealed two missing men. The American officer shouted, "Two men missing." In the meantime two additional men had sneaked off. Now they came running out of a barracks where the musicians practiced, breathlessly carrying their instruments. The American officer then announced, "All present and accounted for."

At times it was apparent that the discovery of these plots was a welcome diversion for the Americans, a kind of challenging interruption of their boring duties. We too understood these nonsensical attempts to be a kind of child's play that could break up our tedious daily existence. When the guards discovered an actual escape, the rest of the prisoners had to be punished. We would be forced to stand for hours in front of the barracks in that hot Mississippi sun until all the buildings and grounds were carefully searched.

Recaptured prisoners would be put in the brig for up to four weeks, after which they were treated as heroes. Among ourselves we made fun of them by suggesting that after the "final victory" they would get a notation in their *Soldbuch*: "A courageous artist who escaped for the Fatherland."

Of course, most of us were quite happy to spend the duration of the war in quiet security, thousands of miles from the front lines. We had a saying, "Be careful that you are one day able to see the homeland again. Be aware that too much good food doesn't make you so fat that you can no longer open your eyes." It's hard to believe, but while people were starving back in Germany we were using flour to line our soccer fields.

After Hitler committed suicide, the entire camp again came under the gaze of the *Pleitegeier*.[15] There it was hanging on the wall of one of the barracks where a speaker, whose name I have forgotten, stood up and praised our heroic leader who had, he insisted, fallen on the front lines during hand-to-hand combat. My dear friend, Paul Schmidt from Krefeld, stood next to me and facetiously suggested that the lyrics of our national anthem would now have to include, "In Bethlehem was born to us a child." In reality it was a macabre situation. The speaker refused to recognize that in a few days his pretense as defender and spokesmen for us would be over. He and the other ardent Nazis would soon be segregated into their own camp. In a fascinating transformation of loyalties, after the speaker's return to Germany, he resurfaced as the editor of a Saarbrücken newspaper advocating the Saarland's return to France.

In February or March of 1945 we learned that the body of a German general, whose name I think was Hans Schubert [*see*

---

[15]Those brave or foolhardy enough to make fun of the official *Reichsadler* icon would refer to it as a *Pleitegeier*. The iconic *Reichsadler* was the Third Reich's fierce-looking eagle which held a swastika in its talons. The word *Pleitegeier* suggests a scruffy-looking vulture circling in search of helpless prey.

photograph], was arriving from a camp for generals so he could be buried with full military honors in a small cemetery outside our camp which held German prisoners who had died during their incarceration.[16]

The camp leaders carefully planned the funeral procession. For some it was a welcome opportunity to show off their National Socialist allegiance; for others it was simply a change of pace from their daily routine. In any case, it was an impressive show. In the forefront marched a brass band, after which came the highest-ranking officers wearing their carefully reconstructed uniforms. The camp leadership laid out the general in his full-dress uniform, including his World War I Turkish medal for bravery, and placed him in an open coffin. The coffin was then covered with the national colors onto which the camp tailor had sewed a swastika. The rest of us looked through the barbed wire at this remarkable procession. At the burial plot one of the officers gave a brief talk which included the usual Nazi slogans and his hope for a final victory—this just weeks before the end. A twelve-man American honor guard fired a final salute. As the coffin was lowered into the earth, the German officers gave the Hitler salute.

The next few days, photographs of the burial appeared in the American press. And this was precisely at the time when American troops were beginning to uncover many of the Nazi atrocities. A wave of indignation swept through the country. Our nearby Memphis newspaper editorialized, "They should have thrown the body of this German general out onto the fields so the buzzards could have picked it clean." Then photographs of Nazi emblems on barracks walls began appearing in various newspapers and magazines, as well as reports about the coddling of the German prisoners, especially as compared to the horrible treatment suffered by Nazi concentration camp victims. This meant an end to the comfortable life in our camp. We begin to receive starvation rations, which meant that the industrious comrades who grew fruit and vegetables in their camp gardens became very popular with the rest of us.

---

[16]General Schubert probably died in Camp Clinton, Mississippi, which was a camp for captured generals.

5
German Political Battles in American Prison Camps

I know of two instances where men were killed in the latrines and thrown into the toilets. No part of them was ever found. They were victims of die heilige Geist [the Holy Ghost], which meant the Nazis running the camp had murdered them because they suspected them of having collaborated with the Americans.

GERMAN POW

I quickly discovered there was more political freedom in the German army than in an American prison camp.

GERMAN POW

AT TIMES, THE AMERICAN prison camps appeared to be a microcosm of the society the captives left behind in Nazi Germany. The first prisoners to arrive in 1943 were members of Field Marshal Erwin Rommel's elite Africa Corps. Many, and especially the officers, were proud and even arrogant. They were convinced Germany was going to win the war, and they often mistook kind treatment as a sign of national weakness. As one Africa Corpsman put it, "If you give us this good bread, it is only to coax us, to corrupt us. If you are treating us so well, it is only because you are afraid of losing the war."[1] These unrepentant officers and NCOs attempted, often with considerable success, to establish the same kind of rigid organization and thought control that had existed in the Third Reich.[2] As a result, brutal confrontations between Nazi and anti-Nazi prisoners often ended up in violence and even murder.

The short-handed American camp officials frequently endorsed the Nazi camp leaders, either because they desired peaceful, efficiently run camps or because they too distrusted radical leftist prisoners. In some camps, authorities allowed prisoners to display National Socialist emblems and photographs, to fly the German flag, and even stage parades to celebrate Hitler's birthday. At Camp Breckinridge, Kentucky, the American camp commander personally led a group of prisoners to church while the mocking Germans lustily sang the Horst Wessel song.[3] The commander at Camp Alva, Oklahoma, insisted that the German prisoners greet him with the same Nazi salute they gave their

---

[1] Daniel Costelle, *Les Prisonniers* (Paris: Flammarion, 1975), 28.

[2] The Geneva Convention stipulated that prisoners be allowed to select spokesmen to represent their interests to camp officials and visiting inspection teams. Early on, these *Lagersprecher*, or Confidence Men as they were called because they allegedly had the confidence of their fellow prisoners, were often hard-core Nazis because they were the most aggressive. According to Sidney Fay, "German Prisoners of War," *Current History* (March 1945), 193–4, such power helped "make the camp a miniature Germany where persecution of anti-Nazis is thorough and violent."

[3] Anti-Nazi prisoners attempted to explain the lyrics of the so-called Horst Wessel song to the American camp commander but to no avail. The chorus of the song, whose actual German title was *Die Fahne Hoch* ["Lift the Banner High"], goes as follows:

Clear the streets for the brown battalions!

Clear the streets for the SA's ranks!

Already millions look with hope on the swastika

The day of freedom and bread is here!

officers, although, at the time, this was not the official *Wehrmacht* salute. Another commander announced, "In a Nazi camp, there is order and discipline—no problems."

Several German prisoners later published accounts of their experiences in the American camps, but no one better described the political conflicts than did former POW Hans Werner Richter in his 1969 novel, *Die Geschlagenen* ["The Defeated"]. Richter, who after the war became a prominent member of the liberal German writers' organization, *Gruppe 47,* vividly described what it was like for anti-Nazi prisoners to arrive in a camp dominated by Nazis:

> Tightly pressed together, like a narrow Guard of Honor, stood the camp prisoners on each side of the street. They all wore the same blue coats and hats which in the darkness had the effect of a gathering storm. They stood there silently. No word of greeting, no sound, nothing came out of their ranks.
>
> "Deserter!" Gühler heard someone near him whisper. He looked astonished into the hostile faces but kept quiet. A menacing feeling crept along the silent walls. They walked faster and faster along the long street.
>
> "Traitor," whispered those surrounding them. "Deserters! Cowards!"[4]

In a later interview, Richter also explained why threatened prisoners did not complain to the International Red Cross whose representatives periodically investigated conditions in the camps:

> It would have been absolutely impossible. I believe I saw a Red Cross representative once, but he was passing so far away. . . . And besides, if we had dared to tell him something, you can imagine what the consequences would have been . . . slaughtered in the night. And as far as the camp authorities are concerned, that would have served only to attract reprisals. For the Americans, it was very simple. Whatever happened among the prisoners was not to be

---

[4]Hans Werner Richter, *Die Geschlagenen* (Berlin: Deutscher Taschenbuch Verlag, 1969), 162; translation by author.

interfered with, according to the Geneva Convention, except in the case of murder, of course."[5]

Especially in the early months, Nazi leaders often controlled camp newspapers, books, religious services, work details, and even the mail rooms. And they took harsh measures against those prisoners they deemed insufficiently loyal, using the threat of physical force or retaliatory acts against their families back in Germany. Historian Judith Gansburg argues, "Among the captives there was more fear and distrust of one another because of politics than there was of their captors . . . and this distrust nurtured Nazism more effectively than Hitler himself could have done."[6] Agreeing with Gansburg, Arnold Krammer concludes, "Many of the larger camps organized midnight tribunals and 'kangaroo courts' which censured and condemned 'traitors' and 'deserters.' Threats of impending execution took the form of premature obituary notices and chicken-bones in the anti-Nazis' bunks, after which the victims waited in terror for the inevitable."[7]

It is impossible to determine the actual number of Nazi-inspired murders and forced suicides in the camps. Numbers range from Krammer's seven murders and dozens of other inci-

---

[5]Quoted in Daniel Costelle, *Les Prisonniers*, 39–40. Arnold Krammer, however, disagrees, citing a letter from Lt. Col. Leon Jaworski of the Eighth Service Command to camp commanders ordering them to report all incidents of violence; *Nazi Prisoners of War in America*, 170, n. 56. A study of the various camp reports indicates that some commanders did report the actual violence, but few described such incidents in political terms. Later, after official government policy hardened toward Nazi leadership in the camps, commanders became more conscientious about protecting their prisoners.

[6]Gansburg, *Stalag USA*, 6.

[7]Krammer, *Nazi Prisoners of War in America*, 170. See also Edward John Pluth, *The Administration and Operation of German Prisoner of War Camps in the U.S. During World War II*, Unpublished Ph.D. Dissertation (Ball State University, 1970), 299–308, and Lewis H. Carlson, "German World War II POWs in America: Cultural and Political Conflicts," an unpublished paper delivered at the National Association of Popular Culture's Annual Meeting, Philadelphia, Pa., April 13, 1993.

dents at some 200 camps,[8] to Daniel Costelle's 167 clandestine executions.[9] Quite naturally, American authorities contended that all such figures were inflated. John Mason Brown, Director of the Special War Problems Division of the Provost Marshal General's Office, insisted, "The general public appears to have a grossly exaggerated idea of the Nazi-criminal aspects of camp life; there have been a total of only two murders and not over ten severe beatings due to political reasons."[10] Equally defensive was Provost Marshal General Archer L. Lerch, who in the spring of 1945 took issue with the "misinformation" the public was receiving from news stories which he dismissed as "fantastic." "There have been only five murders and two forced suicides that could be attributed to Nazi methods," claimed Lerch. "Any prisoner who fears for his own safety need only report to the nearest American officer or enlisted man, and he will be given protection."[11]

Whatever the actual numbers, seldom were camp officials able to identify the Nazi perpetrators. Eventually, however, in three separate cases, U. S. military authorities did arrest and convict fourteen German POWs for the murders of three fellow prisoners; and in July of 1945, two months after all American prisoners were safely out of German hands, these fourteen Germans became the first foreign prisoners of war ever to be executed by the U. S. Government.[12]

Late in 1944, political and military officials, responding to

---

[8]Krammer, *Nazi Prisoners of War in America*, 170, 173.

[9]Costelle, *Les Prisonniers*, 63; Costelle went on to add, "The number of those gravely mutilated, battered, and injured defies estimation."

[10]John Mason Brown, "German Prisoners of War in the United States," *The American Journal of International Law*, XXXIX (1945), p. 213.

[11]Archer L. Lerch, "The Army Reports on Prisoners of War," *American Mercury* (May 1945), 546–7; see also "Address of Major General Archer L. Lerch," *Congressional Record, Appendix*, 79th Cong., 1st Sess., A1024. Lerch became Provost Marshal General in June 1944.

[12]Krammer, *Nazi Prisoners of War in America*, 171–173; see also Richard Whittingham, *Martial Justice: The Last Mass Execution in the United States* (Chicago: Henry Regnery Co., 1971) and Wilma Parnell, *The Killing of Corporal Kunze* (Secaucus, N.J.: Lyle Stuart, 1981).

increasingly vocal criticism from Jewish organizations, prominent journalists, including the progressive German-American press, and several liberal political figures, made a greater effort to segregate unrepentant Nazis and to launch an ambitious reeducation program to prepare select anti-Nazi or nonpolitical prisoners for their return to Germany.[13]

The anti-Nazi elements included a wide variety of groups. On the far left were Socialists, Communists, and radical trade unionists. At the other end of the spectrum were fervent, class-conscious Nationalists who feared Hitler was destroying their Germany. In between were Catholic centrists, moderate Social Democrats, and various non-Germans such as Austrians, Poles, Dutch, Czechs, and even some Russians who, for whatever reason, had fought in the *Wehrmacht*, but who as prisoners wanted to separate themselves from all things German. Finally, there were those prisoners who were largely apolitical or who simply sought to curry favor with their American captors.

Some of the most radical anti-Nazi prisoners had served in Hitler's notorious *999 Strafbataillon* [999 Penal Battalion], which included various political and criminal "undesirables," many of whom had spent years in German concentration camps. When manpower shortages became acute, they were drafted into the army where some fought while others soon deserted or surrendered.

Luca Felix Müller, who had opposed the war on conscientious grounds, deserted during the Normandy invasion. As a prisoner, he continued to oppose all aspects of National Socialism and became an active participant in the reeducation programs. Erwin Schulz, a former anti-Nazi street fighter who had spent years in concentration camps, was drafted into the *999 Strafbataillon*. He deserted in North Africa and continued his rebellious behavior in the American prison camps. Helmut Dillner, on the other hand, had no use for deserters, radicals, or any German soldier who did not honor total military discipline.

---

[13]Gansburg, *Stalag USA*, 6, argues that these reeducation programs enjoyed considerable success; Ron Robin, *The Barbed-Wire College: Re-Educating German POWs in the United States During World War II* (Princeton: Princeton University Press, 1995), ix, concludes that for the most part they were a failure.

HELMUT DILLNER

Born in Kreiz, Thuringia, Helmut Dillner joined the army in 1938 and ended up in a communications unit. He was captured in North Africa on May 12, 1943, and ended up in Camp Brady, Texas, where he picked cotton. Time has dulled Dillner's memory, but he still recalls celebrating Hitler's birthday in 1944 and the contempt he felt for many of the German soldiers who were captured after the Normandy invasion.

I REMEMBER ON APRIL 20, 1944, we had a big march for Adolf Hitler's birthday. That was in Camp Brady, Texas, and at the time we still considered ourselves active soldiers; in fact, we thought we might still win the war. Once you entered the army, it didn't matter what you had been as a civilian. You were now a soldier and you acted like a soldier. We celebrated Hitler's birthday with wine that we had made out of fruit. I worked in the kitchen so I could get whatever we needed. We cut a little square out of the wooden floor in our barracks and fermented it there. Of course, you could smell it when you came in the door. For months we also had been building this tunnel under the fence. On this day, four or five guys escaped and went to Fredericksburg which was a famous German-American town located northwest of San Antonio. Even the mayor spoke German. They were caught but there was no harsh punishment the first couple of times you escaped. You were just put in the stockade on bread and water for a couple of weeks. Nobody punished us for celebrating Hitler's birthday, although some of the guys didn't think we should.

We Africa Corps soldiers refused to have anything to do with prisoners taken after the Normandy invasion. They were always filthy, even though they had been in camps where they could have washed. We didn't like it that they didn't keep themselves clean and that so many were Communists. Some even had

Communist signs. Why didn't they just go to Russia? They would have been happier there. Then they would have found out what communism really was. Not all of them were like that, but some were. I always refused to go on work details with Western Front prisoners.

LUCA FELIX MÜLLER

Born in 1918, Luca Felix Müller is the son of the well-known
Dresden expressionist painter and Communist sympathizer,
Conrad Felixmüller, who greatly influenced his son's own anti-
fascism. Müller was drafted into the army as a veterinarian, but
in 1944, as a matter of principle, he deserted to the Allies in
France. In the United States he was a willing participant in the
so-called "Factory" at Forts Getty and Kearney, where American
authorities attempted to "reeducate" select prisoners in preparation for their postwar return to a democratic Germany. At Fort
Kearney, Müller helped edit *der Ruf*, the well-known progressive
and elitist periodical put out by the German prisoners themselves, and he became head of the archives. After the war Müller
lived in the former German Democratic Republic until the June
17, 1953, popular revolt, after which he defected to West Berlin
where he taught veterinary medicine at the Free University. He
currently lives on Berlin's Wannsee in a home filled with art trea-
sures created by his father and various family friends.[14]

A MAN GOES THROUGH a terrible soul-searching when he is trying
to decide whether or not to desert, but, in the end, he must remain
true to his beliefs. There is no other way. Until recently, I was
always hesitant to tell my fellow citizens that I was a deserter,
and I'll tell you why. At a friend's birthday party I told a World

---

[14]This interview was conducted by Norbert Haase, a German colleague
with whom I co-authored a German version of this book entitled *Warten
auf Freiheit* (*Waiting for Freedom*) (Berlin: Aufbau Verlag, 1996). The
editing and translation are mine.

War II veteran that I had deserted. He nearly fell off his chair. He was a university colleague of mine and we had a good friendship. Since then he will have nothing to do with me. So it is in German society. The average German will always put his personal safety and that of his children above all else. In 1934 I knew Jews in Dresden who ran around town wearing swastikas. Some were even family friends. They would say, "National Socialism is a grand thing! Its minor anti-Semitism will soon die out." To make a political error is forgivable, but to accept inhuman behavior is criminal. I cannot act this way. Before I became a soldier, I even made myself welcome the bombers that destroyed my home town because I so wanted the war to end and the Nazi regime destroyed. Much later I took to the streets of the German Democratic Republic for public demonstrations against the government, and I did the same thing after I defected to West Berlin. I only demanded that some political party did not organize or run the demonstrations. I simply cannot act like the average German. I must be myself. For the average German, patriotic thought plays a greater role than any other. Thank God that has now somewhat changed. The Poles have shown that you can outlive a dictatorship. The Hungarians too, and to a certain extent the Czechs. Then in 1989 the people in the GDR showed that it could even happen in Germany. Since then I have begun to feel a certain national pride.

My father was the Dresden expressionist painter, Conrad Felixmüller, who was also very involved politically. He was a Communist not only on humanistic grounds but because they were the most decisive opponents of World War I, during which he was put into a mental hospital because he was a conscientious objector. He left the Communist Party in 1924 when he learned of Stalin's atrocities. However, he continued to work on Franz Pfemfert's magazine *The Action*, for whom he produced many woodcuts. Naturally, this put him in contact with many of the intellectuals of the day who were also convinced that National Socialism would be a terrible catastrophe for Germany. So I grew up in this anti-Nazi atmosphere. When the Reichstag burned down on February 27, 1933, my father immediately said, "The Nazis started it." The next year, we moved to Berlin because it had become too dangerous in Dresden. My father's fame and success had made the authorities suspicious. When the police raided our house, I was forced to throw our entire collection of *The Action* and a considerable amount of Russian literature into the fire place.

Berlin was then much more liberal than the hinterland. For example, I passed my *Abitur* in Berlin in 1937 without ever having belonged to the *Hitler Jugend*. That would have been impossible in Dresden. In addition, Hitler included four of my father's paintings and forty of his drawings in his infamous exhibit of degenerate art which first traveled to Dresden in 1934.[15] Then things began to go bad for us in Berlin. My father was no longer allowed to show his work. Some friends arranged a commission in England where he stayed from January to June of 1939. He returned to Germany but with the intention of emigrating to England. That would have been possible in July or August of 1939, but that would have meant leaving all his work behind. My younger brother and I were still studying. We expected the war to come, but we thought the West was so well armed that the war could only last a short time before Germany would be overwhelmed. My father was also no hero, and he had to face an uncertain future as an immigrant. So we convinced him and ourselves to let the war come to us. Even after the war began, and the army successfully rolled over Poland and France, I was one of those who thought there was no way Germany could win.

Looking back on those times, only the high officers on the German general staff could have toppled Hitler. I know that several attempted to do so and that they all failed and were punished. But it is incomprehensible to me that they could find no way to distance themselves from the regime. Of course, the Nazis

---

[15]This exhibit of degenerate art *[Entartete Kunst]* ended up on permanent display in Munich as an example of what loyal Third Reich Germans were supposed to shun. These prominent artists were mostly Jewish or leftists, or they were individuals whose work was considered too political, modern, or abstract to be properly nationalistic. In 1937 Hitler formally opened his House of German Art in Munich which he promised would end the "artistic lunacy and pollution of our people." In the spring of 1992 surviving examples of the degenerate art exhibit were collected and put on display in Berlin, although to a much different kind of reception than in 1934.

mistreated many of the officers, but, with few exceptions, they were all very anxious to further their careers. At the time the war broke out, my family knew a colonel on the general staff in Berlin who said to us, "We are nowhere near ready with our war preparations! The war has started much too soon." He and many of his fellow officers knew from the beginning that the war had to end in a catastrophic defeat; yet, they willingly went along with it.

I was stationed near the French town of Falaise where some eighteen German divisions were trapped by the Allies during the Normandy invasion. To the northeast were Canadian troops; to the north British, and in the northwest and south were the Americans. It was a military catastrophe. As an officer of veterinary medicine I was in charge of some 400 heavy draft horses. When a couple of them were killed, I was ordered to buy replacements from nearby French farmers. This allowed me to get away from my unit. With the help of a French farmer whom I carefully approached, I found a tank with a white star on it and turned myself over to what turned out to be Canadian troops. My decision to desert was made easier because I was responsible only for horses rather than men.

I explained to a Canadian intelligence officer I had deserted because I fully expected and wanted Germany to lose the war. The psychological effects of deserting one's country are severe, but the Canadian was very impressed when I told him I had always opposed the war. He told me he had studied at Heidelberg, although he spoke little German because that had been long in the past. I spoke rather fluent English. He took me out of the camp during the day and returned me at night. We encountered French farmers who wanted to go back to their land they had been forced to leave because of the fighting, so I translated for them while still wearing my German uniform.

I was then sent to England and put on a ship for America that had transported food, war materials, and troops to England, but were carrying prisoners on the return trip. We were perhaps 400 soldiers and a couple dozen officers. The Americans followed the correct POW guidelines and separated the officers from the other soldiers. As we sailed into New York harbor in October of 1944, we stared at the Statue of Liberty through the barbed wire that crisscrossed our port-hole windows.

We were put on a train and transported across America to Camp Trinidad, Colorado, where I was to discover I had enjoyed more political freedom in the traditional Germany army than I would in an American POW camp. Trinidad was dominated by uncompromising Africa Corps officers. They required all of us to give the Nazi salute even to American officers. You could even find *Pleitegeier*[16] cut out of tin cans hanging on the barracks walls. In accordance with the Geneva Convention we had our German Confidence Men who represented our interests to the proper authorities. At the top was a colonel from the reserves, but he was surrounded by ardent Nazis, especially from the *SS*, and they set the tone for the camp. So whenever an American officer came onto the grounds, there were immediately two Nazi officers by his side. This was naturally very hard for me to accept.

I was only a lieutenant, but I spoke frankly. When I told some of my fellow officers of the military disaster on the Western Front and that in a few weeks the war would be over, it became very quiet in the barracks. A short time later a captain came up to me and said, "If you think that you can spread defeatism here, you will never make it to the protective custody of the Americans before we shut you up." Then someone else said, "Here, we hold the spirit of Rommel alive! After the war is won in Europe, we will pour out of these POW camps and roll over America." So in this land of the free we were to be ruled by Nazis.

Naturally, all this disgusted me so I decided to contact an American officer. I thought that under the protection of the Americans I could say what I wanted. One evening at dusk I approached the guard house and told the guard, "I want to speak to an American officer." He summoned a chaplain whom I told about my plan to resist because I was being tyrannized by my own officers. He told me to go to the mess hall. I hadn't been there twenty minutes when an American MP approached me with a billy club in his hand. He asked, "Lieutenant Müller? Come with me!" Outside was a covered jeep which took me back to my bar-

---

[16]As mentioned in Chapter Four, the word *Pleitegeier*, which signifies a scruffy-looking vulture circling in search of helpless prey, was used by those wanting to make fun of the official Nazi eagle.

racks. Outside the barracks was another jeep with a couple of guards standing alongside it, and inside by my bed was yet another guard holding a billy club. I didn't understand why all these guards were there. I later learned that those seeking pro-tective custody were often beaten by the other prisoners and their bedding and belongings destroyed. That's why they transported me in a covered jeep and stationed the guards to watch over my belongings. I was told to pack my things and get back in the jeep. They then drove me to the American camp commander who was a Southerner. Even the Americans could scarcely understand him, and with my school English I had great difficulty. I told him about my desire to resist and warned him, "If the Americans do not protect the German rank-and-file prisoners whom they now have under their jurisdiction, they should not be surprised when these men disappear into the blast furnaces just like the French dissenters did during the occupation of the Rhineland." This impressed him. I also told him that most anti-Nazi officers were afraid to express their ideas because they feared the *SS* terror-ists.

Several of us were subsequently sent to Camp Ruston, Louisiana. There were two Austrians and a couple of others who were being removed for various political reasons. Camp Ruston contained a wide range of prisoners, including Communists, Social Democrats, trade unionists, 999ers, Biblical scholars, and even German Nationalists. All were opponents of the regime who had made their views known. There were ideological conflicts, especially between the Nationalists and the Communists, but most of these conflicts remained civilized because of the liberal mood in the camp. There were no political parties as such, and no one brought his old animosities with him.

At Camp Trinidad we had had one newspaper, the *Chicago Sun Times*, but it was tightly censored. In Ruston there were no newspapers and no theater, perhaps because there were too many diverse interests and political beliefs. But there was lots of time for reading, and we profited from discussions with each other. We had considerable freedom, but we also noticed that the military is the same everywhere, and that clearly the American military authorities preferred orderly Germans to those of us who were anti-Nazis.

There was a compound in Camp Ruston which contained Russian officers from Vlasov's army.[17] In the evening they sang their Russian songs. That was wonderful and we talked to them through the barbed wire. When I was a student before the war I had spent some time in Prague where I got to know Jewish friends of my father, and I realized I needed to learn a Slavic language for my basic education. I took advantage of the situation to try and learn Russian from one of these officers who had been a teacher in Moscow. As officers we received $20 a month and I used this to purchase books. I wanted to learn to read Dostoyevsky in his own language, so I spent four hours a day for three months learning Russian.

Later, I learned that the American authorities had agreed to send the Vlasov Army back to Stalin. The U.S.S.R. had even sent officials to Camp Ruston to implore the Vlasov officers to return, but most of them had refused. What happened next was a human tragedy. The Americans first placed the Russian dissidents under guard. Then they loaded them onto trucks and drove them to the harbor. On the way, many of the Russians jumped off the trucks and tried to escape. Even after they boarded the ship, some jumped over the side. They knew they would not survive their return to the U.S.S.R.—and none did.

[In 1944 the Provost Marshal General's Special Project Division launched a reeducation program at Camp Van Etten, New York. It was referred to as "The Factory," where carefully selected German prisoners edited der Ruf, the highly sophisticated prison newspaper. They also reviewed books for prison libraries and took classes in American history, politics, and literature in preparation for their return to postwar Germany. These activities were later moved to Forts Kearney and Getty in Rhode Island.]

---

[17]Russian prisoners could be found in both American and German prison camps. After Soviet General Andrei A. Vlasov's capture by the Germans in August of 1942, he denounced Stalin and recruited fellow prisoners to fight for the Third Reich. Many of these volunteers ended up in American prison camps. At the end of the war, the American government returned the Vlasov prisoners, who strenuously objected, to the Soviet Union where most were executed or disappeared into slave labor camps.

In the winter of 1944 I was among a group of prisoners the Americans selected and sent to Camp Van Etten in upstate New York to participate in a reeducation program. I took over the archives which was very interesting. We received a wide variety of American newspapers as well as transmissions of various European radio programs, all of which kept us informed about the course of the war. We were also preoccupied with the publication of *der Ruf*. We welcomed all this activity as an opportunity to educate our fellow prisoners.

In April of 1945 we were moved to Fort Kearney, and then several of us were selected to go to Fort Getty to be a part of its reeducation program. We eventually became the first class to graduate from this program. The program directors told us, "We want to show you what we Americans understand by democracy." How they did this was interesting, and we enthusiastically participated. Harvard University's Howard Mumford Jones, who was then president of the Academy of Arts and Sciences, headed up the program. Jones insisted, "No one can introduce human beings to democracy when they are behind barbed wire." He taught us our first course on American History and Literature. Henry Ehrmann, who was a German immigrant, taught a course called New Views of German History. We would listen and then write reports.

In July of 1945 I was one of the first sixty-six German prisoners to be repatriated. We sailed back to Europe on an 18,000-ton liberty ship. We were given a complete set of regulations; in fact, the American army had regulations for everything and these applied to their own military prisoners as well as to us. I still remember a couple of amusing examples: "Skylarking and horseplay are strictly forbidden!" and "All formations are to be done on the double." If we were going to our bunks or to work chipping off the rust or even to eat, we had to double-step. And whoever did not double-step received a smart kick in the backside from the guards. We were not prepared for this kind of treatment after being taught about democracy and freedom in the reeducation programs at Forts Kearney and Getty. But this was the military, and to them we were simply ordinary POWs. I later saw the film *From Here to Eternity*, and it showed the American military acting the same way toward their own men. In fact, some of the men fought with each other—even with knives—until they almost killed one another. So that's the only way you can understand what happened to us on the ship returning home. That's how the military treats people. But this treatment affected my attitude toward Western democracies, and also toward the totalitarian systems of the U.S.S.R. and the G.D.R., and it will stay with me for the rest of my life.

ERWIN SCHULZ

Born into a Berlin worker's family in 1912, Erwin Schulz spent several years in the 1930s in concentration camps for his Communist and anti-Nazi activities. In 1942 he was drafted into the infamous *999 Strafbataillon* [999 Penal Battalion], into which Hitler put political prisoners, criminals, and other social "misfits" because of growing military manpower shortages. After deserting in North Africa, Schulz ended up in the United States as a POW who openly fought against fascist elements in the prison camps. Because of his reputation as a "troublemaker," American authorities held up his repatriation to Germany, sending him instead to England where the House of Commons took months to discuss his and other similar cases. Eventually, he was repatriated and settled in the German Democratic Republic, but authorities once again looked on him with suspicion, this time because they feared he had been contaminated by Western ideas.[18]

I STILL HAVE SOME documents pertaining to things that went on during the short time I was the camp spokesman in Camp McCain, Mississippi. We were mostly former members of the *999 Strafbataillon* who had been captured or deserted in North Africa, and now we discovered our freedom was also restricted in the American prison camps. The camp commander ordered us not to participate in any political discussions, including anything about the concentration camps we had been in or about our anti-fascist activities. Then he closed down our camp newspaper.

The military mind is similar wherever you are. It is always

---

[18]As with the Luca Felix Müller interview, Norbert Haase conducted this interview, although the translation and editing are again mine.

intolerant of any views or individuals outside of its own narrow sphere. For example, we certainly knew discrimination in Germany, but we also found it in the United States. We discovered in Mississippi and Alabama that blacks were considered to be lower than low. We occasionally went out on work details with them, and they were not treated any better than we were. Like us, they might just as well have been surrounded by barbed wire.

Before it was banned, we used to post our newspaper on the barracks wall because it was the only way we could keep our fellow prisoners informed. For example, Fritz Liebscher had been a political prisoner in Buchenwald, and he described his experiences for our newspaper. When one of the recently arrived prisoners read one of his articles and made the unfortunate remark that Liebscher's wife and children should have been exterminated with the rest of the inmates, Liebscher hit him right in the face. This young, ignorant man picked himself up and ran off to the guards saying we had threatened and beaten him and God knows what else. The camp commander ordered Liebscher to stand on the parade grounds with no hat in the midday sun. This was Mississippi where the temperature was often over 100 degrees. The guards, who had a mental picture of German "supermen," stood behind him with their machine guns at the ready.

We all knew each other from our anti-Nazi activities, and we knew Liebscher. So we decided to do something about his plight. We announced we would refuse to cooperate in any way, including work, until he was no longer forced to stand in the sun. We argued that such treatment was similar to that meted out by the Nazis in the concentration camps. The discussion raged back and forth. Then the commander decided to put Liebscher into the isolation barracks, and he received no further punishment.

As a result of the Liebscher incident, I was terminated as camp spokesman. There were certain elements in the camp that collaborated with the Americans, and they said I had instigated the work stoppage. We were then ordered not to mention Buchenwald or anything else that was politically controversial.

We were branded as troublemakers and segregated from the others behind our own barbed-wire fence. This was called the Communist compound, and we were not allowed to talk to prisoners outside our compound. In truth, we saw ourselves as anti-fascists who wanted to work together against the Nazis. We consisted of Social Democrats, Communists, trade unionists, and all kinds of other radicals representing a wide spectrum of political opinion. Some of these men had refused to cooperate with camp officials; others had been denounced for one reason or another; and a good many had been threatened or beaten up by fervent Nazis in other camps. They were all put in our compound. The Americans collected information on us which then accompanied us wherever we were sent. They also restricted our privileges. This naturally made many of us upset. My file stated I was a "fanatical Communist" and a "troublemaker." Later, in a camp in England, I worked in the office and took this information out of my file. There were still powerful Nazis in this camp, and if they had discovered who I was, who knows what they might have done. A number of anti-Nazis had been murdered in the American camps so I knew it was better to stay alive than to have such a record.

I was born October 13, 1912, in Berlin where I attended elementary school. As a ten-year-old in 1922 I became a member of *Fichte* which was Berlin's largest workers' sports club. My father did not belong to an organized political party, but he was a union member. These were bad times, and I was unable to get any kind of apprenticeship position when I turned fourteen. I tried different firms but found nothing. Finally, I went to work for Jonas and Company as a salesman. I was supposed to receive training but I never really did. It was simply that I had something to do rather than just hanging out in the streets. For a time I was a member of a labor youth union, but there was then chaos in the trade union movement, and the various factions were continuously at odds with one another.

By 1930 there was no work at all. For an entire year I had nothing but occasional small jobs. It was simply hopeless. Without knowing much about theoretical matters, I went to lectures, and I became increasingly involved in the labor movement. I had also participated in the famous 1929 May Day street struggle against the fascists.

After the Nazis came to power in 1933, I joined other dissidents in distributing pamphlets against rearmament. I was also involved in other political demonstrations and activities, and in 1935 I was arrested and sentenced to five years in Luckau prison for instigating crimes of high treason. Many of the inmates in

Luckau had received long sentences because of similar accusations, and I can assure you it was not a comfortable life. You can't imagine the hatred that was directed toward us.

After two years in Luckau, I was sent to various other concentration camps before finally being released in 1940. Then I was rearrested and interrogated by the *Gestapo*. I was again released, but I was constantly harassed and kept under strict police surveillance. Every time I went out I wondered if I would ever come home again.

These arrests and my years in prison naturally made me very cautious and suspicious. By the time I was drafted into the *999 Strafbataillon* in December of 1942, I had learned to distrust anything that smacked of the military. We knew that there were certain officers whose job it was to spy on us 999ers. In my heavy mortars unit we had a sergeant who had attended one of the special Ordensburg schools to train elite Nazi students. He was quite cunning but we knew about him. We were convinced that our superiors were our enemies so we were always very careful not to say anything incriminating. In North Africa six or seven soldiers who had mentioned they wanted to be captured by the Canadians were arrested, court-martialed, and shot. A group of Jehovah's Witnesses were also shot. As a warning, our company had to stand by and watch while they were murdered.

No one wanted to end his life in this manner, so Otto Linke and I decided to desert. Our heavy mortar unit was sitting on a totally exposed hill which made for an impossible military situation. Artillery shells were landing all around us, and we were torn to pieces. We were simply canon fodder so Otto and I decided to carry out our plan. There were Italian troops on one side of us and German troops on the other. By this time the Italians also had lost their will to fight; unfortunately, we had no contact with them, and they were also segregated from us after we became prisoners.

Our troops began to retreat and in the confusion it was difficult to tell who was deserting and who was simply among the missing. Otto and I hid in some bushes. We said to each other, "Finally, on this first day of May 1943 we begin our lives as free men." The next day we turned ourselves over to some Moroccan troops who were delighted to get our weapons. They then turned us over to de Gaulle's troops who put us in a small temporary prison camp in the rear lines. While we were there a chaplain stuck his head in our tent and told us that an anti-Nazi had just been murdered and that we should be careful.

After short stays in camps in Bizerta and Oran, we were moved to Casablanca where we were put on a hospital ship bound for New York which contained a large number of wounded American soldiers. Some of the German prisoners on board fantasized that U-boats would attack and liberate us. While sitting in the mess hall and filling their bellies with tremendous amounts of food, they bragged, *"Wir machen die Amerikaner kaputt!"* ["We'll destroy the Americans!"]. These fools had no idea of the economic might of the United States.

After our arrival in America, we were sent to Camp Aliceville, Alabama. We 999ers were easily recognizable through our open discussions. The German army had been rolled back from Stalingrad and defeated in North Africa. It was now clear that Germany would lose the war, so we felt we could talk more openly. We considered the Allied troops to be our friends, and in no way did we want to cause the Americans any problems. We talked openly about how we wanted nothing to do with the outspoken fascists, but the Americans handled us just like the most impassioned Nazis. When we naturally fought against being lumped together with them, we were labeled "troublemakers." Anyone who demanded his rights under the Geneva Convention was also considered a disciplinary problem. At night we always posted a watch because the situation with the other prisoners was very tense. The *Gestapo* elements threatened us just to prove how powerful they were. What the Americans wanted was discipline. We were supposed to salute all officers, but we had enough of that kind of thing and we refused to salute them. So again we caused trouble.

We tried to get our own anti-Nazi barracks in Aliceville. We wanted the camp authorities to segregate the *Gestapo* elements and their faithful followers so they would not be able to influence the younger prisoners who had never heard anything but Nazi propaganda. But the Americans turned everything upside down. Instead of the Nazis, we were isolated into a rather primitive compound for a couple of months and then sent to Camp McCain, Mississippi, which was an anti-Nazi camp.

In Camp McCain we were joined by various prisoners from other camps. We knew some of them from North Africa or from our own incarceration in other camps. These men later became part of the Fort Devens contingent. I was voted the camp spokesman, probably because I was not an official member of any political party. But after some disagreements and conflicts I was replaced. When I asked the Americans about this, they told me I could remain compound spokesman if I so desired. So I became the compound Confidence Man, and we had no camp spokesman.

As the representative of the prisoners, I felt like a shop steward, settling differences in a factory. The Americans wanted quiet and order, and as few problems as possible. For example, if someone felt he was being threatened, I was supposed to say to the Americans, "This man feels endangered. What can you do about it?" Some of the men wanted musical instruments, sports equipment, and books. Because we were considered a punishment camp, we were denied such amenities, although other camps certainly had them. So back and forth I would have to go. That got on the Americans' nerves and they would say, "You'll have that soon" or "They don't have that in other camps" or "We have already proposed that." I also wrote formal letters to the American officials making these requests, but they would just hold on to them, unless a Swiss inspection team was coming; then they would return them to us along with their good intentions to act soon.[19]

Along with those of us who had long been anti-Nazi, we had some German officers who had passed themselves off as anti-fascists during their American interrogation. They arrived in our camp wearing all their uniform insignia and decorations. We had nothing like this; in fact, most of us didn't even have uniforms. Those of us who had long suffered from Nazi abuse in Germany and who had even been threatened while POWs were not enthusiastic about the arrival of these new officers. We looked at them suspiciously and asked, "What do these Nazis want here?" As Confidence Man, I told these officers that we were anti-Nazi opponents of Hitler, and as such we didn't want them running around showing

---

[19]The Swiss legation in the United States represented Germany's interests during World War II. Its representatives, along with the International Red Cross, made periodic inspection visits to the prison camps at which time prisoners could supposedly voice complaints.

off all their military decorations. Some of these officers angrily argued that enlisted men could not talk to them like this, and that according to the Geneva Convention they were entitled to orderlies to shine their boots and generally look after them. But by this time we didn't recognize officers as being any different than the rest of us. There were also some who had come from good Catholic or Protestant homes and now were rediscovering their religion. Finally, there were those who didn't want to offend the Americans so they could get home as quickly as possible to resume their former careers. My talk to all of them was short and sweet. I told them they had to remove all their military decorations, and they did.

Although Nazis were not an important element in McCain, we wanted to inform outside individuals about their dominance in other camps. Any contact with outside sources was naturally forbidden, but without the knowledge of the American camp officials, we were able to communicate with certain sympathetic German Americans and prominent journalists. Finally, in 1944 such information began to come out in the open, when writers like Vicki Baum and Dorothy Bromley began publishing articles.[20]

When we arrived at Fort Devens in 1944, the various anti-Nazi groups agreed to select Herbert Tulatz as their camp spokesman. They felt that I could not get the approval of the Americans for that position so they agreed on Tulatz. He won the election although I don't know what the vote was. Then some time later we wanted to replace him with Erwin Welke, but this resulted in a battle with the American authorities who kept delaying the election. Without approval we distributed a flyer calling for Welke's election. The American camp commander asked, "Who published this flyer?" I stepped forward and told him I had. At first, he want-

---

[20]On August 19, 1944, Vicki Baum published a controversial story in *Collier's* magazine. Allegedly based on facts she had gathered from the prisoners themselves, Baum's "Land of the Free" presented a fictional Austrian prisoner, Gottfried Schlegel, who had suffered terrifying Nazi abuse which the American camp commander largely ignored. Earlier in the year, Walter Winchell had also told of Nazi camp dominance on his radio broadcast of March 5, 1944, as had Dorothy Dunbar Bromley, in her "War Prisoners Include Nazis and Anti-Nazis," *New York Herald Tribune*, April 12, 1944.

ed to punish me, but then he asked if I would also design a flyer for the other candidates. I told him, "President Roosevelt never made election propaganda for the conservatives, nor they for him."

We had a variety of classes at Fort Devens, but there was nothing in the study plan about trade unions or desirable social reforms. English, German, French, mathematics, and American history were considered safe subjects, but we had nothing about the history of the Weimar Republic or anything controversial. It was a narrow curriculum, and the German prisoners themselves had helped design it. Of course, there were certain inducements and privileges if one were willing to cooperate.

Some of us were sent from Fort Devens to Camp Stark, which was located deep in the New Hampshire wilderness. That must have been May of 1944; in any case, there was still snow on the ground. There were about 250 of us. Once again we were a mixture of Communists, Social Democrats, trade unionists, and those who had no precise political ties. There were also a number of prisoners whom the Americans considered to be criminals.

It was wonderful to be out in the forest cutting down trees. We thought, "The war will soon be over and this is a great place to spend our remaining time." There were no complaints—until a new commander, who was a Polish American, arrived. When he introduced a quota for how many trees we had to cut down, we began to resist. Then he extended our working hours and no longer counted our travel time. There were many other little irritating things he implemented just to annoy us. If he had really wanted to increase production, he could have done so in a much more positive way.[21]

While we were in Camp Stark, we learned from the American newspapers that Ernst Thälmann had been killed in a concentration camp. Thälmann was a prominent Communist who was certainly known to all anti-Nazis, so we decided to stage a memorial service. The service included speeches of old friends, and then we sang radical union songs. This really upset the camp commander. He thought he had a mutiny on his hands, and he became very nervous.

---

[21]The new commander was Captain Alexandium Kobus. For a much more positive treatment of Captain Kobus and a glowing description of Camp Stark, see Allen V. Koop, *Stark Decency: German Prisoners of War in a New England Village* (Hanover & London: Press of New England, 1988).

After the end of hostilities in 1945 the Red Cross wanted a list of former political prisoners. There were some 300 of us who had served something like 2,000 years in German prisons and concentration camps. The Red Cross was going to recommend that those on the list be granted an early release for their return to Germany. But there was considerable disagreement over where we would be sent because of the political problems in eastern Germany. We were afraid, however, that the Nazis would get home before us.[22] We thought if we had to stay, they should stay with us, and we would try to reeducate them.

In the spring of 1946 I was sent to Belgium and then on to a camp in Shelby, England. Some of us wrote letters to top government officials and to certain members of the British labor movement asking them to exert pressure so we could be sent home as victims of fascism.[23] My mother even wrote such a letter to the commander of Shelby. Our cases were eventually debated on the floor of the House of Commons.

There were no 999ers in Camp Shelby, but I had some good luck. I introduced myself to the intelligence officer who was a Viennese Jew, and I ended up working as a typist in his office. I typed up the daily menus for the officers' mess. Also in the camp were English conscientious objectors who had refused to carry arms in the war. With my little English and their equally limited German we were able to communicate with each other. We also received books from Walter Janka, a former publisher who sent us reading materials from Mexico. I can still remember reading Anna Seghers' anti-war novel *The Seventh Cross* straight through the night. For the young prisoners this was something very new, and we naturally had many discussions. They had never heard of such books.

I was finally repatriated to Germany in October of 1946. We were briefly placed in a mustering-out camp where some of the intractable Nazi officers and NCOs now talked about joining the Western Allies to wage war against the U.S.S.R.

---

[22]Schulz and his colleagues' fears were justified. In the fall of 1945 the first large contingent to be sent back to Germany included many ardent Nazis and others who were classified as "useless."

[23]"Victim of Fascism" or *OdF [Opfer des Faschismus]* became an official designation in postwar Germany.

6
American *Sonder* Prisoners

It just so happens we were American soldiers who were in the Holocaust, but we can't get our government to admit it.

AMERICAN POW

The first thing I saw at Dachau was a bunch of walking skeletons. I was put in a building very close to the cooking facilities for the SS troops. There weren't many of us in that building, but we were the Sonderkommandos.

AMERICAN POW

DURING WAR THERE ARE always cases in which captors target certain prisoners for extraordinary and horrifying treatment. Among those POWs selected by the Germans for "special" treatment were a number of Jews, a few "incorrigible" troublemakers, and those suspected of being special agents or spies rather than regular soldiers. Whatever the rationale, these men were removed from their fellow prisoners and put into special work or concentration camps usually reserved for slave laborers, political prisoners, Jews, and other "undesirables." John Foster, Don Coulson, and Sandy Lubinsky were three of the relatively few American prisoners who suffered this singular, horrifying treatment. Coulson ended up in Dachau because he refused to cooperate with his German captors. Lubinsky was singled out as a Jew and sent to the slave labor camp at Berga. And Foster, who was suspected of espionage, was tortured and ended up in a hospital overlooking Buchenwald. The German word "*sonder*" denotes "special," but in the context of the concentration and slave labor camps it referred to the lowest of prisoners or slave laborers, meaning those designated for "special" assignments or even a "special" death.

JOHN J. FOSTER

John Foster is not sure why he was so mistreated by the *SS* or why he was sent to a hospital outside of what he thinks was Buchenwald. Perhaps it was because he was carrying a map of his home town, the streets of which sounded like military designations. Or perhaps it was because he and his Airborne unit were mistakenly dropped so far behind German lines. In any case, the torture he suffered during interrogations and his searing memories of stacked Jewish bodies and burning flesh have caused him permanent physical and psychological problems. Alcohol became a serious problem as did violent rages. He was unable to get any kind of permanent civilian job. He now receives fifty percent disability for post-traumatic stress disorder, but nothing for his recurring physical problems which he also traces to his war wounds and the abusive treatment he suffered as a prisoner.

YOU FIGHT A WAR, and then you fight your government harder than the war to get what you've got coming. After I came home I got to thinking about all that I had seen, and it began preying on my mind, but I was never asked to testify by any organization. My original discharge papers state that I was in Buchenwald, but no one ever asked me what I saw. As a matter of fact, they didn't even know what kind of camp it was.

I parachuted into Holland on September 17, 1944, with the 82nd Airborne as part of Operation Market-Garden, and was captured about five days later. Market-Garden was a large-scale American and British air and land offensive which tried to move around the northern end of the Siegfried Line. The Allied Forces were to seize bridges across a series of Dutch rivers, the last of which was at Arnhem on the Lower Rhine, and then move on into

Germany. That's what the movie *A Bridge Too Far* is all about. We were flown in by C–47s, but they dropped us in the woods about fifty or sixty miles beyond our initial target near the town of Groesbeek. We got shot up pretty bad, and we were trapped. The Germans in front of us were retreating, and there were also Germans behind us. So we were caught in between. Most of our guys were killed during the fighting before we were overrun. I had hurt my back when I landed in a tree coming down and couldn't feel my legs; in fact, I didn't have any feeling in them for about three months. I also took a bullet in the back and some shrapnel before we surrendered, but because I was so numb, I'm not sure when or how this happened.

My buddies Bill Reed and Jim Batstone carried me to a barn because I couldn't walk. The Germans then took them away, and I was left with five other wounded guys. They soon moved us to another place, and that's where the SS troopers began interrogating us.

Maybe the reason they treated me so badly was that I had this map of the new bus routes of Port Huron, Michigan, where I was raised. I had also been captured behind enemy lines wearing a uniform that we had intentionally camouflaged with dirt so no insignias were showing. That map had Military Avenue on it, as well as Lapeer Road, Twenty-Fourth Street Viaduct, Electric Avenue, and Lakeside Road. I guess they thought it was some kind of military map. I just had it in my wallet. I never thought anything about it. But when they took us to this barn, they took our wallets, and they found it. I was lying on my back on the ground trying to explain, but there wasn't anyone who could speak English. That's when they tortured me the first time. One of them stuck his bayonet into my right knee cap. All I could say was *"Nix versteh, Nix versteh."* Then he jabbed me again.

They next strung me up by my index fingers. I've still got those scars. They look like fish gills. Then they tied me to a chair, blindfolded me, stripped me to the waist, and poured hot wax over my shoulders. I first felt something cold; then I felt something real hot, and I passed out. After it was over, I discovered they would lay a cold cloth on your shoulders with slits in it so the wax would run in certain ways onto your skin. I've still got these crisscross scars. This went on for about twelve hours. Finally, somebody came in who could speak English. He was dressed in black, wearing a kind of black derby hat, but his uniform was that of a regular *SS* trooper with the swastikas on the front. He asked me, "Are you an American?" I told him I was. He then asked me my name and I told him, along with my rank and serial number. He said, "I see you are from the 82nd Airborne." I said, "Yes." I just answered the questions he asked me, and that saved my bacon. Otherwise those other guys would have killed me. He made them stop torturing me, and he had them put some grease on my fingers and bandaged them. He also must have been responsible for sending me to the hospital overlooking Buchenwald.

They loaded the six of us into the back of a truck. I didn't know the other five guys. They were from another outfit called the "Railsplitters." We rode at least two days and one night in that truck. We ended up in Buchenwald in that little hospital. I knew it was Buchenwald because we could look out the window of the hospital from the second or third floor and we could see a clear field of bodies about two or three blocks away. They were naked, and they were using bulldozers to bury them.[1]

Our hospital was located just outside the compound, and you could smell the sweet, sickening odor of burning flesh. I didn't realize how serious it was at the time. Naturally, we were afraid we would be going out in that field with the rest of the bodies. Two of the other five guys did die from their wounds. Because of all we had seen, I've often wondered why they didn't kill the rest of us instead of shipping us out to another prison camp.

I was in that hospital six or seven weeks. We were in a twenty-by-twenty-foot room with six cots. If there were any other Americans there, I never saw them. A nurse took care of us. The Germans never spoke to us in English, but we could talk to each other. Each day we could look out the window and see bodies

---

[1] It is possible this hospital was next to some other concentration camp. Not surprisingly, Foster was unclear about specific details at the time, and he still is. He did mention, however, thinking that he saw a sign with Buchenwald on it just before arriving at the hospital. The hospital released Foster in November of 1944, and he was sent to Stalag 11-B at Fallingbostel, just west of the Bergen-Belsen concentration camp.

being moved around. They brought some bodies in that were wrapped up in this brown paper like you use to wrap up meat. They looked like they were frozen; at least, they were stiff as boards when they took them off these wagons. I saw literally hundreds of these bodies. Anybody who tells me the Holocaust didn't happened, simply does not know what he is talking about.

DON COULSON

Feisty, impudent, sarcastic, and incorrigible, Don Coulson ended up in Dachau as a "political prisoner" because he clearly had an attitude problem—especially during interrogations. In Dachau he became a *Sonderkommando*, transporting bodies to the crematoria. He tells chilling stories about killer dogs, brutal guards, and the smell of death. For forty years, Coulson refused to talk about his experiences except to disinterested government authorities. But President Ronald Reagan's 1985 visit to Bitburg, Germany, to commemorate a military cemetery in which a number of *SS* soldiers were buried, changed Coulson's mind.[2] After all, it was the *SS* that was responsible for the horrors he witnessed and suffered, and now it was time to speak out.

I WAS DRAFTED INTO the Army Air Corps in November of 1942 and ended up in England as a clerk. I wanted to get into combat, but nobody would listen. So I went on a couple of night missions with the British. They didn't mind; in fact, I guess they would have taken an all-American crew if they could have found one. When my commanding officer found out, I told him the truth. He told me he would not say anything if I promised not to do it again. I told him I couldn't make that promise. So he sent me to what the

---

[2]The German Government originally suggested that President Reagan make his 1985 speech at the site of one of the former death camps, but that would have been uncomfortable for the president. In separate earlier conversations with Israeli Prime Minister Yitzhak Shamir and Nazi-hunter Simon Wiesenthal, Reagan claimed to have photographed the horrors of the death camps at the end of the war. In reality, Reagan never left the States during World War II, and political advisers did not want to remind the media of this embarrassing story.

British called a "bomb-aimer's school" near Liverpool, and I became a bombardier on a B–17. The British were using the Sperry bomb sight, but I came back and used the Norden which made a helluva lot of sense. I don't know how the hell we won the war. I know the big boys claimed great accuracy for the Norden bomb sight. Well, I think you could hit a target maybe the size of Finland, but I don't think you could hit Helsinki. Then I got my eardrums loused up on our second trip on D-Day and they wouldn't let me fly anymore.

After I got out of the hospital back in England they put me on a gun for base defense. It was a 75-mm, but no one taught me how to shoot it. If the Germans bombed the base, we were supposed to shoot back at them, but otherwise we were not to shoot. I was on that gun by myself, and I didn't even know how to put a shell in it. So I got a patriotic wild hair in my fanny and asked for the infantry—and they gave it to me—Lord, did they give it to me.

I joined the Ninth Infantry Division. They said they would give me a little training, so I was sent down on the Salisbury Plains to a British base. I got to dry fire an M–1 a few times. Then they gave me three rounds to zero it in. That was my training. I was sent over to northern France in late September of 1944.

In France, I was assigned to K-Company of the 47th Infantry, and I immediately got into trouble. In my home town of Tulsa, Oklahoma, cab drivers were the local bootleggers, pimps, and everything else that was the bottom of the barrel, and who should be my first squad leader but a Tulsa cab driver. When he tried to assign me to be a forward scout, I told him, "Boy, your ass sucks wind." He then proceeded to tell me, "Maybe you flyboys can talk like that in the Air Corps, but you can't in the infantry." I asked him, "What are you going to do, send me into combat?" He promised to make me sorry. So he assigned me to be an ammunition bearer. I was supposed to carry Browning Automatic Rifle clips. He must have put a dozen bandoliers over my shoulder. I could hardly walk. Within five minutes of our first battle, our BAR man got hit. I told the assistant BAR guy to pick up the gun and start firing. He refused because it was drawing too much fire. So I gave him the bandoliers and I became the BAR man.

I then got hit in the thumb and sent back to England pretty close to where I started. They just wrapped my thumb up and sent me back. I don't know why an aid man didn't do it in the front lines. I was in England just long enough to drink a couple of beers and back I went into combat. I was then assigned to a Headquarters platoon, and that's where I met "friendly fire"; in fact, that's the reason I became a prisoner of war.

It was early December, and three of us went on this recon mission somewhere close to Malmédy. We were not supposed to engage the enemy—just find out what we could. We ran across a tank-refueling depot there. There must have been two acres of gasoline and oil drums scattered in among those tanks. So we torched it. We moved back about 200 yards to a little stand of trees where we watched those drums explode in the air like a giant fireworks show. Some fat-ass, little son-of-a-yankee-mammy was sitting on a hill with an artillery piece and, seeing the fire, figured it was a target of opportunity. One of his short rounds got us. I woke up in a German aid station. I never saw the two guys who were with me again. I must have had 35 or 40 small pieces of shrapnel in my head and shoulders. For ten years after I got home, those little pieces tried to work themselves out.

After I woke up, I was interrogated. I guess I caused them a lot of trouble because I never quite told the truth. I had learned as a kid, if you run across a pathological liar, you should just tell a bigger lie. First the interrogator asked me, "What is your arm?" He meant what branch of the service I was in. I told him it was an appendage that hung from my shoulder. He got a little disturbed about my answer. I wasn't supposed to make it easy for those people, and I wasn't too sure I was going to get out alive anyway. We had heard rumors that they might very well kill us. So I had a kind of Katy-bar-the-door attitude. What the hell, if I was not going to make it, I was at least going to cause all the trouble I could. He then asked me again: "You know what I mean. What is your arm?" This time I answered, "It's a shoulder appendage that's got fingers on the end of it." He gave me a real nasty look and said, "I'll ask you one more time, and if you give me the same answer, I'll cut off your arm and hand it to you." I thought, "Well, hell, I better not give him the same answer." So I told him I was in the underground balloon corps. That left him kind of wide-eyed, and he asked, "What is that?" I told him, "You Germans wouldn't understand this because you don't have oil wells, but in Oklahoma, when water seeps into an oil well, they pack it with Duncan Cement which hardens when it gets wet. The

Americans and the British have started tunneling under the English Channel, and they inflate these thick, hard, rubber balloons and pour Duncan Cement around them; then, they deflate the balloons and pull them out. You know, we were damned near all the way across the channel when Churchill and Stalin got on Roosevelt about launching the invasion. Hell, we were almost there." I've never in my life seen anybody with such an incredulous look on his face. He just went running out the door to get the *Kommandant*. When he came back, his face was as red as a spanked baby's butt. That got me my shoulder broken. He aimed his rifle butt at my head, but I ducked, and he got my shoulder instead. He knocked a few pieces of bone off of it. Like I said, I didn't want to make it easy for them, and I didn't.

From there I was sent to Halle, Germany. I got there in a motorcycle sidecar, in which I was forced to ride head down with my feet up in the air where the guard could see them. We traveled only at night. In Halle I was kept in some kind of engineering school where the SS interrogated me for about a week. They put a few knots on my head to go with my broken shoulder. This one bastard had a leaded riding crop. It must have been twenty-five years before the scars from that disappeared off my back. If I get a sunburn, you can still see the outlines of those scars. I kept up my pathological stories as long as I could. I didn't think I was going to get out alive, so I decided to keep confusing the issue.

I was then sent to Stalag 11-A at Altengrabow just southwest of Berlin. The first thumping I got there was by this real nice German fellow. He called a bunch of us in and pointed to a map and said he was going to update us on what was going on in the war. He pointed to the map and said that such-and-such a division was here while others were over there. Well, some of our guys started saying, "No, no, we're over here." About the third time that happened, I told them, "If you bastards keep telling him what he wants to know, I'm going to have you all shot as traitors. And if the Russians get here first, I'll see to it that they shoot you." See, I understood what he was trying to do. Well, he got powerfully unhappy about this.

They tried to make me work at Stalag 11-A, and I got the hell beat out of me because I refused. Bombs had destroyed the railroad yards, and they wanted us to go out and repair them. I told them, "Some of my buddies probably lost their lives making those holes, and I'll be damned if I'm going out there and fill them up for you." They threatened not to feed me, but, hell, I went from 187 to 93 pounds anyway so how much more weight could I lose?

I was put in solitary confinement several times, and it was mostly for baiting the guards. In fact, that's what finally got me sent to Dachau. A few of the guys in camp had chocolate bars like those that came in Red Cross packages. A guy gave me one. I was willing to kill for it, but I still cut off little bits of it and threw them at the guard dogs. When a dog would lunge for that piece of chocolate, he would give the guard holding his chain a terrible jerk. That was just one of the things that got me in trouble with the guards. Then one of the guards got to talking about what was going to happen when the war was over and the Germans were in New York. I told him, "Boy, you better get your head out of your ass because when Roosevelt, Churchill, and Stalin get through partitioning Germany, there's not going to be enough left for you to piss on." Well, he ran off to tell the *Kommandant*. He called me in, and accused me of causing unrest among the guards. He thumped me around a bit, and I got what they call a slight cerebral atrophy—which causes a little catch in my speech. I'm not sure what he hit me with—probably a rifle butt. I just know I was unconscious.

A few days later I was on my way to Dachau. They stuck me again in a motorcycle sidecar. In fact, my German rides were all half upside down in that damned sidecar. I didn't know where I was going, but the *Kommandant* had told me I had lost my military status and was now considered a political prisoner for having caused unrest among the guards.

The first thing I saw at Dachau was a bunch of walking skeletons. I was put in a building very close to the cooking facilities for the *SS* troops. There weren't very many of us in that building, but we were the *Sonderkommandos*. I figured they were not going to leave any witnesses, so I was making my plans for when I had to go over this little bridge to the crematorium. I figured I would try to take one of the guards with me down into the creek to see if we could drown each other.

Every day was about the same for the *Sonderkommandos*. We got up before daybreak for roll call. If there was anything on earth you could count on, it was one of those damned roll calls about six times a day. Then we had to go over to this shed and get our hand-

carts on which we piled the bodies. About ten o'clock we got a liter
of what we called Skilly, which was boiled rutabaga without any
salt or pepper. That had to last us until dark. For supper we got
about a half liter of the same and a little square of *Knäckebrot*,
which was a very crisp, dry cracker. That was it for the day.

I never saw another American in Dachau. The guards had
already killed off most of the Jews. We had Gypsies, homosexuals,
some people from the Balkans, lots of their own political prisoners whom they kept isolated, and a few Jews. I talked a little with
some of these people. A lot of them could speak English. I never
learned enough German to do more than get something to eat and
get slapped. Most of the guards could speak English, although
there was not a single one of them in Dachau who ever exhibited
any basic decency.

I was in Dachau about a month before it was liberated. I never
came in contact with those who were gassed, but I knew what was
going on. Most of the bodies I picked up were those the guards had
beaten to death or the dogs had killed or had simply starved to
death. The last days we were simply unloading freight cars filled
with bodies that had come from other camps that evidently didn't
have big enough crematoriums to keep up with the dead. There
was an outbreak of typhus and spotted fever that was killing
them by the hundreds so these other camps were shipping them
to Dachau. The bodies would arrive, some 200 to a boxcar, and
then we would unload them, put them on wagons, and take them
over to the crematorium. I didn't put any bodies in the crematorium, but I piled them up so other workers could put them in.

There were two groups that we had to pick up that still haunt
me. One was a group of young Balkan officers—I don't know from
which country. Somehow, they had displeased the *SS* guards. I
don't think they were Serbians because they, like the Jews, had
pretty much already been killed. The guards took them into a little yard, maybe 50 by 50 yards, and turned the dogs loose.
Afterwards, we literally picked up pieces of flesh everywhere.
This one guard said, "We should have used kids to train the dogs;
the adults don't put up enough fight."

The second time had to do with another group of those junior
officers. The guards put them into that same yard, and they decided to put on a show. They didn't use dogs this time; instead, they
used burp guns, and literally chopped them into hamburger meat.

And, again, we had to clean up the mess. For years after, I had nightmare after nightmare about all this.

There's another incident that I've never been able to erase from my mind, although I know I did the right thing. There was this little Frenchman who worked with me on one of those carts. One of the dogs had torn the muscles out of his leg. One morning, when we were supposed to go get our cart, he couldn't even get out of bed—his leg was swollen so badly. His name was Etienne—but I called him Tiny. He begged me to kill him. He said he didn't want to go out there and let the dogs tear him apart which is what happened if you could no longer work. I told him, "Never mind, I'll help you get out there." I got behind him and pulled him up on his feet; then, while he was kind of relaxed, I snapped his windpipe. He knew immediately what had happened, and he kind of turned and put his hand on my face and patted me a couple of times. That got me—and it still does

[Coulson begins sobbing.]

I've never told this story before to anyone.

So when Reagan went to Bitburg and talked about the honor of soldiers on both sides at that cemetery where the SS were buried, well, I hated that bastard from that moment on. Every SS soldier was an ideologue. Not a one knew anything about humanity. There were two kinds of SS officers: the one wanted to kill you right away while the other insisted on first torturing you.

SANFORD "SANDY" LUBINSKY

In clear violation of the 1929 Geneva Convention, the German commander of Stalag 9-B at Bad Orb singled out Sanford Lubinsky and approximately 80 other Jewish POWs and sent them to the slave labor camp at Berga. There, they and some 250 other American prisoners worked under such horrifying conditions that approximately twenty percent of them died.[3] When Lubinsky was liberated, he weighed only eighty pounds. Since then he has suffered many physical and psychological problems. To compound his enduring agony, the United States government has shown little interest in his story; in fact, Lubinsky is still battling the bureaucracy to get the recognition he believes he deserves. Only in 1991, after the death of his wife, did Lubinsky decide to speak publicly about his experiences.

I WAS CAPTURED DURING the Battle of the Bulge at Clervaux, Luxembourg. The whole month of November we were pushing toward Aachen trying to take the Huertgen Forest. It was a farce. Just guys getting killed by the hundreds. There was snow and mud everywhere. Everything was just a mess. We were supposed to move out for a rest to Clervaux. We were almost all suffering shell shock. Well, we never got that far. We thought we had the Germans on the run. Of course, Hitler had all his forces marshaled for that surprise attack. I think we pushed them back on the first day about four miles, but then we started to fall back. On December 17 they just overran us. I was with the

---

[3]See Mitchell G. Bard, *Forgotten Victims: The Abandonment of Americans in Hitler's Camps* (Boulder, Colo.: Westview Press, Inc., 1994), 77–78.

Pennsylvania Twentieth-Eighth National Guard Infantry, and we were caught right in the middle of things. I was knocked out by a concussion grenade and hit by fragments from a mortar. I was unconscious when the Germans went through. I came to that night. I could hear them in the distance yelling at each other. A couple of us moved down to the railroad yards to try and get back to Bastogne. But on the morning of the eighteenth we were captured.

The Germans marched us back from the front and loaded us onto boxcars. I was hit in the head once but not otherwise mistreated. In fact, I was treated really well by the interrogation officers. All I did was give my name, rank, and serial number. They offered us some bread and even some wine. They weren't mean. This was the *Wehrmacht*. They were regular soldiers just like we were. But when they marched us back, we went past some of the *SS* types, and they were rough. I didn't know it, but I had this one round of ammunition in my pocket, and I pulled it out. This one guard raised all kinds of cain with me over this. He hit me in the head with his revolver butt. I thought I was going to die right then and there, but he sent me on.

At the time, we thought that would be our worst experience, but for some of us things got much worse. Of course, our mental state was very, very bad. We were depressed, and there was nothing we could do about that. We knew no one was going to rescue us. Some of the guys cried. At age twenty-seven, I was old enough to know that whatever will be will be. You just had to go along with the flow. If you ran or did anything dumb, you would be killed. Of course, I was really hurting from my wounds, but you didn't want to drop by the wayside because if you did, the *SS* would finish you off. The *Wehrmacht* took prisoners, the *SS* did not.

They gave us a small can of goose liver and put us in these boxcars. For water we only had what was in our canteens. We were in those boxcars two or three days until we arrived in Stalag 9-B at Bad Orb on December 21 or 22. There they separated the officers from the noncommissioned officers and the enlisted men, and we did get some soup. I remember one guy tried to steal some meat. He was taken out and shot.

We were there for close to four days when the *Kommandant*, whose cousin was in charge of the slave labor camp at Berga, ordered the Jews to line up separately.[4] Anyone who had the "H" on his dog tags had to line up—"H" standing for Hebrew. There were two or three Christian boys who tried to trade dog tags with the Jewish guys, but we were warned that anyone caught without a dog tag would be shot.

All told there were 387 of us.[5] A colonel and a chaplain wanted to come with us, but the Germans wouldn't allow it. They told us we were going to a nice camp. We had heard plenty of stories, and we were plenty worried. I figured it was really bad news. I thought, "Well, I lived a Jew, I might as well die a Jew." We all agreed that if they started to kill us, we would put up one last defense and try to take a few of them with us.

They put us into boxcars again, and this time they really loaded us up. There were also political prisoners on this train. We were kept in those boxcars at least four days without any food or water—none. It got so bad we even tried to drink our own urine, and that just doesn't work. We had no way to filter it—just drink it plain. I was lucky enough to be by the one small window in the side of the car, and I could look outside and see what was going on. We were strafed twice. The boxcar ahead of us was badly shot up and quite a few of the boys were killed. When we arrived at Frankfurt an der Oder, it was really bad. We were bombed in the railroad yards, first by B–17s and then by British Lancasters. They lit up the sky like fireworks. I looked out and could see the rails just twisting in the air. The concussion made you first feel

---

[4]Many American Jewish POWs suffered verbal abuse in the German camps; however, the vast majority were not segregated or singled out for "special" treatment although they certainly feared the possibility.

[5]The actual number of American POWs at Berga varies. With the many deaths plus a number of escapes, the Berga prisoners had no way of keeping an accurate count. Bard puts the number at 350, approximately 80 of whom were Jewish. The others were "prisoners considered troublemakers, those they thought were Jewish and others chosen at random;" Bard, *Forgotten Victims*, 74. Almost nothing else has been published about Berga, with the exception of an article in the May 1, 1983, Fort Myers, Florida, *News-Press* which featured interviews with four other Jewish-American Berga survivors who described the same kinds of appalling and deadly conditions as does Lubinsky.

like your body had contracted inside itself and then in the next moment it felt like your body had exploded outward. We figured that was it. Our guards had run off to protect themselves and left us locked up. We were just sitting there. That was much worse than being shelled. You just knew you were going to die. I don't know how, but we lived.

After we finally arrived in Berga, they took the European Jews out of these mines and put us in their place.[6] In the meantime, we had guys who were dying from dehydration which, of course, kills you faster than no food. Some of the guys had eaten snow, and had terrible diarrhea. There was hepatitis and pneumonia. We became so weak, but we had to march to these cold, dark underground caverns where we worked seventeen hours a day. We discovered later the Germans were building an underground armaments factory.[7]

I was put on a five-foot drill used for boring holes in the rock. The drill weighed over 100 pounds, and there I was trying to hold it over my head and drill this hole into the rock. At the time I was one of the strongest guys, but I was getting weaker all the time. Every time I had to set the drill down, I would catch it from the guards. The one would hit me with the black snake, which was a whip, and the other would hit me in the back with a club or a shovel. We'd drill these holes, and the Germans would set dynamite in them and set it off. They didn't care whether we were out of the way or not. Some of the guys got hit by flying rocks. Afterwards we would haul out the loose rock.

None of the guards ever showed any compassion. We were simply *verdammte Juden*—nothing else. We should have been treated as soldiers. One of our guys was terribly sick—he was already dying—and they dragged him outside and threw cold

---

[6]According to Bard, "Unlike the POWs in most camps, who were not required to engage in forced labor, the inmates of Berga were expected to perform the kind of work used by the Nazis to kill Jews slowly"; *Forgotten Victims*, 79.

[7]The Geneva Convention prohibited the use of POWs to work where any kind of war materials were being produced. Of course, the singling out of Jews and the transferal of any American prisoners to the Berga slave labor camp were also violations of the Geneva Convention.

water on him. This was in January or February. He was dead the next day. Some of the guys were on burial detail. They would just take the bodies out in a cart and dump them in this big hole. That's what they did with this poor guy.

Our daily ration was a piece of bread that was maybe an inch to an inch and a half thick. Much of the time we didn't even get ersatz coffee. It was just hot water. The guards just laughed at us. They would throw scraps of potato peelings into the latrine area— which was all slippery and slopped up as you can imagine, and some of the younger guys would dive for scraps of potatoes. The older guys would try to stop them. There was no water to wash anything off. Of course, they all got terribly sick. That was the same as taking poison. We knew they weren't going to live, and they didn't. But that's how hungry they were.

We had two men from New York, and they were good men. One was named Golden. I don't remember the other's name. We didn't have any doctors, but they tried to take care of the sick guys as best they could. They would bathe a guy down if he had a fever, but that's about all they could do. These two guys could speak good German, and they finally escaped. A day or two later they brought them back—dead. They had shot them and then hung them from a pole with their hands and feet tied, just like they were carrying a dead deer. They wanted to show us what happened when someone tried to escape.

We were so smelly and foul that I once slept for two nights with a guy before I realized he was dead. All of us had diarrhea. When we were marching to work, we couldn't just get out of line if we had to go. And we never had a chance to wash. Still today I can't stand the smell of anything filthy. From our barracks we could see the bodies of Jews, Russians, and others piled up like cord wood. They just couldn't burn them fast enough. The hunger, lice, cold, filth, and dying did terrible things to our minds. We got to where we didn't care whether we lived or died. It was so easy just to give up. Some of the guys did, and you couldn't blame them. What kept me going? A couple of times I felt myself dying. I was so weak I knew I was going to pass out, but I begged the good Lord not to let me be buried over there. So what kept me alive was that I wanted to die back home. And, of course, I wanted to see my wife and child again. Out of the 387

Americans who left Bad Orb, fewer than 100 of us made it out alive.[8]

After the war we never could get our military authorities to believe that we were part of the Holocaust. Back in 1946, the authorities wanted me to come over to identify the Berga *Kommandant* on charges of war crimes, but I wasn't able to go.[9] But that was the only time I was contacted. We've all tried to get the story out, but it's a tough, uphill battle. It's tough to get through the politics. Sometimes the truth is harder to come by than a lie. Nobody wants to believe that the *SS* had anything to do with us. We are not looking for any special favors, but it just so happens we were American soldiers who were part of the Holocaust, although we can't get our government to admit it.

---

[8]Although no one knows the precise number of Americans who died at Berga, Bard concludes that approximately twenty percent died in the camp itself or during a forced march to escape the closing Russian troops; *Forgotten Victims*, 103.

[9]In October 1945, Berga camp commander Erwin Metz and his superior, Ludwig Merz, were tried, convicted, and sentenced to death; however, in 1948 General Lucius Clay commuted Merz's sentence to five years incarceration and Metz's to life imprisonment; then in 1952 the U. S. War Crimes Review Board further reduced Metz's sentence to fifteen years. Naturally, Berga survivors fought against these decisions, but by then Cold War politics had changed official U. S. attitudes toward German war criminals; Bard, *Forgotten Victims*, 124–125.

7
Liberation and Repatriation

When I was liberated the doctors told me I wouldn't have made it another three days.

AMERICAN POW

After the war we were sold down the river as slaves.

GERMAN POW

IN LESS THAN PRECISE language, Article 75 of the Geneva Convention stipulates, "Repatriation of prisoners shall be effected with the least possible delay after the conclusion of peace." For the vanquished German government this posed no problem, and shortly after the cessation of hostilities, American POWs were on their way home.[1] Many of these men, however, would suffer psychological after-effects once they resettled in civilian life. None received any kind of debriefing or transitional care. Most were quickly mustered out of the service and left to their own devices to deal with painful memories, inexplicable and debilitating anxieties, and even acute antisocial behavior. Even today, a half century after the fact, many still feel the physical and emotional

---

[1] There were problems for some of the American prisoners liberated by the Russians. Some ended up in the U.S.S.R., but after brief delays, most were sent to Odessa where they boarded ships for their return home.

effects of their incarceration, and not a few of them believe they have been ignored or mistreated by the Veterans Administration.

For German prisoners, the immediate postwar experience was far different. Although many eventually would also suffer post-traumatic stress disorders, their immediate problem was repatriation itself. After "the conclusion of peace," only a minority were sent directly home to Germany. The majority remained in the United States for up to fourteen months, after which most were sent to England or France, where some remained until 1948.

The 1944 Morgenthau Plan, which would have reduced postwar Germany to a pastoral state, called for reparations "by forced German labor, outside of Germany." In 1945 the Allies discussed this possibility at the Yalta and Potsdam conferences, as well as at the San Francisco Conference where delegates suggested that France, Holland, Belgium, Luxembourg, Yugoslavia, and Greece bid for the postwar services of a minimum of three million German and Italian prisoners for rebuilding their respective countries. French delegates announced they would request two million German workers, and the Russians called for between five and ten million. By the end of the European war, the Allied Powers had thus committed themselves to using German POWs for rebuilding those countries destroyed by Hitler's aggression.

Certainly the publicizing of Nazi atrocity stories, especially the graphic films and photographs of concentration camp victims and starving American POWs, provided further impetus for this punitive use of German prisoners. According to a May 1945 Gallup poll, eighty-two percent of the American public favored requiring German prisoners to spend two or three years to help rebuild the destroyed cities of the U.S.S.R.[2] Representative George Bender of Ohio agreed, declaring that "the time has come when they should be sent back to Europe to rebuild . . . the lands they devastated. . . . It would remove from idleness a group of dangerous, arrogant men who might otherwise one day form the nucleus of a new menace to the world."[3] Organized labor, veterans'

---

[2]*Washington Post*, May 6, 1945, 5B.

[3]Pluth, *The Administration and Operation of German Prisoner of War Camps in the U.S.*, 406. See also "Asks Rebuilding by Nazis," *New York Times*, May 1, 1945, 6.

organizations, and a few vocal politicians, concerned about job opportunities for returning U.S. soldiers, also urged the immediate repatriation of all German prisoners.

Other American voices, however, warned against the immediate shipping of large numbers of prisoners back to Germany. The *Washington Post*, which considered the use of postwar POW labor "a violation of both the spirit and letter of the Geneva Convention," nevertheless worried about possible military dangers of an immediate repatriation: "To send the German prisoners home at the cessation of hostilities or soon thereafter seems highly impracticable and even dangerous," warned its April 24, 1945, editorial. "Returning prisoners might soon band themselves into *Freikorps* which could subsequently be united into a private army." American military officials in Europe also requested the cautious repatriation of German POWs because "they are probably the only large group of Germans who are well fed and who are still strongly Nazi."[4]

Various American business and farming interests wanted to retain the prisoners for other reasons. Their labor was cheap, dependable, and reasonably well-organized. The U.S. War Department complied, and shortly after VE-Day, it made 140,000 prisoners available to private contractors for use in agriculture and industry.

In late June of 1945, Provost Marshal General Archer L. Lerch announced prisoners would begin returning to Europe in July. In a "Proclamation to POWs," published in the July issue of *der Ruf*, Lerch attempted to explain his repatriation plan to worried German prisoners who had heard rumors about enlisted men being retained for additional time while officers, including many ardent Nazis, would be going home.[5] Lerch assured them, "The

---

[4]"Return of Rabid Nazis Opposed," *New York Times*, May 31, 1945, 14.

[5]Some of the German prisoners who participated in the War Department's reeducation programs felt especially betrayed. One bitterly disappointed POW accused Lerch of "selling us down the river like slaves" and concluded there was now little difference between German and American military aims. Another prisoner called it "the greatest hoax that was ever perpetrated"; see Pluth, *The Administration and Operation of German Prisoner of War Camps in the U.S.*, 408–409.

American government might send back to Europe those who do not deserve our confidence and who show they are unwilling to learn from disaster . . . but these men will not go back to Europe as free citizens. They will have no privileges. They will be prisoners still."[6]

By the end of November, just over 73,000 German prisoners had been repatriated, approximately 50,000 of whom the War Department classified as "useless" POWs, which meant officers and noncommissioned officers who could not be required to work, those who were sick or mentally incompetent, and rabid Nazis who were considered untrustworthy. And what of the enlisted men who remained behind, including some who had long opposed National Socialism? They would be the last to leave the United States, and then tens of thousands of them would end up in France or England instead of their homeland.[7]

The emotion and relief that every American POW felt at his moment of liberation have already been chronicled or implied in previous narratives, and the long-term repercussions of captivity for these former prisoners will be dealt with in Chapter Eight. This chapter begins with the story of Joseph Demler, whose liberation photograph in *Life* magazine produced such understandably negative reactions on the part of Americans that it, along with countless other atrocity stories, photographs, and films, contributed to the growing demand to severely punish Nazi war criminals. Unfortunately, such shocking revelations also resulted in harsher treatment for German POWs in the United States, including the decision not to send the majority of them immediately back to Germany. Kurt Pechmann and Ludwig Norz were among the thousands of German prisoners sent to France and England, and both naturally resented this clear violation of the Geneva Convention.

---

[6]"The First Fifty Thousand: A Proclamation to POWs," *Der Ruf*, July 15, 1945, No. 8; quoted in Krammer, *Nazi Prisoners of War in America*, 236.

[7]After the war, France received 700,000 German prisoners and England 175,000, but the majority of these men came from the Allied-held prison camps in Europe.

JOSEPH G. DEMLER

The most unforgettable photograph of a World War II American POW appeared in Life magazine on April 16, 1945 *[see photo insert]*. The emaciated body of nineteen-year-old Pfc. Joe Demler looked frighteningly similar to those of Hitler's concentration camp victims. Such an image contrasted sharply with what Americans believed was the humane and healthy treatment received by German POWs. Like so many American soldiers captured during the Battle of the Bulge, Demler was certainly mistreated, but his condition was exacerbated by pneumonia followed by acute pleurisy which reduced his weight to less than seventy-five pounds.

WHEN I WAS LIBERATED the doctors told me I wouldn't have made it another three days. They didn't have any scales, but they estimated my weight at somewhere between seventy and seventy-five pounds. That was March 29, 1945, when the First Army's Ninth Armored Division liberated us from Stalag 12-A in Limburg, Germany. There was no celebration in the camp's makeshift hospital where I had spent the last couple of months. We were too far gone for that. We were just lying there on our bunks, which is where the *Life* photographer snapped my picture.

A bunch of American officers came into the hospital. I can remember seeing every rank from a second lieutenant to a two-star general. They ordered rations be brought to us immediately—raisins, cereals, canned meat—all kinds of things. Some of the fellows gulped the food down but vomited it right up. Their stomachs were too weak to take it. The guy lying in the bunk next to me didn't get to enjoy his food at all. He was alive when we were liberated but died before the food was brought in. In fact, not many of us made it who were in that hospital.

[The most common killer of American prisoners in Germany was pneumonia, often brought on by a lack of food, inadequate clothing and shelter, overwork, and a particularly harsh "Middle Passage" to the permanent camp. Joe Demler suffered all these debilitating conditions.]

I was captured December 29, 1944, during the Battle of the Bulge. It was only my fourth day on the front lines. We were in this old house when these German tanks started blasting us with their 88-mm cannons. Once they had us zeroed in, there was nothing we could do. We had no support and were completely outnumbered, so we had to surrender. We filed out of the house with our hands high over our heads. The Germans lined us up, searched us, and took all our personal belongings. They then began marching us back toward Germany. That first night we slept in a barn beside the road. We had no blankets—nothing—just the clothes on our back, and we darn near froze. For three days we marched in this cold without any food. Finally, on the third day we arrived in the town of Prüm which was about forty miles into Germany. There we finally got some thin barley soup and a small portion of black bread. We stayed in Prüm about a week, sleeping in a bombed-out hospital with no heat. The Germans put us to work repairing the local rail yards which had been bombed by Allied planes. We worked mostly at night, to dodge the bombers, but even then we got bombed and strafed. We also cleaned out bombed-out air-raid shelters in a nearby town. That meant digging out bodies as well. The Germans gave us a little cheese and a few crackers each day. They also kicked us and sometimes butted us in the ribs or head with their guns.

We were then moved to Gurlstein where we did the same kind of work. By this time we were about 1,500 prisoners. They kept us in a warehouse with no heat, water, beds, or blankets. Increasingly some of the boys began passing out. They just couldn't take it. With almost nothing to eat, the hard work and constant exposure were too much. At night the snow came through the roof so if your clothes were wet from working, they never dried out. Our building had no latrine and many fellows had dysentery. Conditions were simply terrible.

I too began to feel weaker. I could see myself getting thinner and thinner. Then I began to have chills and feel pains in my right side. But I was luckier than a lot of the fellows. Many of them just collapsed and died.

On January 23, 1945, I developed pneumonia. It was three days before I could get permission to see a German doctor. He gave me some white pills and that was it. The Allies continued to bomb us, and the Germans began moving out the sick and wounded. The fellows who were too weak to hike were loaded on wagons; the rest of us had to march to the train station. It was cold that night, and raining like the dickens. The Germans made us stand in the open for six hours. Then they loaded us into boxcars where we were so crowded that we didn't have room to lie down; we just sat on the bare floor. We were on this train three or four days without any food. Whenever Allied bombers came over, the German train crew would unhook the locomotive and take cover in the nearest tunnel, leaving our boxcars standing there as targets. Lots of boys died in those crowded boxcars, including one right next to me.

We finally arrived at Stalag 12-A in Limburg where each of us was given a piece of bread and a hunk of sausage. I got off the train and walked through snow to the hospital that had been set up for prisoners. It was in an old, bomb-damaged shed, and it was run by two American doctors, Major Henry Huber and Captain Charles Gallup, who had been captured by the Germans. They had few supplies, little medicine, and only a few instruments, but they did the best they could. Captain Gallup was an especially good doctor and a swell guy. I remember once he got some chocolate bars from his home in Los Angeles and gave them all to his patients. If it hadn't been for him, I would surely have died. He took one look at me and said, "Son, you have pleurisy. You're going right to bed and you're going to stay there." And I did—until I was liberated.

I was in that hospital two months. All we had to drink was "Jerry coffee," which was made from burned barley, and hot green water which they called "tea." For food we had thin soups, black sawdust bread, and a few potatoes. There were no regular meals. Some Red Cross food got through, but the Germans stole most of it. I didn't smoke so I swapped my cigarettes for extra food; maybe that's one reason why I made it.

I can't begin to describe the conditions. I never once had my clothes off in three months. Our socks rotted on our feet. There were no sanitary facilities, and our bunks and bodies simply crawled with lice—big red ones. You would pick them off your body and out of your hair and crush them between your fingers, but they'd come right back. Finally, my head was so full of lice Captain Gallup took his scissors and cut off all my hair. The docs did the best they could, but lots of fellows started leaving this world and going to the next. When I was liberated, only three of the original eight men in my double-tiered bunks were still alive.

[After his March 29, 1945, liberation, Joe Demler spent the next eight months in various military hospitals.]

One of the first things they did after liberation was to delouse us. Then they transported us in ambulances to American field hospitals. There I received blood transfusions and penicillin until I was strong enough so the doctors could operate. The doctors said my pleurisy had developed into empyema which is the buildup of fluid in a body cavity. I ended up in a good American hospital at Verdun. The doctors removed a rib to put in a drain, after which they drained four quarts of pus from my chest. I was there five days, then ended up in the Forty-Eighth General Hospital in Paris, where a Lieutenant Colonel Robert Shaw of Dallas, Texas, was the doctor who took care of me. Many Americans would learn his name on November 23, 1963, when he tried to save President Kennedy's life after he was shot. He was a marvelous doctor, and he started building me back up before I could be flown back to the States where I spent the rest of my convalescence at Kennedy Hospital in Memphis, Tennessee. I was released from the service in November of 1945 and almost immediately received a thirty percent disability for what I had gone through. Years later my disability was raised to 50 percent, but there are some POWs with similar ailments who receive 100 percent.

I really don't know why I made it. It was simply survival of the fittest. I wanted to live and somehow I made it. Without this desire you don't make it. I also said a lot of prayers; in fact, I still pray every day for all my fellow prisoners who died during captivity.

KURT GERHARD PECHMANN

Kurt Pechmann's positive POW experiences in the United States stood in sharp contrast to the painful ordeal endured by Joe Demler; however, after the war it was Pechmann who suffered deteriorating conditions. Born in Kunan (Chonjna), Silesia, in what is now Poland and trained as a granite cutter, Kurt Pechmann fought on the Russian front where he suffered severe frostbite. During his convalescence in Germany he guarded prisoners, which was an interesting preparation for his own later experiences as a POW. In the United States, Pechmann spent most of his time in work camps in Wisconsin where he and his fellow prisoners even staged a strike. After the war, Pechmann emigrated to the United States and became a citizen. He presently lives in Madison, Wisconsin, where he is a monument maker. A few years ago, he and his son designed the State of Wisconsin's Vietnam War Memorial.

WHILE I WAS A POW in Wisconsin, I wrote my mother that I didn't know whether I would ever be able to see her again because my eyes were growing shut. She went to the local doctor in our little town back in Germany to ask what the problem might be. I was only trying to make a joke. When I was captured I weighed 128 pounds. After two years as an American POW I weighed 185. I was just trying to say I had gotten so fat you could no longer see my eyes.

I was captured on November 6, 1943, by the British who turned me over to the Americans. This was the so-called Gustav Line just north of Naples. We were only eighteen fighting men, and there were probably 800 or 900 British against us. What could we do? We had one heavy machine gun, one light machine gun, and the rest were just rifles. I will never forget the night I was captured. Anyone who didn't go through it, couldn't know what that was like. It was so dark you couldn't see your hand in front of your face. We had planted mines in front of our lines, and that night one of the British soldiers stepped on one of them. I'm sorry, but war is war. They bombarded us with everything they had for four hours. I was out in no-man's-land in a foxhole on watch. Actually, I fell asleep. I woke up when everything got quiet. My buddies were back in a cave. One guy came out to relieve me and yelled, "Kurt, Kurt, are you alive?" They figured I was goulash. They couldn't believe I was still alive. By this time we were more or less surrounded. The only way out was down the side of the mountain where we were entrenched. Then they blocked that. Next hand grenades started exploding all around us. What do you do? You just lie flat in your foxhole, and that's where they got me. All at once you say, "Don't shoot. Don't shoot." I got caught with another guy at eleven o'clock at night. When the rest of our guys got caught in the morning, we threw our arms around each other because we were so happy to see each other again. Then one of the British soldiers took me back up the mountain to show him where our mines were. With a rifle in your back, you don't know how trigger-happy that guy is. I wanted to tell him there were mines everywhere. I didn't speak any English and he didn't speak any German, but the word is almost the same: *mines* or *Minen*. Then some Germans up on the mountain heard the word *Minen* and began shooting at us. I yelled, *"Kameraden, nicht schiessen. Nicht schiessen. Wir sind Gefangener"* ["Comrades, don't shoot! Don't shoot! We are prisoners!"]. I shouldn't have said anything, but I didn't care anymore. I was a prisoner and I wanted to save my own neck. My enthusiasm for war was over.

We landed in Norfolk, Virginia, where we showered and got deloused. They blew this pink powder all over our bodies. They boiled our clothes in a big steam kettle. Some guy said, "Throw everything away. Throw everything away. You get everything new in America." And we did. Everyone got a brand-new quilted blanket, two packs of cigarettes, an army razor, and a can of Spam. That was our nice welcome to America. Nobody ever mistreated me in America. Not once did I get hit or verbally abused.

I eventually ended up in a work camp at Barron Rice Lake in northern Wisconsin. About 200 of us were put in a cow pasture. In Germany we could never strike or refuse to work, but we did at

Barron Rice Lake. We were supposed to receive ten cents an hour,[8] which meant about twenty dollars a month in camp money. We also got three dollars a month from the German Red Cross. We had not received any wages from our previous camp. Perhaps because we had moved around so much, the money never caught up to us. We had been using IOUs which allowed us to buy cigarettes, ice cream, and beer at the PX. But now the commander told us that without money we could not charge anymore. We told him, "No money, no charging, no work." So we refused to work. The commander asked us if we had learned about striking in Germany. We told him, "No, in Germany strikes are not allowed. We learned this in America." At the time, the pea harvest was just starting and the farmers needed us in the worst way. A day and a half later, about eleven o'clock in the evening, the commander came to us and said, "Boys, I got the money here so go back to work." That's all we wanted, so we went back to work. The guards quietly thanked us for going on strike because their pay records had also been lost somewhere and they were not getting paid.

There was just one strand of barbed wire around that camp. Nobody wanted to escape. Why should we? In the meantime, we had made German-American friends. They would come to the fields to visit us. They used to bring their dogs to the camp for us to care for while they went on vacation. One couple brought us their great big St. Bernard. Mario was his name, and he understood only German.

We worked in several small towns in Wisconsin, and we enjoyed it because it was interesting and got us out among the civilians. We also had movies four or five times a week. They were always in English. At first, they showed us strictly American war movies so we complained. We told them we knew all about war. Then we got other kinds of films. We learned a little English from the movies, but in the canning factories some of the people spoke German and many of the German-American farmers did as well.

---

[8]Actually, German prisoners received a maximum of eighty cents a day in scrip, plus ten cents to be used for toothpaste, shaving materials, and other personal items. Prisoners could also put their wages into a savings account which supposedly could be converted into hard currency after repatriation. In reality, this did not work, largely because of the tremendous postwar inflation in Germany.

*[Pechmann was one of the unfortunate German prisoners
American authorities sent to France for three additional years of
hard labor, often under dehumanizing conditions.]*

The one thing America did wrong occurred at the end of the
war. According to the Geneva Accord, every POW could choose his
own home town to which he had to be repatriated within three
months of the end of the war.[9] But the U.S. shipped many of the
POWs to England and France. The war was over with Germany
on May fifth, but I continued to be assigned to various Wisconsin
work camps until the following year. Then the Americans sent me
from Hartford to Milwaukee and from there to Camp Shanks,
New Jersey, to prepare to ship out to Europe. They took away all
our old clothes. Everyone was given three pairs of new socks and
underwear and almost new outer clothing with PW stenciled on
it. At that time, I had accumulated thirty-eight pairs of socks. The
guards would sometimes throw away old socks with holes in
them, and I would turn them in to the quartermaster and get a
brand-new pair. That's the way I collected socks. I wanted to take
them back to Germany, but they were all taken away from me.

On board they told us we were going to land at Le Havre
because the German harbors were all destroyed and that we
would go from there by train to Germany. That was all baloney
because the harbors in France were also destroyed. There were
5,000 of us on that big troop transport. When we went past the
Statue of Liberty, many of us had tears in our eyes because we
had fallen in love with America. We knew how good we had it in
the States, but we didn't know what to expect in Europe.

In Le Havre the Americans turned us over to the French
troops. The Americans had given us food rations for a week, but
the French guards took these away and left us with only one day's
rations for three days on the train. It had been a long time since
the guards had eaten such good food, and I'm sure they enjoyed
our rations. We went by train to a big German POW camp just
outside of Paris. It was rotten there. They tried to take everything

---

[9]Among the prisoners there were always rumors about what the Geneva
Convention did and did not say about repatriation. As already mentioned,
the Code called for repatriation to "be effected with the least possible
delay after the conclusion of peace."

away from us. But instead we threw everything we could into a big pit and burned it rather than give it to the French. That included cigarettes, presents for our families, after-shave lotion, shoe polish, everything that would burn. We called it the Pit of the Eternal Flame. Cigarettes by the thousands went in there.

The French took everything else we had away from us. They took our blankets and uniforms and gave us dirty, filthy French clothing, shoes, and blankets. I was in that camp for about two months. To eat we had something like greasy cereal for breakfast. I preferred to go hungry rather than eat that stuff. They also gave us three beets a day and some colored water which they called coffee. It didn't take long for me to lose all my American fat.

I worked on one farm where the farmer was a German-hater. There were four of us and he treated us just plain rotten. He got us up at 3:30 in the morning. We had to feed the livestock, clean the stalls, and then we went to breakfast. Right after breakfast we went to the fields and spread manure by hand and did other farm work. Two of us were in charge of forty-eight cows. We milked them by hand three times a day. We did not get one cup of coffee or a glass of water, although we did steal milk from the cows. All the farmer gave us to drink morning, noon, and evening was apple cider. I was on that farm at least a year. One day this farmer hit one of our guys for trying to make an electric heater because we had no heat. He had taken one of those clay roof tiles and filed notches in it with a saw blade. Then he wound wire around it. For this he was punished. That night I sneaked out and went to the police department in the town which was about three kilometers away. The constable was sleeping and told me to come back in the morning. So I spent that night outside of town in a field and went back in the morning. The chief searched me and found some letters I had written to our camp commander which I wanted to smuggle out. It was illegal to take our mail, but he still took my letters. Then he threatened to hit me. Finally, he sent me back to the farm. In a nearby town there was another POW whom we would occasionally see on the way to the fields to work. I gave him a letter to take to our camp commander. About two weeks later the commander came to the farm and interrogated the farmer. We were sent back to our camp, and because that farmer had physically punished a prisoner and had not fed us properly, we were told he would never get another POW.

I was sent to another farmer where we had it pretty good. I then volunteered to become a civilian for two years and signed a contract to do this. This meant I had to work as a laborer. In the meantime, I got a letter from my girlfriend that invited me to go to the wedding of her sister. Of course, I had signed that contract which stipulated I could not go to Germany, but the farmer agreed to let me go for two weeks. As soon as I got my papers and got across the German border, I said to myself, "Good-bye, you'll never see me again." That was 1948, and it was my first time back in Germany in almost five years.

LUDWIG NORZ

Ludwig Norz was born in 1926 in Rotenburg, in southeast Germany. Any hopes for an aspiring career as an architect were dashed when he was drafted into military service in 1944. Captured on March 20, 1945, less than seven weeks before the end of the war, Norz landed in New York on VE-Day; nevertheless, he was to spend more than three years as a prisoner of war. Sensitive, ambitious, and intelligent, Norz tried to make the best of his time in camps in Arizona, Washington, and Montana, but he was understandably bitterly disappointed when at the end of the war the United States sent him to England instead of home to Germany. Norz's lengthy narrative serves as a good summary of what a Germany prisoner had to go through both during and after hostilities.

Front-line soldiers like Norz understood that whether they lived or died usually depended much more on chance than on whether or not they were courageous and capable warriors. By the time of his capture, the German army was in chaos, losses were catastrophic, and a private's willingness to fight on no longer existed.

OUR DIVISION SPEARHEADED THE initial attack in mid-December of 1944 into the Saarland. From what I know, it was a full-strength division of about 20,000 men. After two weeks, we were down to 150 men. When they refilled the regiment, I was one of the replacements. That brought us not quite to full strength, but I think we had about 18,000 men. During the next two weeks, about seventy-five percent of those 18,000 became casualties. After that, everything just fell apart. I didn't really know how bad it was going to be until the actual fighting. We were nothing but cannon fodder.

While out on patrol I was shot by French resistance fighters. I was shot through the hip, so I couldn't use my legs. For awhile I just lay there by myself. Then I pulled myself along the ditch with my hands. I knew what would happen if the French Underground found me, and I knew it was just a matter of time before they would. I guess it was adrenaline that kept me going. I wanted to go in the general direction where the others had gone. I didn't get far before I heard machine gun fire. Soon a German motorcycle with a sidecar showed up. The passenger was shooting in the direction of the village. Then he reached down and hauled me into the sidecar. Evidently, some of our young guys had run into a group of fighting SS—as opposed to the other kind—and told them I was back there. So they came and rescued me. I don't know why I was so fortunate. I was taken to a German field hospital where they fixed me up. That bullet took out a big chunk of my bottom, and there was considerable nerve and tissue damage, but miraculously no bones were damaged. I don't why I was so lucky, but I do know if you are a nonbeliever, you certainly become one after an experience like this.

A few weeks later I was back at the front, and by then everything had disintegrated. We were just wandering around, more or less on our own. We were on the west side of the Rhine, and we wanted to cross back over the river and go home. But the army still had its rules. You still had to report. If you were found without authorization more than three miles from your unit, you were subject to a court-martial. At night, when you wanted something to eat, you reported to the nearest military installation and told them you were lost. They would then reassign you.

On March 19 a few of us made our way to Kaiserslauten and reported to the commanding officer. The next morning he wanted to put us into a fighting unit, but morale was gone. Nobody was in a fighting mood. In fact, nobody had been in a fighting mood for a long time. We had long known the war was over. A major told us we would never be allowed to give up. He was a typical Prussian officer, and he told us we were going to fight to the last man. I can still see everybody standing around him in a rebellious mood. We looked at each other, and just closed in on him. Nobody said anything; we just quietly surrounded him. He looked at us, shut up, and walked away. The next day, after we were captured, we were standing around, and who comes marching up with his hands stretched high in the air, but that major. In spite of our predicament, we just laughed.

That was March 20, 1945. The U.S. Army had cut us off at the Rhine, and we could no longer get across the river. We were surrounded and more or less just waiting to be captured. There was no longer any organized fighting. The Americans simply herded us together like a bunch of cattle and corralled us in this big field. We Germans had our *Frontkämpferpaket* which were something like the American K-Rations. They contained cigarettes, candy or chocolate, and crackers. We were supposed to get one a day. We had received one for Christmas, but our officers then told us there were no more. After we were captured, the Americans brought our rations in by the truckload, and we got three a day. So we were eating our own rations those first few days of imprisonment, and they served us quite nicely.

[Like most prisoners, Norz was interned in several transition camps, where he was also interrogated, before finally being put on the last POW ship bound for the States.]

I don't know how many prisoners were there—I'm guessing maybe 25,000 because they just kept coming in. It was cold and raining. Morale was very low, and it didn't help that those first few days we had to sleep in the mud. We didn't have adequate protective clothing. But at least the weather turned nice during the daylight hours so we could dry out.

After a few days we were sent to a camp in France near Stenay. We were there for a couple of weeks under similar conditions to those in Kaiserslauten, and that's where I was first interrogated. There must have been twenty tables lined up in an open field, and at each sat an interrogator. Keep in mind there were 20 or 30,000 prisoners so this was simply mass production. A captain interrogated me, if you could call it that. He simply asked name, rank, serial number, and where I was from. I told him Tübingen. He said, "Tübingen? I know Tübingen. I studied there for four years." I could tell he liked the place. He asked how Tübingen had survived the war. I told him all right although one of his favorite student hangouts had been damaged. The interrogators were looking for members of the SS and the Nazi Party. Since I had not been a member of either, I wasn't worried. After all, what could I tell them? By that time the war was all but over.

I was next sent to Cherbourg. Things were a little better there. We lived in tents, had regular food, and were a little better organized. We even had some health care. I was told there were 55,000 prisoners in that camp. Rumor had it that one last transport was going to the States, and that a number of German prisoners would be on it. I was one of about 2,500 who got on that final POW ship.

We arrived in New York Harbor May 7, 1945. The next day was VE-Day, so we got off the boat to a giant celebration. We were then put on a train for about five days and ended up in Florence, Arizona, just outside of Phoenix. We spent four weeks in Florence, supposedly for quarantine. A few guys escaped, but they were quickly picked up. The guard who returned them said, "You fools. You stick out like sore thumbs there on the desert." He told them if they had stolen a car they might have made it, but they were on foot.

[Before he was transferred to various work camps, Norz had time to seek out positive relationships and to reflect on the need for self-improvement.]

While we were in quarantine in Arizona we had nothing to do. We didn't have to work or anything. All we did was walk around the fence and exchange experiences. It was difficult to keep occupied. I thought to myself, everybody has a career, an education, and life experiences. I was young and without all that so I thought, "Why not use this time." So I picked the brains of my fellow prisoners every chance I got, and I learned a great deal. Everyone was willing to talk because we had so much time. One man was older than most of the others. He was very quiet and an obvious gentleman. His name was Dr. Meier, and he sort of took me under his wing. He had been a judge, but because he had fallen out of favor with the party, he was drafted into the army as a private. He was a very fascinating man, and I learned a lot from him. Unfortunately for me, after about three weeks he was singled out, and sent to Fort Eustis, Virginia, for the reeducation program, and then sent home to be a part of the new government where he eventually again became a judge.

We talked about the future, and he reinforced many thoughts I already had. He had a young daughter, and he wanted her to come to the United States. I felt the same way. My dad had gone through World War I and had lost everything after the war. Now the same thing was starting all over again. I wanted to get away from all that. I wanted something better for my family. I wanted more security. I also wanted to live in a more open society.

I think the quest for self-improvement is traditional in German culture. It was built into the system. For one thing, we had good schooling. You were expected to be a useful member of society, and to at least have a trade. If your parents could afford it, you went on to higher learning. But on the other hand, there was the class system. It was difficult to break down the barriers and go on to the next level. Yet, everyone was expected to contribute. You also had to be disciplined. Where that comes from, I really don't know. It was just the way things were. Years ago, Germans even legislated cleanliness, until it became a national habit. This thing about being self-motivated and striving for improvement developed the same way.

Unfortunately, I was never in a camp where one could take classes. I heard about it, but after that first quarantine camp, I was always in work camps. I did occasionally get to see a movie, but that was about it. Later, when I was a POW in England and allowed to mix with the public, I became serious about learning English.

[Although the war with Germany was officially over, American authorities continued to assign Norz and his fellow prisoners to various work assignments. Because the hours were often very long, their guards sometimes tried to make working conditions more tolerable, but guards, like camp commanders, could vary greatly.]

Our treatment in the American camps got worse right after the end of the war. Some of the Africa Corps prisoners told us that when they first arrived, they had a very good life. The Americans told them they were guests of President Roosevelt rather than prisoners of war. They had the best of everything considering their circumstances. They were not forced to work. But as the fortunes of the German army declined, so did the treatment and the food. These same prisoners told me when the Battle of the Bulge was raging, the treatment and the food improved, but afterwards everything once more got worse.

In June of 1945 some of us were sent to Glasgow, Montana, where we worked in the sugar beet fields. A regular army guard would take us out from our base camp. He and the farmer would figure out how much we were to do each day. Sometimes there would be a discussion. I had the impression the guard would try to convince the farmer to have us do a little less because our work quota would change from day to day. It usually took us until seven or eight in the evening. Then we would go back to the base camp. We brought our own food. We had nothing to do with the farmer. I understand some prisoners lived on farms, but we were always in these 100-man details. Sometimes a farmer would give us something to eat or cigarettes, but they were not required to do so.

We had good and bad guards. Some looked out for us, and I think coaxed the farmers to give us something extra to eat. We were young guys, and we were always hungry. We had long working days, and we worked seven days a week. We were supposed to get eighty cents a day in wages, most of which was put into an account in our name. We were given a small amount to buy toothpaste, shoe polish, and cigarettes, although cigarettes were rationed. There was no beer. When I finally got home in late May of 1948, I received the remainder of my money. It amounted to twenty Reich Marks. We then had to exchange our Reich Marks for the new Deutsch Marks. I ended up with five D-Marks for three years' work.[10]

Sometime in the summer of 1945 we were sent to Fort Lewis, Washington, which was a good assignment. Some of us worked as lumberjacks, and some in the four large mess halls. Most of my time was spent in the kitchen. We did everything except cooking. There were regular army cooks for that. We cleaned up, and often we served the food. That was sometimes a problem, especially after a directive came out that we were not to eat steak and some of the other better foods. But we never went hungry, especially considering where we came from and what we had gone through. The cooks in the kitchen always made sure we got our share, and that included putting steaks aside for us. We did work long days. There were troops constantly coming in from the Pacific, and they had to be fed. I can remember some days going to the kitchen at four in the morning and staying there until two the next morning, but normally our work day ended about seven in the evening.

---

[10]At the time, five D-Marks were worth a little more than one dollar.

I knew nothing about my family, and this was hard. We were not allowed to write. This was a violation of the Geneva Convention, and it was not the only one. There was a standard form when you got captured that went to the International Red Cross which was supposed to send it on to our families. I don't know when mine finally arrived. My family didn't know where I was. No one was reporting MIAs at that time because everything had collapsed. In December of 1945, I was in a hospital in Arizona with a very high fever, and all the patients had a chance to send a telegram home for Christmas. Someone told us the Vatican paid for this. I sent mine, but it did not arrive until the following October. By then I was in England and already in contact with my family because the British allowed us to write and receive mail.

When I was outside the camps working, I saw the way people lived. What we experienced in the camps was one thing, but what interested me was the vastness of the country and the openness of American society. In those days, the German class system was so much more rigid. I had a brother who was thirteen years older than I. He was at the top of his class in school. He wanted to go on to the *Gymnasium* and on to college, but to do so he would have had to go to Tübingen to make his *Abitur*. Most unfairly, he was denied acceptance at Tübingen because my father was only a baker. It was not even camouflaged. It was that class thing. Ironically, the Nazis gave my brother the chance to become an engineer when they were seeking out talent to rebuild Germany and to prepare for war. The government had somehow discovered his school records and encouraged him to study engineering. They even paid for his studies. So he got his college education and his engineering degree, but for the wrong reason.

[Norz is still upset that he and thousands of other German prisoners were not sent home at the end of the war; after all, thirty-six of the thirty-eight months Norz spent as a POW occurred after Germany signed an unconditional surrender on May 7, 1945.]

After Fort Lewis, we went back to Montana and the sugar beet crop. Winter came early in 1945, and we dug out sugar beets from under the snow and ice. In December we were sent back to Florence for the cotton crop. We stayed there until March of 1946 when we thought we were being sent home. We had heard that the Geneva Convention stipulated that every POW was to be sent

home twelve months after hostilities ceased.[11] This was commonly talked about in the camps, although we did not have an official
copy of the Geneva Convention.[12] Because the Germany government no longer existed, we also thought we were supposed to be
represented by the International Red Cross. James Bacque, who
later wrote *Other Losses*,[13] concluded that the International Red
Cross was prevented from representing us. I am not sure about
this, but we clearly had no representation. I don't know why we
were not sent directly home. Some say the American government
made a deal with France and England to send them German
POWs to rebuild their economies. In any case, thousands of us
were sent to France, England, and Belgium. I was among those
sent to England, although we still thought we were going home
until the day before we landed.

We boarded a boat in San Francisco and sailed via the
Panama Canal. While going through the Canal, we had to go
below deck so we wouldn't see the military installations, but there
was nothing we would have been able to do. After we got back on
deck we saw three captured German ships. One of them was the
Prince Eugenia that was later sent to the Pacific for the atomic
tests.

The American authorities told us we would have transportation to Frankfurt but would have to get home on our own from
there. Later they told us something was wrong with the engines
so we had to put into Guantanamo Bay, Cuba. We were there for
two or three days. We joked about them guarding us because no
one would have jumped overboard when we thought we were on
our way home. They must have somehow thought we knew about

---

[11]Again, the actual phrase in the Geneva Convention was "with the least
possible delay."

[12]This too was a violation of the Geneva Convention which mandated that
a copy be posted in every POW camp.

[13]James Bacque's *Other Losses: The Shocking Truth Behind the Mass
Deaths of Disarmed German Soldiers and Civilians under General
Eisenhower's Command* (Rocklin, Cal.: Prima Publ., 1991) is a very controversial book which holds General Eisenhower responsible for the postwar mistreating and eventual deaths of thousands of POWs incarcerated
on German soil.

not going home to Germany so they figured they had to guard us. But nobody knew. They finally told us the evening before we were supposed to get off the ship that for technical reasons we were going to England. They told us the North Sea was still mined and that we would be shipped home from England within three months. That was April of 1946. I got home in May of 1948, more than two years later, and almost three years after the end of hostilities. I was one of the last Germans to get home who had been imprisoned in the United States, but a cousin of mine was kept in France until the end of 1948. Fortunately, he spent most of his time on a farm and was treated reasonably well, much as were French prisoners who worked on German farms during the war. Some who were kept in France never made it home. A brother-in-law of mine did not die as a prisoner of war, but he did die three days after he came home. He was over six feet tall, with an athletic build, and weighed about 200 pounds. He was trying to make it home at the end of the war, and he almost made it. He could have walked home in a day because we lived not far from the French border. But he stopped to see his brother who had not served in the army because of a physical disability. At the time the French were still trying to find German soldiers who they thought might be hiding out. There were severe penalties for hiding a former soldier, but his brother wanted to ignore the order and hide him. My brother-in-law said, "No, I can't do that to you. It's too dangerous, and I can't live off the little food you have for yourself and your four children." So he turned himself in—just a day's walk from home. He came home a year later with a group of about 5,000 prisoners who were in pretty much the same terrible shape he was. He weighed seventy-eight pounds. There was nothing left of him. He was put into a hospital, but it was too late to save him. History does not record him as having died in a French prison camp, but he did.

Everything was different in England. In the States, every camp commander seemed to conduct his camp the way he wished. No two camps were alike. The British apparently had clear-cut directives how to run their camps. You knew what to expect. If you had been in one camp, you had pretty much been in all of them. For the most part we worked road construction in England. In the middle of December 1946, we were told we might be able to get out of the camps for Christmas; however, there was one stipulation. You could go out afternoons between one and four, but only if a civilian sponsored you. Your sponsor actually had to come into the camp, sign you out, then bring you back and sign you in. Surprisingly enough, there were a lot of people who showed up to take a POW home with them. This was how we first made contact with the civilian population.

One such contact was unforgettable. On a Sunday morning our German camp leader came into the barracks and asked, "Does anyone want to go on a picnic?" Sure, everybody wanted to go. He told us he had invitations for only twenty, but there were 600 or so of us. He suggested we draw straws, and I drew one of the twenty. Had I known in advance what was waiting for us, I wouldn't have wanted to go. As it turned out, it was fortunate I didn't make such a decision. There were about twenty Jewish couples who took us on a picnic and gave us the time of our lives. I'll never forget it. They were all German Jews who had fled Germany. That was a sobering experience. They treated us as if nothing had happened. They just wanted to give us a good time. Since then we have met other Jewish people who didn't know us or Germany, and we had to be careful. This is understandable. But what is so striking is that these people who really had to suffer didn't hate us.

These outings were later expanded to Saturday evening, and, as the days got longer in the spring and summer, our time was extended to daylight hours. Of course, by that time anybody who wanted out could get a sponsor, and even that requirement was ended in the late spring of 1947 when you could go out on your own within a three-mile radius of the camp. This was terrific after all that time of being a closely watched prisoner. You were still clearly marked as a POW so you couldn't hide even if you wanted to. We had people sometimes come up and invite us home or give us something. Sure, we were up against a lot of war propaganda and hostility, but there was also a lot of good will. These people came to regard us as different than just prisoners. It may have started out as simple compassion to ease our lives, but we quickly came to see each other as human beings, and then simply as friends. And, of course, such experiences fundamentally altered our attitude toward England.

I was finally repatriated in May 1948. There were always a lot of rumors, but until the early spring of 1948, hardly anyone got sent home. Maybe one or two a month would be sent from our camp, but these were mostly farmers or miners. Nobody else. Those in the professions had already been sent home before we were sent to England. Then all of a sudden in the spring of 1948, twenty or thirty or even more were being sent home every week. Rumor had it the summer Olympics of 1948 played a role. There were supposed to be requests by some neutral governments that England send the rest of the POWs home, or they would not participate. Whether that's true or not, I don't know.

When I think back on my experiences, I learned that the world was larger than Germany. I was brought up in the narrow, traditional German way. But the world is different. In fact, I now consider nationalism to be the worst thing man ever devised. It keeps us away from those who are different than we are. It forces us to associate only with those who are supposedly just like us. You don't reach out and learn from other people. Unfortunately, we haven't learned a thing in 2,000 years. Look at what's happening in Europe now. We thought this couldn't happen again. How many wars are now going on in the world? Over 100. We haven't learned a damned thing.

8
Legacy

Survivors challenge us to reconnect fragments, to reconstruct history, to make meaning of their present symptoms in the light of past events.

JUDITH HERMAN, PSYCHIATRIST[1]

Nobody helped us with our transition to civilian life. The U.S. Army retrained its guard dogs but there were no programs for us POWs. I guess your family was supposed to be your psychiatrist.

AMERICAN POW

WHAT MOST AMERICANS KNOW about World War II prisoners of war, they have unfortunately learned from the commercial, all-encompassing images of American popular culture rather than from the former POWs themselves. Of course, this fact in no way diminishes the actual legacy of the ex-prisoners; indeed, it only strengthens the need to tell their stories to the general public.

Clearly, a close study of what a POW had to endure during and after his incarceration has considerable relevance for the military and for any future prisoners, but the challenge of coping with the harrowing experiences of internment has a fascinating relevance for all human beings. Raised to believe that normal and

---

[1]Herman, *Trauma and Recovery*, 3.

healthy people must establish some semblance of control over their lives, and nurtured by countless popular culture examples of unconstrained fictional heroes, how does one react when that control is clearly taken away? This final chapter will compare and contrast fictional depictions of the POW, especially as Hollywood projected them for mass audiences, with the actual long-term consequences of captivity experienced by those former prisoners whose stories appear in this book.

Popular cultural portrayals of the POW seldom addressed the long-term effects of imprisonment, except in the action-packed Vietnam POW/MIA revenge films so popular in recent years. To make heroes out of ex-prisoners, Americans wanted to believe they came back better men—that captivity, as Elliott Gruner writes, became "the true test of the American self—a test passed with flying colors."[2] The men in this book do not talk about such challenges, although some of the officers insist imprisonment had no permanent effect on them. The former enlisted men are more introspective. Most know they have been deeply scarred by their experiences. Many have experienced problems with alcohol, family abuse, holding a job, and various physical infirmities. Many have spent years silently trying to excise their painful memories. Most agree that captivity was the central experience of their lives, but not because it somehow redeemed them or made them into more noble Americans. Their legacy can be found in their struggle to retain a sense of decency and self-worth in the face of truly horrifying and debilitating circumstances. Indeed, theirs is the legacy of survival itself.

When former prisoners returned to the United States, many were as confused and disoriented by their reception as they were by their sudden taste of freedom. Their families, friends, neighbors, and the media embraced them as triumphant heroes who would quickly resume their rightful place in society. But many of these men did not feel like heroes. After the initial excitement of

---

[2]Gruner, *Prisoners of Culture*, 147. The idea of incarceration as a crucible for conflicting cultures goes back to the Indian captivity tales of Colonial America. However, even the early Puritans noticed that those captured by Indians acted differently after their return from captivity. Cotton Mather attributed this "strange" behavior to witchcraft or an infection by the devil; see Doyle, *Voices from Captivity*, 70.

being home, they commonly felt empty, out-of-place, and beset by anxieties. In no way were they prepared to resume their former responsibilities or take on new ones. Compounding this difficult readjustment were the countless novels, biographies, autobiographies, popular histories, and, above all, films that depicted the life of a soldier or prisoner in terms to which they could not relate.

POW movies such as *Stalag 17* (1953), *Bridge on the River Kwai* (1957), *The Great Escape* (1963), *Von Ryan's Express* (1965), and *Victory* (1981), as well as in the long-running and very popular television series, *Hogan's Heroes*, did not reflect the reality of actual internment. In fact, such depictions were likely to leave the former prisoners feeling a strong sense of guilt and inadequacy. In these fictional accounts, the POW waged incessant war on his dim-witted captors, escaped at the slightest opportunity, sabotaged and killed when necessary, and always acted in ways that reflected his noble stature, his faith in God, and the superiority of the American way of life. For this resilient and independent agent, adversity was something to be conquered, like the enemy himself. In such portrayals, as film historian Philip Landon points out, the prison camp itself became a familiar stage on which the American male fulfilled his heroic and noble destiny:

> The lasting popularity of POW films rests on their mythic narratives rather than their historical authenticity. Enclosed in barbed wire or surrounded by impenetrable jungle, the prison camp becomes as much a "mythic space" as Monument Valley in a John Ford Western or the urban streets and nightclubs of the gangster film.[3]

---

[3]Phil Landon, "From Stalag 17 to the River Kwai: The World War II POW Film," an unpublished paper delivered at the National Association of Popular Culture's Annual Meeting, New Orleans, April 10, 1993. For further discussions of World War II films see Lewis H. Carlson, "For You the War Is Over: Film Images of World War II POWs," in Lewis H. Carlson and Kevin B. Vichcales (eds.), *American Popular Culture at Home and Abroad* (Kalamazoo, Mich.: New Issues Press, 1996), 177–192; Robert Fyne, *The Hollywood Propaganda of World War II* (Metuchen, N.J.: Scarecrow Press, 1994); and Colin Shindler, *Hollywood Goes to War: Films and American Society, 1919–1952* (Boston: Routledge, 1979).

No more mythical figure endures in American film than John Wayne, who so often portrayed heroic soldiers.[4] The fact that Wayne had never been in actual combat did not diminish his credibility with adoring audiences, although it certainly did with many of those who knew the horrors of war firsthand. Larry Guarino, who spent eight terrifying years in a North Vietnamese prison camp, tells the story of sitting next to John Wayne at a dinner to honor former POWs. In the course of the festivities, Guarino turned to Wayne and said, "Duke, I tried to think about how you might have handled the interrogators. So when they asked questions I told 'em to go to hell. When they asked me to do something, I told 'em to stick it up their asses . . . And do you know what, Duke? They beat the shit out of me."[5]

Billy Wilder's extremely popular *Stalag 17* (1953) is a representative example of Hollywood's version of the POW experience. Based on the play by Donald Bevan and Edmund Trzcinski, who actually had been prisoners in Austria's Stalag 17-B, this film, like most of its successors, claimed to be grounded in fact.[6] It is fiction, however, and contains many of the myths found in most subsequent POW films. Landon argues that *Stalag 17* is actually a *film noir* with William Holden playing the cynical loner, apparently at odds with the kind of camaraderie and mutual support that is needed to survive.[7] It is also a confusing mélange of bad slapstick, featuring sinister and comic Germans, apparent betrayal, abortive and successful escapes, redemption, and the inevitable triumph of good over evil.

Stalag 17 is one of the few POW films in which the leading participants are not officers but enlisted men, albeit portrayed in accordance with contemporary stereotypes: many are short in stature, deficient in intelligence, lacking in social graces, and

---

[4]Among John Wayne's World War II films were *Reunion in France* (1942), *Fighting Seabees* (1944), *Back to Bataan* (1945), *They Were Expendable* (1945), *Sands of Iwo Jima* (1949), *Flying Leathernecks* (1951), *Operation Pacific* (1951), and *The Longest Day* (1962).

[5]Quoted in Gruner, *Prisoners of Culture*, 88.

[6]The long-running TV series *Hogan's Heroes* was a spinoff from *Stalag 17*.

[7]Landon, "From Stalag 17 to the River Kwai."

obviously blue collar. Typical examples are Duke, with his round, Southern European face and guttural speech; Stanislaw Kusavo, a.k.a. Animal, whose loutish behavior would seldom be practiced by an Anglo-Saxon officer; and his mousey Jewish sidekick, Albie. William Holden's Sgt. Stepton naturally represents a higher type, as does the only American officer in the camp, who is the tall, well-mannered, good-looking product of a prominent American family.

As the film opens, Holden, who is living well by trading with the guards, explains his less than exemplary behavior: "It is everybody for himself [and] I'm going to make myself as comfortable as I can." He is suspected of tipping off the Germans about one of the many escapes that are a dominant motif in most POW movies. But the viewer knows better; after all, those who betray their country do not win Oscars. By the end of the film, Holden predictably joins the team, helps the officer escape, restores harmony among the men, and exposes the real traitor, who turns out to be a tall, clean-cut blond who is not an American at all but a German plant who fooled the Americans because he spent his formative years in Cincinnati.

Ceaseless resistance is a given in films such as *Stalag 17*. Prisoners are always baiting the dull, overweight, clownish guards or sabotaging the best-laid plans and spit-polished jackboots of the German *Kommandant*. In the final analysis, such films trivialized the POW experience or played it for laughs, without any serious attempt to portray life "in the bag" as it was for most inmates or even for the men who were guarding them. Hollywood could never do justice to the shock, pain, confusion, and even shame that commonly accompanied becoming a prisoner of war. Robert Engstrom (Chapter One) was so bewildered after his capture in the Battle of the Bulge that he traded his boots the second night of captivity to a German guard just for the chance to get in out of the cold.

Ex-POW and novelist Kurt Vonnegut, Jr., writes, "We are what we pretend to be, so we must be careful about what we pretend to be." Popular fictional images too often led Americans to believe that imprisonment brought out the best in their fighting sons. Manly courage, an indomitable will to survive, and a unquenchable spirit of independence were acknowledged characteristics of a superior culture and people. In reality, most POWs did not battle valiantly against evil adversaries. They simply endured, often under the most humiliating of circumstances. Vonnegut's novel *Slaughterhouse-Five*, which in 1972 was made into a successful film, presents an unforgettable portrait of Billy Pilgrim, an American soldier and POW who is the antithesis of popular culture's traditional hero. Billy is awkward, inept, and non-involved. He has lost all sense of dignity and he escapes only by taking fanciful flights back and forth in time. Bertram Copeland Rumfoord, a retired Air Force Reserve officer, millionaire, and Harvard history professor, is forced to share a hospital room with Vonnegut's anti-hero. Disgusted by Billy's delirious mumbling about wanting to quit and surrender, Rumfoord derisively tells him, "I could carve a better man out of a banana."[8] Perhaps, but Billy's combined use of apathy and fantasy to escape the vicissitudes of a situation he cannot control will seem perfectly rational to many ex-prisoners.

Most former prisoners understood that their depictions in the popular culture of the day had little to do with their own experiences; nevertheless, such portrayals made their transition to civilian life more difficult, especially if feelings of guilt, anxiety, and depression characterized their postwar lives.

Commercial and fictional images seldom examined the enervating tedium, loneliness, mental anguish, and senseless deaths that characterized internment for most POWs. Nor did these fictional accounts acknowledge that such experiences not only affected a prisoner's existence during his incarceration, but often became a painful burden he carried with him the rest of his life.

It was, however, not only memories of incarceration that affected a prisoner's postwar readjustment. His reception by those who never shared such experiences could have a critical psychological effect. Talking through his experiences was frequently the best therapy for overcoming the trauma of imprisonment, but often this could only be accomplished with buddies who had also been POWs. It was not that family members were disinterested or unsympathetic, although sometimes they were, but that they could never really understand how incarceration had so fundamentally changed their loved one.

---

[8]Kurt Vonnegut, Jr., *Slaughterhouse-Five*, 164.

Like most former prisoners, Louis A. Pfeifer, whose POW experiences led to a personal hell from which he still has not recovered, received no debriefing or any other kind of transitional care before being mustered out of the service. Left to his own devices to deal with his ordeal, Pfeifer describes how impossible it was to share his experiences with his family:

> When I now think back on some of the things I saw, I become even more bitter than I was then. I kept all my experiences to myself for a long time. I didn't even tell my wife. My own kids wonder why I am so negative and cynical. People tend not to believe things of this nature. Some of the things I saw were so terrible even I have trouble believing them. When I try to tell my kids, they just can't seem to understand. Maybe I do a bad job of telling them. The Veterans Administration doctor wrote down that I have a lot of deep anger. Well, maybe he's right.[9]

One of the reasons the former prisoners did not want to talk about their days in captivity was the negative stigma that accompanied becoming a prisoner of war. Louis Grivetti (Chapter Three) explains:

> You didn't tell anybody that you had been a POW. If you did, they would always ask, "Why did you let them capture you? Why didn't you fight?" I put twenty-one years in the army, but not a handful of people ever knew I was a POW. I carried this guilt complex for years. My wife didn't even know I had been a POW until she looked at a postcard from the government stating that I was going to receive a dollar a day for the time I had been a prisoner. She wanted to know what the government was talking about.

---

[9]Pfeifer parachuted into France on the night before D-Day and was captured the next day. Perhaps it was because of his German name or because some of his captors thought he was Jewish, but few American prisoners were so badly mistreated. Interview with the author.

Many American prisoners brought considerable resentment home with them. Often they directed their anger toward themselves or their loved ones. At other times they targeted specific institutions such as the Red Cross or the military itself for what they perceived as inadequate support. Sometimes a specific incident would set off their rage, as it did for Robert Engstrom when he encountered German prisoners who evidently had received good treatment during their American incarceration:

> I'll never forget coming back to this country and seeing German POWs at Fort Kilmore, New Jersey. They were working in the kitchens and as waiters, and they had obviously been well fed. Our officers had warned us not to overreact. They didn't want us jumping over the counter and attacking them. They told us, "Just take it easy. Don't do anything stupid." Well, we hit that first chow line, and there were all these big, husky, healthy-looking Germans. I tell you, it was a shock. There we were, a bunch of emaciated runts, nothing but skin and bones. I had dropped from 165 to 118 pounds. Naturally, we wondered how this could have happened. We were angry. They obviously had enjoyed more than enough to eat, and we had not. They had been well treated, and we had suffered.

Former prisoners often received long furloughs before being discharged. The excitement of being reunited with their families carried them through the first couple of days, but then many of them, such as John Pavkov, turned to alcohol to drown out painful memories:

> There was no kind of care after we returned to the States. No one told us what to expect. The army simply sent me home on a seventy-two-day furlough after which I ended up broke and an alcoholic. The first two days I was just tickled pink to be home. I stayed in the house and visited with my mom. Then I started going out drinking. I wouldn't leave the bars. If anyone in my family wanted to see me, they had to visit me in the bars. My brothers would come down and try and get me to go home. At first I refused, but they finally forced me to go home and physi-

cally stopped me from going out. They really helped me, but for two years it was really bad.[10]

Initially, Glenn Miller (Chapter Three) also drank heavily, although alcohol was only a temporary solution:

After I got back to the States, I spent the summer in the Roxy Bar and Grill in Lima, Ohio, with fellow soldiers on leave. It was great. Everyone seemed to be coming home even though the war in Japan was still going on. We were heroes. Everyone wanted to buy us drinks. They all asked how the Germans had treated me. Most could not believe anyone could exist on a daily allowance of one slice of bread and some watery soup. We veterans got along great with each other. We could talk to each other without having to explain anything. We simply understood each other. We usually met at the Roxy about eleven in the morning and began to have a few beers. By afternoon we were flying high. We broke for supper at home and then returned to the Roxy by eight in the evening. We would close the Roxy at one A.M. and go outside the city limits where bars stayed open until three. Then we would go to an all-night restaurant for breakfast and finally back home to sleep to get ready for the next day. This went on virtually every day for my sixty-six-day furlough. I had a few dates which broke up the routine but my memory of that summer is filled with booze until I realized I was running out of money. It was really a great way to forget.

---

[10]John Pavkov was a medic who after parachuting into Normandy on D-Day was almost immediately captured. He suffered many hardships in the camps, but most stressful was trying to care for wounded and sick fellow prisoners without sufficient medical supplies. As he tells it, things were particularly bad for the prisoners arriving in Stalag 4-B at Mühlberg after the Battle of the Bulge: "We were burying them all night long. They died because they had spent days in a boxcar with frozen feet and lungs, dysentery, and no food. They just kept dying, and without supplies there was nothing we could do to save them." Interview with author.

For Sandy Lubinsky, who had suffered so much in the Berga slave labor camp (Chapter Six), the first days home were filled with a sense of emptiness:

> When I first came home, I had no feelings. I couldn't even cry. I carried bread in my pockets for at least a year and a half. If I heard a sound, I would go around the house with a big knife in my hand to see what it was. I had nightmares. My nerves were shot. I had heart palpitations. My moods would swing radically

Prisoners who stayed in the service benefited from the established regimentation that provided a structure within which they could function. As Daniel Soria put it, "I know it helped me that I remained in the service. After I got back to the States, I went back to the National Guard where I started and where I had lots of buddies."[11] Those who were quickly mustered out to civilian life were mostly left to their own devices, often with negative results. One who simply tried to eat his way back to normality was Don Coulson (Chapter Six):

> When I was liberated from Dachau, I weighed only ninety-four pounds. I did spend some time at the Hart Springs Army/Navy Hospital, but I just couldn't eat anything. They said I was getting better, and they gave me a convalescence furlough, but I really think they sent me home to die. I just couldn't hold anything in my stomach. The day I got home my mother made some corn bread and beans. I thought, "Shit, if this is going to kill me, I'm still going to eat it." I ate the hell out of that, and sure enough I got sick and threw everything up. But I went back and ate some more, and threw up again. I didn't care. I just went back again and again.

---

[11]Daniel Soria jumped into France with the 101st Airborne the night before D-Day. He was captured three days later. Soria spent thirty-nine years in the military, retiring as the Command Sergeant Major of California. Interview with the author.

Whatever difficulties the former prisoners had to endure in the immediate postwar years, none could anticipate the long-term effects of a condition which in the aftermath of the Vietnam War would be labeled post-traumatic stress disorder (PTSD).[12] Characterized by chronic nightmares, frightening flashbacks, debilitating depression, and antisocial behavior, recent studies now indicate that approximately twenty-five percent of World War II combat veterans suffered unmistakable symptoms of traumatic stress, but among POWs the percentage was close to ninety.[13]

Psychiatrist Leslie Caplan, who as a POW suffered one of the long, deadly marches during the final weeks of the war in Germany, contends that examining doctors should not employ conventional medical practices when trying to help former prisoners: "We left a trail of slime and blood across Germany so horrible that conditions cannot be evaluated by customary medical criteria." Caplan recalls that at the time of liberation practically all POWs suffered some degree of malnutrition, gastritis, dysentery, respiratory and skin diseases, arthritis, frost-bite, and nervous disorders. Caplan, who is now a part-time VA consultant and full-time Clinical Professor of Psychiatry at the University of Minnesota, insists, "Every POW should automatically be service-connected for these ailments or any ailments related to them. All he should have to do is prove he was a prisoner of war."[14] Among the long-term effects, Caplan includes inability to maintain proper weight, general nervousness, excessive sweating, visual defects, including optic atrophy, cardiac and gastro-intestinal problems, and bone defects. In addition, acute malnutrition and captivity-related maladies contribute to such diseases as arte-

---

[12]The term PTSD first appeared in psychiatric journals in 1980.

[13]David Gelman, "Reliving the Past," *Newsweek*, June 13, 1994, 20–22; see also *Detroit Free Press*, April 27, 1995. Of the more than 100 former American POWs interviewed for this book only two insisted their captivity had no lasting effect on them, and both of these men were long-time career officers.

[14]Quoted in Stan Sommers, *American Ex-Prisoners of War, Inc., National Medical Research Committee, The European Story, Packet No. 8* (Marshfield, Wisc., 1980), 33.

riosclerosis, hypertension, neoplasms, allergies, cirrhosis of the liver, peptic ulcers, and anemia. One VA study concluded that World War II POWs were nine times more likely to suffer a stroke than combat veterans generally, and because of these infirmities their life expectancy is considerably less than that of the general population.[15]

According to psychiatrist Judith Herman, those subject to PTSD "are always on the alert for danger." In addition, they exhibit "an extreme startle response to unexpected stimuli." They are also troubled by "numerous types of sleep disturbance [and] take longer to fall asleep, are more sensitive to noise, and awaken more frequently during the night than ordinary people."[16]

Before counseling and psychiatric help gradually became available in the 1980s, most former prisoners had no way of knowing why seemingly insignificant incidents could trigger irrational rages. Daniel Soria remembers how a sudden noise or someone ordering him to do something could set him off:

> I can still remember walking down the street with my wife, and hear a car backfire or a kid throwing a firecracker, and I'd hit the goddam deck. I'd hit that sidewalk like I knew what I was doing. That was just a reaction.
>
> Mentally we were really screwed up. I remember when I got married, my mother said, "She's too good for you." That's why I got married. I should never have got married. We carried it around for a long time. I hear all this stuff about the Vietnam veterans. I guess we had the same goddam problem but didn't know it.[17]

Often it was a specific and particularly horrifying memory that tormented an ex-prisoner. For Louis Pfeifer, who was forced to work with slave laborers, it was the haunting image of starving children:

---

[15]Sommers, 35–37; see also *Ex-POW Bulletin* (Feb. 1996), 2.

[16]Herman, *Trauma and Recovery*, 36.

[17]Interview with the author.

There were a bunch of children housed close to us. I mean little kids. They had these big eyes and big stomachs. I think they were the children of Polish or Jewish slave laborers. There was a big yellow star on the side of their barracks. When we marched by on our way to work, we could see them looking out their barracks' windows. They were obviously starving. It still bothers me terribly when I read or hear about innocent children suffering and dying because of what adults do to each other in wars. The kids are innocent victims. If adults want to carry on like idiots, fine, but don't victimize the kids. Why should they take a beating? But I was also an innocent victim, and I didn't like it either.[18]

A strong sense of guilt about the death of a fellow prisoner, whose name he cannot remember, continues to torment Pfeifer:

One night one of the boys died in our barracks. We took him outside and buried him between our barracks and the latrine which was only a few feet away from the fence. He was a young guy, maybe nineteen or twenty. He just died. I didn't know his name and I still don't. There are still a lot of guys missing from World War II, and he's probably one of them. I often wondered if his parents ever found out what happened. But there are so many things on your mind that you don't really keep track of other guys. Under those conditions, it becomes every man for himself. You don't go around knocking somebody else in the head, but you keep what you've got, and you don't share.[19]

Guilt, real or imagined, certainly played a dominant role for many of these men. First there is the continuing guilt for having been taken prisoner; then, there is the guilt for what you might have done differently or for how you might have helped someone; finally, there is the guilt for having survived when so many of

---

[18]Interview with the author.

[19]Interview with the author.

your buddies did not. Daryle Watters was a glider pilot who has never forgiven himself for the death of his copilot:

> There is definitely a sense of guilt for having been taken prisoner of war. That goes without saying. All of us suffer this irrational sense of guilt. Combat is the first part of this. First of all you get a buddy killed who has done nothing wrong, like the guy sitting in the copilot's seat when we went in over Holland. He had obeyed all the rules, was a good soldier and a decent human being, and he gets killed. I had almost nine months as a POW to think about whether I could have flown my glider any differently. I flew straight and level like a dummy so that flak gun could get us. But I didn't get killed; he did. What could I have done to have saved him is a very normal human response. I even wrote his name down and smuggled it out of the camp. I had to find out if he indeed had been killed. And he was. This thing just nagged at me during all those lonely months in prison. What did I not do in my training? You're fighting the war for your buddy, not for the country or the president. So if you feel you did something wrong, it's going to nag at you.[20]

Watters, who later would spend considerable time trying to help fellow ex-prisoners deal with PTSD, first had to excise his own postwar demons:

> When we finally got home, all of us were Section 8s to one degree or another [psychologically unable to cope]. I know when I went back to college my grades went way down from what they had been before the war. I seemed only to have an attention span of about thirty seconds. I think the

---

[20]Daryle Watters flew a glider into Normandy on D-Day, one of the most extraordinary and dangerous assignments of the war. Three months later, during the invasion of Holland, the tow plane cut Watters' glider loose short of the target, and he and his men were taken prisoner and shipped to Stalag Luft 1 at Barth. Interview with the author.

guys who stayed in and went back to familiar duties and had all the support system of their buddies around them recovered much more quickly than did those of us who immediately got out of the service.

A fellow who had served on the parole board and had lots of experience evaluating the mental state of civilian prisoners noticed the first time he met me that there was something wrong. I'm not sure what he saw. Perhaps a vacant stare, a lack of social skills, and all the character- istics of someone who had become too introverted—which was not my nature.

When things got too difficult, I would get out the deck of cards and began playing solitaire just like I did when I was a prisoner. Or if I couldn't study, I would just go fish- ing by myself. I would never keep the fish. I'd always turn them loose. I always had to have an out. Then there were the nightmares that everybody talks about. Twisting and turning and four hours sleep a night and waking up in a cold sweat. Sometimes I'd wake up and be trying to stran- gle my wife which was very dangerous because I had all that commando training. I could just as well have broken her neck.[21]

No one recognized such symptoms immediately after the war. Ex-prisoners, like veterans generally, suffered silently, unaware why certain everyday situations seemed so traumatic. Many of them have only recently sought help, perhaps because in retire- ment they have lost the structured routine of daily work that may have helped keep those feelings at bay, or perhaps because their fellow countrymen are no longer so judgmental about such afflic- tions. John Foster (Chapter Six) describes the extreme behavior that finally forced him to seek help:

What got me finally to go to the VA hospital was that I couldn't sleep at night, and I was having these horrible nightmares. They were so real that I'd wake up in a cold

---

[21]Interview with the author.

sweat. Certain things still happen today that trigger a flashback and a feeling of terror. I also have a hard time remembering things—I'm now rated with a forty percent loss of memory. If I didn't have all this written down, I wouldn't be able to talk to you. I was also abusing alcohol, and I became so violent that I even tried to kill my own son. All this was going on, but I didn't really know why. I finally got help, and the VA did grant me a fifty percent PTSD disability payment, but because their recognition of PTSD was something new, they said they didn't have to pay me anything retroactively. And I've never received any disability for my physical wounds even though I have never been able to pass a physical examination that would allow me to do any kind of physical labor.

For many of the men the problem was not just getting to a Veterans Administration hospital but the VA doctors who were supposed to treat them. Robert Engstrom (Chapter One), for example, was so dissatisfied with the results that he simply fell back on his own resources:

A couple of years ago I got really jumpy. I didn't know what was wrong. We were wintering in Tucson, and somebody told me I should check with the local Veterans Administration hospital, so I did. The main guy there sent me to this lady who was about sixty. She told me she was Dr. So-and-so. We talked, and she wrote some stuff down. I told her that from time to time I was getting very nervous. I had never been too jumpy before, but I was getting hyper, and my wife was becoming concerned. When we came back home to Michigan, Tucson transferred my records to the VA hospital at Fort Custer. I went there a couple of times, but then I gave up. I just didn't show up for my last appointment. I decided I'd make it on my own.

Even worse than unsatisfactory treatment was to encounter a VA doctor who refused to acknowledge that a patient's psychological problems could be traced back to his incarceration. As Daryle Watters put it, "They seemed to think you had to have a flak

wound and a physical scar before you were entitled to compensation."[22] Louis Grivetti (Chapter Three) agrees:

> The first time I went for what they call a protocol physical was at the Veterans Administration in Louisville, and the doctor treated me with considerable contempt. While he was examining me, I would try to tell him certain things, but he didn't want to hear anything of the sort. He'd say to me, "Shut up. Do you want me to finish your papers or not?" He'd just stare at me and then write something down. You can't tell the wellbeing of a person by just looking at him.
>
> A short time later, I went to my first POW reunion and met an official from Washington. When I told him what had happened with the doctor at the VA in Louisville, he said, "You should have stood up and busted him in the mouth and walked away." He then told me to go back and request a new protocol physical, which I did. But I ran into this same doctor, and this time we had words. About a week later I had to go see the psychiatrist. The first thing he asked me was, "What's this about you giving Dr. So-and-So a hard time." So I had to go through my whole story again. But this doctor was a Vietnam veteran, and he told me, "Don't worry, I'll take care of you." I presume he's the one who got me the thirty percent disability for PTSD.

The initial step in treating PTSD was simply getting these men to open up. This was seldom easy, but once they began talking, most felt better about themselves. Louis Pfeifer attempted to expunge his harrowing memories about the tortured children in the slave labor camps by talking about the war and captivity to high school students. For Louis Grivetti, it was joining his local ex-POW chapter that helped him end his silence:

> Now I can talk about my experiences. I think the change occurred when I joined this ex-POW organization. We get

---

[22]Interview with the author.

together and share our experiences. Somebody who has not been in that situation cannot comprehend what the hell we're talking about. I even became commander of the Daniel Boone Chapter of the Ex-POWs Association in Lexington, Kentucky. When we began, we would try to get a different person each month to talk about himself. For some of the guys it was very difficult. Some would break down before they could finish, which I have myself. But we try get it all out in the open. Last year this female psychiatrist even got our wives to attend with us. By getting them to talk about the different things that we do, the doctor was able to explain a lot of things our wives did not understand.

For Sandy Lubinsky (Chapter Six), it was the death of his wife and a sense of his own mortality that got him talking about a past he had tried so hard to forget:

I'm just happy I can now talk about it. If you had called me three years ago, I wouldn't have been willing to talk to you. But I feel different about life now. Losing my wife in 1991 had something to do with it. I'm getting older, I'm going to die soon, and I know it. I firmly believe we have our heaven and hell here on earth, and I've certainly had my hell. So I don't know how much worse it can get.

Talking, therapy, and supportive family and friends all helped the former prisoners, but many also believe they deserve some kind of official recognition for what they have endured. This has been a long, difficult struggle. Beginning in the last year of World War II, there have been numerous attempts to honor ex-POWs with some kind of service decoration, but military leaders have consistently opposed such efforts, and the public itself had to be educated. The horrors of captivity were brought home to Americans during and especially after the Vietnam War when numerous ex-prisoners published their memoirs, went on speaking tours, or allowed their experiences to be portrayed on film. The Iran hostage crisis, which began on November 4, 1979, and lasted 444 days, also changed many perceptions of what it meant to be incarcerated by a hostile foreign power. In 1985, in the face

of continuing military opposition, Congress finally created the Prisoner of War Medal, and many states subsequently began to issue free license plates with "POW" inscribed on them. There were those, of course, who continued to object to any kind of recognition. One such critic insisted that the United States was the only country in the world to honor those surrendering to the enemy. Others have suggested that POWs represent failed missions and are thus an embarrassment to the pride and success of the American armed services.[23] Louis Pfeifer has an answer for such critics:

I had problems getting the free license plates ex-POWs are entitled to. My wife finally contacted the Secretary of State's Office in Topeka, Kansas, but the man she talked to really insulted her. He told her the reason there was nothing about having been a POW on my discharge papers was because it was less than honorable to have been a prisoner. I wonder if he would have said that if he had ever been one.[24]

And what of the former German prisoners of war? Most agree they did not suffer the same degree of physical or psychological impairment from their actual incarceration as did their American counterparts. However, combat certainly had a devastating effect on many of them. Some were badly wounded, and none was immune to the long-term effects of having spent months—even years—on the front lines. In addition, many of their problems were exacerbated after the end of the war, either because of additional time spent in English or French work camps or because of the devastation and political problems they encountered when they finally returned to Germany.

Guilt was a double-edged sword for many German POWs. On the one hand, some felt ashamed of having been captured, although this was not the case for most German soldiers taken prisoner after the Normandy invasion, when they knew all was lost. On the other hand, what of Hitler and the atrocities of the

---

[23]See Doyle, *Voices from Captivity*, 292–3.

[24]Interview with the author.

Third Reich? Did not every German have to share in the responsibility for this nightmare? Kurt Pechmann (Chapter Seven), who later would design and build the State of Wisconsin's Vietnam War Memorial, describes how his thinking evolved from his moment of capture through his later incarceration in the United States:

> That night I slept in the open among the British soldiers, but I couldn't escape. The next morning they brought us down for questioning. They asked us what unit we were in. They already knew the answer so why hide it. They took us back to a makeshift POW camp. A British captain who spoke fluent German asked me if I was a convinced Nazi. I told him, "That's a good question. I have to be honest with you. If you had grown up in Germany, you would also have been a victim of the one-sided propaganda. You only hear the German party line. They run everybody else down, so you become convinced you are the best people." We were not allowed to listen to foreign radio stations. If you did so and were caught, you might very well be sent to a concentration camp. And, as a young guy, you could care less about politics. So you were convinced your country was the best. But shortly after I arrived in America as a POW, I became convinced that there was no such thing as *Deutschland über alles*. There are other countries that are also good.

With his belief that captivity had fundamentally changed his life for the better, Eberhard Ladwig (Chapter Three), who later became a successful botanist and teacher in the former German Democratic Republic, excised any sense of guilt:

> Contemplating all that happened to me—learning about a different kind of life, reading that book on Jewish thought, personally meeting Jews, Austrians, and others who were different, and having lots of time to think—made me realize, I never felt myself so free as when I was in captivity.

For Oskar Schmoling (Chapter Two), whose American captors stood him up against a wall for an apparent execution, it was better just to try and forget everything. Of course, such experiences simply do not disappear:

You try to forget. It was war. War was fair to no one, so you could not expect much from anybody. There was mistreatment on both sides. I try to treat my POW experience as if it never happened. This included not talking about it, not even to family or friends.

Luca Felix Müller (Chapter Five), who had fought against Nazi oppression even before he became a prisoner of war, ended up in the German Democratic Republic, where he once again chose to fight against a rigid, totalitarian government. Eventually, he escaped the GDR to take up residence in West Berlin. With so much pain in his life, Müller is still disappointed that the United States did not take early action against Germany's concentration camps and for its naivete at the end of the war:

When the Americans liberated Buchenwald and other concentration camps, they were astonished, horrified, and shocked. But they must have known about these thing, much earlier. When I was in Prague in 1934, we talked about the horrors of the concentration camps. What happens under a totalitarian government is incomprehensible to those who live in a liberal, democratic society. And this was also true for many Germans. It was unbelievable and therefore incomprehensible. For the average American, including the GIs who witnessed the carnage at the end of the war, all this was new but certainly not for American political leaders. They knew about the concentration camps from immigrants. How much they knew about the ovens in Auschwitz and other extermination camps is perhaps arguable. But something could have been done earlier. In Fort Kearney we saw a film about Auschwitz with an English narration. We were then asked to write down our reaction. I had never heard the name Auschwitz; in fact, I wrote down "Auschnick." I knew nothing about Auschwitz. Naturally, we knew that the Jews, including many of our Jewish friends in Berlin, had been picked up and sent to Litzmannstadt and other concentration camps. But more we did not know. The average American also knew nothing more. But high-ranking government officials must have been playing a kind of secret game.

They could have discovered what horrible things were going on if they had wanted to. But of course we Germans also did not want to know what was really happening.

The Americans were also politically naive. They thought they just had to knock the stuffing out of the enemy and then go back home. The Morgenthau Plan was an example of this kind of thinking.[25] They really had no idea what we Germans should do after the war. This can partly be explained by American history and by a people who are preoccupied with themselves and their own land. They can afford to do this because they occupy their own continent. The Americans were woefully naive about Europeans' historical struggles over borders and nationalities. This is one reason why Roosevelt allowed Yalta to go the way it did. The Soviets understood what they had to do and they prepared accordingly.

Josef Krumbachner (Chapter Four) also believes the Americans could have done more at the end of the war to counter the Russian threat:

Looking back, we experienced the kindness and basic humanity of most Americans. However, after the war it was difficult for us to understand the naive good faith which resulted in them making so many bad mistakes in Europe. We could not understand why they refused to use their unique world power to establish a postwar world in which future conflicts would not be inevitable. I still remember a huge banner that stretched across a street in Winston-Salem, the tobacco city, where after the capitulation some of us worked. In huge letters were the words, "CAMEL LEADS THE WORLD." But this meant more than simply Camel cigarettes. We thought of that old saying: "Too much good will leads to license and abuse."

---

[25]The Morgenthau Plan would have destroyed all of Germany's industrial might, turning the country into a virtual agricultural state.

Like survival itself, where one ended up in Germany upon repatriation was often due as much to chance as to any kind of planning. Guenther Oswald (Chapter Three) was one of the lucky ones who escaped being sent to the Russian zone:

When we were repatriated, we were divided up according to the zone we were to be shipped to in Germany. The group going to the Russian zone was very small. I had fought in Russia, and I wouldn't have gone there either. I knew better than that. A young lieutenant who was one of our fellow prisoners got up and made a speech in favor of repatriating to the Russian occupation zone. He praised everything there in comparison to the other zones. He convinced quite a few men and they agreed to go to the Russian zone. I had several addresses from those who went. I wrote letters, but most of them were answered by wives or parents. They had no idea where their husbands or sons were. Maybe a year later, I met a former captain who had been with us. He told me that those choosing the Soviet zone ended up in Russian labor camps

Old Nazi fighter and concentration camp inmate Erwin Schulz (Chapter Five) eventually ended up in the German Democratic Republic where he discovered that his past struggles against National Socialism did not help him with a regime that thought him "contaminated" by his exposure to Western ideas:

Once returned to civilian life, you were supposed to have it easier if you could prove that you had been part of the resistance or if you were an *OdF*.[26] But it was no real advantage. Oh, you got a few more food coupons but nothing much else. In no way did we get to live high on the hog. But at the time we were satisfied just to have a higher priority ration card. I also became a member of the VVN.[27]

---

[26]*Opfer des Faschismus* was a special designation for "Victim of Fascism."

[27]*Verband der Verfolgten des Naziregimes* (Association of Those Persecuted by the Nazi Regime).

This was supposed to help those of us who had fought against Hitler, but it was closed down in 1953 which was a big mistake.

Those of us who had been in Western prison camps were eventually thrown out of our government jobs in the German Democratic Republic. We who were anti-Nazis and old 999ers were simply not trusted because the government thought we had been contaminated by the West. The ex–999ers in West Germany also had their problems, although Herbert Tulatz later became an official in the labor movement, and Erwin Welke served as a member of the Bundestag. But in the East, if you didn't have contacts, you had trouble finding any kind of position.

Most of the men in this book agree that along with the war itself, being a POW was the central experience of their lives. Even those who insist they were unaffected have not entirely removed the experience from their conscious and subconscious minds. Prisoners on both sides of the Atlantic remember an incident or two when they were especially well treated, but many, and certainly most Americans, are more likely to recall what it is they are trying to forget. Some 5,000 German ex-prisoners returned to the United States after the war to take up permanent residence and eventually become citizens. At least that many have visited the United States, including the sites of their former prison camps. A sizeable number of their American counterparts have also returned to search for their prison camps, but few, if any, have decided to remain in Germany. Nevertheless, there are Americans who recognize the positive as well as negative lessons they absorbed from the suffering and anxiety that was their daily existence.

Glenn Miller (Chapter Two) argues that something can be gained from any experience, however dreadful it appeared at the time:

You learn from any experience. Just being in the army was a maturing thing. I think the army did more for me in terms of just appreciating the fact I could compete with other guys physically, mentally, and socially. The POW experience? Well, I can't leave food on a plate. I even have

problems leaving any gravy. I have to get a piece of bread and sop it up. My wife says I learned that I could take more than I thought I could. I did gain a lot of confidence, but that was because I had to.

Clifford Fox (Chapter Three) described his captivity in almost glowing terms:

I think this experience changed me as a human being. Since then it's been easier for me to accept setbacks because I've seen so many people who could not handle adversity. It also changed my attitude about people. We Americans tend to think we're the greatest, but there are great people all over the world. So being a POW made me more tolerant of others. It also made me more apprecia- tive of what I do have. The old saying "Life is what you make it" is pretty much true. You can be sad and depressed, or you can decide to just go on when things don't go the way you want them to. I wouldn't take any- thing for my POW experiences, but I sure would not want to go through them again.

Danny Abeles (Chapter Two) learned to appreciate the small- er things in life:

The little things we take for granted are so important. Take something like toilet paper. When you have to use cellophane wrappers from cigarettes you realize what a luxury toilet paper is. Just try living without it for ten or eleven months. We take these things for granted, and when you don't have them, boy do you miss them. After I got home, I was always opening the refrigerator door. My mom would say, "Go ahead and eat something." I'd tell her, "No, it's just nice to know there's food there." I still cannot stand to waste any food. I remember when I would have given my right arm for what we now throw away.

Robert Engstrom continues to struggle with thoughts of guilt and survival:

I still ask, "Why me?" I go over to the chapel at Michigan State University and almost all my class is on those bronze plaques. The twins got killed in Africa before they were over there six weeks. At least fifteen out of the twenty-one in my ROTC class never came home. I just don't know why it had to be me that survived. I sometimes feel I should be over there with them.

Ludwig Norz (Chapter Seven) understands the role chance played in determining who survived and who did not, but he also believes in something beyond chance:

I'm not sure what effect the POW experience had on my subsequent life. I know you can't get it out of your system, and not just life as a POW, but life as a soldier as well. The war experience is always there and having been a prisoner just intensifies such feelings. All this becomes part of your makeup, and each of us deals with it differently. There were times when I was ready to explode because of the seeming injustice of it all. After Vietnam, Americans learned what stress can do to a soldier. If there is such a thing as post-traumatic stress disorder, and I think there is, we too were afflicted. We just had to try and deal with it on our own.

But there were also parts of the POW experience that were positive. You do learn patience and a degree of tolerance. You have to go through a series of stages. You look at life and the world differently. You learn that things are not black and white. You also learn about the role of chance. My regiment was decimated. Almost everyone was killed, but I got out alive and was sent to America. My next door neighbor and a cousin were POWs in Russia, and they didn't get back to Germany until 1954. But there is something beyond chance. If I didn't have a very abiding belief that all of this will somehow be put right on a different level of existence, I would have snapped long ago.

Because of his POW experiences Guenther Oswald (Chapter Three), who later emigrated to the United States, learned a

strong sense of tolerance and an even stronger desire and appreciation for free institutions:

> The way it was for East Germans under communism was the same as it was for us under the Nazis. Both were dictatorships where one was not free to say or do what he wanted. I went back to Germany only one time after I emigrated, and that was in 1983. My wife and I went to Boizenburg which was just over the East German border because my youngest brother was still there. We had a family reunion. My oldest brother had emigrated to Argentina, and he and his wife also came back, as did some other relatives. We three brothers walked to the outskirts of the city and into a forest where we begin to talk about the German Democratic Republic and its way of life. My youngest brother quickly said, "Shhhh, don't talk so loud. One doesn't say anything against the conditions." And that was in the forest. That's the same way it was when we were growing up under Hitler.

Whether German or American, these former prisoners understand they have survived the terrifying experience of having been prisoners of war, and the more fortunate among them are determined to challenge any lingering sense of guilt. Tough, uncompromising ex-paratrooper George Rosie (Chapter Three) puts it so very well:

> POW stories never end. In 1974 when the 101st Airborne Division Association was holding its annual meeting in San Mateo, California, I went down early to breakfast one morning, and in one of the booths a man was sitting all alone. I asked him if he wanted company. He nodded, so I joined him. He introduced himself as Cecil Hutt. We talked for a little while, and I looked up, and Joe Beyrle [Chapter Four] was standing by the cashier. I waved him over and introduced him to my breakfast companion. Hutt said it was his first reunion. Joe and I asked him why. He answered, "Actually, I was a little ashamed. I was captured on D-Day." I looked at Joe, smiled, and said, "Well,

you sure picked two great guys to join for breakfast. Joe and I were both captured on D-Day as well." Few men expected to be wounded, killed, or captured. We did feel some frustration at first. But our option was simple. We had the choice of dying or being captured. It's now a half century later, and we're still here!

Bibliography

AMERICAN POWS IN GERMANY

Monographs and Nonfiction:

Bard, Mitchell G. *Forgotten Victims: The Abandonment of Americans in Hitler's Camps*. Boulder, Colo.: Westview Press, 1994.

Barker, A. J. *Prisoners of War*. New York: Universe Books, 1975.

Baron, Richard, Abe Baum, and Richard Goldhurst. *Raid! The Untold Story of Patton's Secret Mission*. New York: G. P. Putnam's Sons, 1981.

Brickhill, Paul. *The Great Escape*. Greenwich, Conn.: Faber, 1950.

Burgess, Alan. *The Longest Tunnel: The True Story of World War II's Great Escape*. New York: Grove Weidenfeld, 1990.

Cohen, Bernard M., and Maurice Z. Cooper. *A Follow-Up Study of World War II Prisoners of War*. Washington, D.C.: Government Printing Office, 1954.

Des Pres, Terrence. *The Survivor: An Anatomy of Life in the Death Camps*. New York: Oxford University Press, 1976.

Doyle, Robert C. *Voices from Captivity: Interpreting the American POW Narrative*. Lawrence: University Press of Kansas, 1994.

Durand, Arthur A. *Stalag Luft III: The Secret Story*. Baton Rouge, La.: Louisiana State University Press, 1988.

Foy, David A. *For You the War Is Over: American POWs in Nazi Germany*. New York: Stein & Day, 1984.

Franklin, H. Bruce. *M.I.A. or Mythmaking in America*. Brooklyn, New York: Lawrence Hill Books, 1992.

Fussell, Paul. *Wartime: Understanding and Behavior in the Second World War*. New York: Oxford University Press, 1989.

Gansburg, Judith. *Stalag USA: The Remarkable Story of the German POWs in America*. New York: Thomas Y. Crowell, 1977.

Gruner, Elliott. *Prisoners of Culture: Representing the Vietnam POW*. New Brunswick, N.J.: Rutgers University Press, 1993.

Homze, Edward. *Foreign Labor in Nazi Germany*. Princeton, N.J.: Princeton University Press, 1967.

Howes, Craig. *Voices of the Vietnam POWs: Witnesses to Their Fight*. New York: Oxford University Press, 1993.

Irving, David John Cawdell. *The Destruction of Dresden*. New York: Ballantine Books, 1985.

Kehlenhofer, Guy L. *Understanding the Former Prisoner of War: Life after Liberation. Essays*. St. Paul, Minn.: Banfil Street Press, 1992.

Moore, Bob, ed. *Prisoners-of-War and Their Captors in World War II*. London: Berg, 1996.

Motley, Mary Penick, ed. *The Invisible Soldier: The Experiences of the Black Soldier, World War II*. Detroit: Wayne State University Press, 1975.

Shoemaker, Lloyd R. *The Escape Factory*. New York: St. Martin's Press, 1990.

Terkel, Studs. *The Good War: An Oral History of World War II*. New York: Pantheon, 1984.

Trials of War Criminals before the Nuremberg Military Tribunals. Vols. 11 and 13. Washington, D.C.: U.S. Government Printing Office, 1952.

Vulliet, Andre. *The YMCA and Prisoners of War During World War II*. Geneva: International Committee of the YMCA, 1946.

Weingartner, James. *Crossroads of Death: The Story of the Malmédy Massacre and Trial*. Berkeley, Calif.: University of California Press, 1979.

Memoirs, Biographies, and Oral Histories

Abdalla, John. *Allen King, World War II American P.O.W.* Memphis: Oral History Research Office, Memphis State University, 1989.

Beattie, Edward W. *Diary of a Kriegie*. New York: Thomas Crowell Co., 1946.

Beltrone, Art and Lee. *A Wartime Log*. Charlottesville, Va.: Howell Press, 1995.

Bing, Richard L. *You're 19 . . . Welcome Home: A Study of the Air War Over Europe and Its After Effects*. Self-Published, 1992.

Carpenter, Willis and Roberta. *I Was the Enemy*. Millersburg, Ind.: Privately printed, 1990.

Chernitsky, Dorothy. *Voices from the Foxholes: Men of the 110th Infantry Relate Personal Accounts of What They Experienced during World War II*. Uniontown, Pa.: Privately printed, 1991.

Collins, Douglas. *POW*. New York: Norton, 1968.

Cox, Luther. *Always Fighting the Enemy*. Baltimore: Gateway Press, 1990.

Daniel, Eugene L. *In the Presence of Mine Enemies: An American Chaplain in World War II German Prison Camps*. Charlotte, N.C.: E. L. Daniel, 1985.

Davis, George J. *The Hitler Diet, As Inflicted on American POWs in World War II*. Los Angeles: Military Literary Guild, 1990.

Diggs, J. Frank. *The Welcome Swede*. New York: Vantage Press, 1988.

Dillon, Carrol F. *A Domain of Heroes: An Airman's Life Behind Barbed Wire in Germany in World War II* (Privately printed, 1995).

Dobran, Edward. *P.O.W.* New York: Exposition Press, 1953.

Duke, Florimond. *Name, Rank, and Serial Number*. New York: Meredith Press, 1969.

Ferguson, Clarence. *Kriegsgefangener 3024, POW*. Waco, Tex.: Texian Press, 1983.

Frelinghuysen, Joe. *Passages to Freedom*. Manhattan, Kans.: Sunflower University Press, 1990.

Hamann, Lorin W. *A Prisoner Remembers World War II*. Elkader, Iowa: L. W. Hamann, 1984.

Harrison, Jack S. *Flight from Youth: The Story of an American POW*. Madison, Wisc.: J. S. Harrison, 1973.

Harsh, George. *Lonesome Road*. New York: W. W. Norton & Co., 1971.

Hatch, Gardner (Chief Ed.). *American Ex-POWs*. Paducah, Ky.: Turner Publishers.

Hopewell, Clifford. *Combine 13*. Dallas, Tex.: Merrimore Press, 1990.

Howell, Forrest W. *Whispers of Death: Yankee Kriegies*. Moore Haven, Fla.: Rainbow Books, 1985.

Kimball, R. W., and O. M. Chies. *Clipped Wings*. Dayton, Ohio: R. W. Kimball, 1948.

Lister, Hal. *Krautland Calling: An American POW Radio Broadcaster in Nazi Germany*. Austin, Tex.: Eakin Press, 1989.

Meltesen, Clarence R. *Roads to Liberation*. San Francisco: Oflag 64 Press, 1990.

Newcomb, Alan. *Vacation with Pay: Being an Account of My Stay at the German Rest Camp for Tired Allied Airmen at Beautiful Barth-on-the-Baltic (Stalag Luft 1)*. Haverhill, Mass.: Destiny Publishers, 1947.

O'Donnell, Joseph P. *The Shoe Leather Express: The Evacuation of Kriegsgefangener Lager Stalag Luft IV, Deutschland, Germany*. Robbinsville, N.J.: J. P. O'Donnell, 1982.

O'Donnell, Joseph P. *Luftgangsters*. Robbinsville, N.J.: J. P. O'Donnell, 1982.

Sage, Colonel Jerry. *The Man the Germans Could Not Keep Prisoner*. Wayne, Pa.: Miles Standish Press, 1985.

Sampson, Francis. *Paratrooper Padre*. Washington, D.C.: Catholic University of America Press, 1948.

Sexton, Winton K. *Back Roads to Freedom*. Kansas City, Mo.: Lowell Press, 1985.

Spivey, Delmar. *POW Odyssey: Recollections of Center Compound, Stalag Luft III and the Secret German Peace Mission in World War II*. Attleboro, Mass.: Colonial Lithograph, 1984.

Stone, James F. *A Holiday in Hitlerland*. New York: Carlton Press, 1970.

Victor, John A. *Time Out: American Airmen at Stalag Luft 1*. New York: R. R. Smith, 1951.

Westheimer, David. *Sitting It Out: A World War II POW Memoir*. Houston: Rice University Press, 1992.

Zemke, Hubert. *Zemke's Stalag: The Final Days of World War II*. Washington, D.C.: Smithsonian Institute, 1991.

Zemke, Hubert. *Zemke's Wolf Pack*, as told to Roger A. Freeman. New York: Pocket Books, 1988.

Novels:

Giovannitti, Len. *The Prisoners of Combine D*. New York: Bantam Books, 1957.

Klaas, Joe. *Maybe I'm Dead*. New York: Gollancz, 1955.

Simmons, Kenneth. *Kriegie*. New York: Thomas Nelson & Sons, 1960.

Vonnegut, Kurt. *Slaughterhouse-Five, or the Children's Crusade*. New York: Dell Publishing Co., 1969.

Westheimer, David, *Von Ryan's Express*. New York: New American Library, 1964.

Westheimer, David, *Song of the Young Sentry*. Boston: Little, Brown, 1968.

Unpublished M.A. Theses:

Burbank, Lyman B. *A History of the American Air Force Prisoners of War in Center Compound, Stalag Luft II, Germany*. M.A. Thesis, University of Chicago, 1946.

Goldman, Ben. *German Treatment of American Prisoners of War in World War II*. M.A. Thesis, Wayne State University, 1949.

GERMAN POWS IN THE UNITED STATES

Monographs and Nonfiction:

Bacque, James. *Other Losses: An Investigation into the Mass Deaths of German Prisoners at the Hands of the French and Americans After World War II*. Toronto: Stoddart, 1989.

Bartow, Omer. *Hitler's Army*. New York: Oxford University Press, 1991.

Böhme, Kurt W. *Geist und Kultur der deutschen Kriegsgefangenen im Westen*. Munich: Ernst und Werner Gieseking Verlag, 1968.

Christgau, John. *"Enemies": World War II Alien Internment*. Ames, Iowa: Iowa State University Press, 1985.

Cooper, Herston. *Crossville*. Chicago: Adams Press, 1965.

Costelle, Daniel. *Les Prisonniers*. Paris: Flammarion, 1975.

Gansberg, Judith M. *Stalag, USA: The Remarkable Story of German POWs in America*. New York: Crowell, 1977.

Gottschick, Johann. *Psychiatrie der Kriegsgefangenschaft: der Gestellt auf Grund von Beobachtungen in der USA an deutschen Kriegsgefangenen aus dem letzten Weltkrieg*. Stuttgart: Gustav Fisher Verlag, 1963.

Hartmann, Erich. *In the Camps*. New York: W. W. Norton, 1995.

Jung, Hermann. *Die deutschen Kriegsgefangenen in amerikanischer Hand— USA*. Munich: Ernst und Werner Gieseking, 1972.

Keefer, Louis E. *Italian Prisoners of War in America, 1942–1946. Captives or Allies?* New York: Praeger Publishers, 1992.

Koop, Allen V. *Stark Decency, German Prisoners of War in a New England Village*. Hanover, N.H.: University Press of New England, 1988.

Krammer, Arnold. *Nazi Prisoners of War in America*. New York: Stein and Day, 1979.

Krammer, Arnold. *Public Administration of Prisoner of War Camps in America Since the Revolutionary War*. Monticello, Ill.: Vance Bibliographies, 1980.

Lewis, George Glover. *History of POW Utilization by the U.S. Army, 1776–1945*. Washington, D.C.: Superintendent of Documents, U.S. Government Printing Office, 1988.

Maschke, Erich, ed. *Zur Geschichte der deutschen Kriegsgefangenen des Zeiten Weltkrieges*. Bielefeld: Verlag Gieseking, 1972–3.

McCarver, Norman L., and Norman L. McCarver, Jr. *Hearne on the Brazos*. San Antonio, Tex.: Century Press of Texas, 1958.

Moore, John Hammond. *The Faustball Tunnel*. New York: Random House, 1978.

Powell, Allan Kent. *Splinters of a Nation: German POWs in Utah*. Salt Lake City: University of Utah Press, 1989.

Robin, Ron. *The Barbed-Wire College: Reeducating German POWs in the United States during World War II*. Princeton, N.J.: Princeton University Press, 1995.

Smith, Arthur L. *Heimkehr aus dem Zweiten Weltkrieg. Die Entlassung der deutschen Kriegsgefangenen*. Stuttgart: Deutsche Verlags-Anstalt, 1985.

Whittingham, Richard. *Martial Justice: The Last Mass Execution in the United States*. Chicago: Henry Regnery Co., 1971.

Memoirs, Biographies, and Oral Histories:

Andersch, Alfred. "*Amerikaner – Erster Eindruck*," in *Flucht in Etrurien. Zwei Erzählungen und ein Bericht*. Zürich: Diogenes, 1981.

Andersch, Alfred. *Die Kirschen der Freiheit. Ein Bericht*. Zürich: Diogenes, 1968.

Andersch, Alfred. *Einmal wirklich leben. Ein Tagebuch in Briefen an Hedwig Andersch 1943–1975*. Zürich: Diogenes, 1986.

Andersch, Alfred. *Gesammelte Erzählungen*. Zürich: Diogenes, 1990.

Andersch, Alfred. "*Sechzehnjahriger allein*." In *Erinnerte Gestalten. Frühe Erzählungen*. Zürich: Diogenes, 1986.

Dalderup, Leo, and John Murdoch. *The Other Side: The Story of Leo Dalerup*. London: Hodder and Stoughton, 1954.

Faye, Clark. *As You Were: Fort Custer*. Galesburg, Mich.: Kal-Gale Publishing Company, 1985.

Gaertner, George, with Arnold Krammer. *Hitler's Last Soldier in America*. New York: Stein and Day, 1985.

Greulich, Emil. *Amerikanische Odyssee*. Berlin: Deutscher Militärverlag, 1965.

Heidenkamp, Ulrich. *PW in Texas: ein Erlebnisbericht*. Berlin: Minerva-Verlag, 1947.

Heym, Stefan. *Nachruf*. Frankfurt am Main: Fischer, 1990.

Hoerner, Helmut. *A German Odyssey: The Journal of a German Prisoner of War*. Golden, Colo.: Fulcrum, 1991.

Hornung, Manfred. *PW*. Vienna: Eduard Wancura Verlag, 1959.

Jaworski, Leon. *After Fifteen Years*. Houston, Tex.: Gulf Publishing Co., 1961.

Mulligan, Tim. *Lone Wolf*. New York: Praeger, 1994.

Pabel, Reinhold. *Enemies Are Human*. Philadelphia: The John C. Winston Co., 1955.

Parnell, Wilma Trummel, with Robert Taber. *The Death of Corporal Kunze*. Secaucus, N.J.: L. Stuart, 1981.

Sager, Guy. *The Forgotten Soldier*. New York: Harper & Row, 1971.

Novels:

Greulich, Emil. *Keinen wird als Held geboren*. Berlin: Verlag Neues Leben, 1961.

Heym, Stefan. *The Crusaders. A Novel of Only Yesterday*. Boston: Little, Brown, 1948.

Malewitz, Edward C. *Thanks, Mrs. O'Brien*. New York: Vantage Press, 1977.
Richter, Hans Werner. *Die Geschlagenen*. Munchen: K. Desch, 1949.
Swarthout, Glendon. *The Eagle and the Iron Cross*. New York: The New American Library, 1966.
Unger, Douglas. *The Turkey War*. New York: Ballantine, 1988.

Other Sources:

Arndt, John, ed. *Microfilm Guide and Index to the Library of Congress Collection of German Prisoner of War Newspapers Published in the United States from 1943–1946*. Worcester, Mass.: Clark University Press, 1965.
Monroe, James L. *Prisoners of War and Political Hostages: A Select Bibliography Report A10–1*. Springfield, Va.: The Monroe Corp., 1973.
Wehdeking, Volker Christian. *Der Nullpunkt: Über die Konstituierung der deutschen Nachkriegsliteratur (1945–1948) in den amerikanischen Kriegsgefangenenlagern*. Stuttgart: J. B. Metzlersche Verlag, 1971.

Unpublished Ph.D. Dissertations and M.A. Theses:

Choate, Mark. *Nazis in the Pineywoods: The Story of German POWs in East Texas during World War II*. M.A. Thesis, Stephen F. Austin State University, 1987.
Corbett, Edward C. *Interned for the Duration: Axis Prisoners of War in Oklahoma, 1942-1946*. M.A. Thesis, Oklahoma City University, 1967.
Doyle, Frederick Joseph. *German POWs in the Southwest U.S. During World War II: An Oral History*. Ph.D. Dissertation, University of Denver, 1978.
Pluth, Edward John. *The Administration and Operation of German Prisoner of War Camps in the U.S. During World War II*. Ph.D. Dissertation, Ball State University, 1970.
Proud, Phillip J. *A Study of the Reeducation of German Prisoners of War at Fort Custer, Michigan, 1945–1946*. M.A. Thesis, Western Michigan University, 1949.
Speakman, Cumins E. *Re-Education of German Prisoners of War in the United States During World War II*. M.A. Thesis, University of Virginia, 1948.
Tissing, Robert Warren, Jr. *Utilization of Prisoners of War in the United States During W. W. II, Texas: A Case Study*. M.A. Thesis, Baylor University, 1973.
Walker, Richard Paul. *Prisoners of War in Texas during World War II*. Ph.D. Dissertation, North Texas State University, 1980.
Williams, J. Barrie. *Re-Education of German Prisoners of War in the United States During World War II*. M.A. Thesis, College of William & Mary, 1993.